155·4

Child-centred

Play Therapy

SECOND EDITION

Janet West MA

ARNOLD

A member of the Hodder Headline Group
LONDON • NEW YORK • NEW DELHI

First published in Great Britain in 1992
Second edition 1996 by Arnold,
a member of the Hodder Headline Group,
338 Euston Road, London NW1 3BH

British Library Cataloguing in Publication Data
A catalogue record for this book is available from the British Library

Library of Congress Cataloging-in-Publication Data
A catalog record for this book is available from the Library of Congress

ISBN 0 340 65253 5

5 6 7 8 9 10

Composition in 10/12 Palatino by Gray publishing, Tunbridge Wells, Kent
Printed and bound in Great Britain by Athenæum Press Ltd, Gateshead, Tyne & Wear

Contents

Foreword to the first edition

My own initiation into play therapy began during the 1939–45 war when, as a lecturer at the (then) University College of the South West, I spent all possible free time working at the Exeter Child Guidance Clinic. We must never forget the immense debt owed by the UK to the influx from the continent – chiefly from Vienna and Berlin – of so many skilled psychiatrists and experienced child therapists, fleeing from the Nazi menace. Some were in transit to the States but a large number remained. At Exeter we had our rich share, and among them Dr S. H. Foulkes who was later to establish the Institute of Group Analysis in London. At the clinic he tried out methods of group therapy, working with Eve Lewis, a pupil of Flugel. Dr Foulkes was the first of my four personal analysts, but it was Eve who trained me specifically in play therapy.

This period was the heyday of experimental child psychotherapy in Britain. We studied avidly the earlier works of Anna Freud, Melanie Klein and Michael Fordham. Later I visited Margaret Lowenfeld's centre in London, and spent a fortnight observing Dr Winifred Rushforth's inspired work with children and adults at the Davidson Clinic (later the Salisbury Centre) in Edinburgh. In particular we were fortunate in having, near Exeter, Irene Champernowne's Withymead Centre, a place of exciting exploration into a variety of therapeutic media including art, craft, drama, music and movement. The need was great; apart from local children suffering from the 'Baedeker blitz', the South West was full of evacuees, mainly from the East End of London, needing help.

Most problems arose from acute crises: traumas from the London raids – one little girl had totally repressed her memory of being buried alive for 24 hours because her mother considered it wiser to deny and forget; separation from families and in particular the absence of fathers – a pattern reinforced by two succeeding generations of war; culture shock, sometimes combined with class shock, which affected also those mothers and teachers who came with the children from the close, warm and lighted (if often appalling) slum conditions of an inner city to what they felt to be the cold, dark and empty countryside with its large animals, strange food, lack of shops and cinemas, and incomprehensible values. But, although these were the main precipitating factors, which always change through time, the underlying personality disorders, then being discovered, recognized and intensively researched, are fundamental and appear to remain constant.

All that I learned was put into practice after the war when for five years I worked part-time as play therapist at the Leicester Schools Psychological Service under Olive Sampson who had shared our interests at Exeter. My main job in teacher training enabled me, throughout the 1950s and early 1960s, to offer optional courses for students from the University and other local colleges

in child guidance, play and art therapy. However, during the more behavioural and drug-oriented 1960s and 1970s, interest in the psychodynamic and child-
centred approaches declined, with the exception of a few clinics.

I was therefore delighted in 1978 to find that Janet West, a former probation
officer who held the position of Student Training Officer at the Leicester Family
Service Unit, was not only interested but showed a remarkable natural flair for
play therapy, combined with deep empathy for those damaged children whom
she met in her work. So I taught her all I knew, supervised her cases for many
years, and we have worked closely together ever since. I cannot speak too
highly of her intuitive understanding of young children and of the results of
her careful, long-term commitment to each unique individual child, the interaction and experience differing in every case. She has read, studied and experi-
mented far beyond the basics that I could offer her, taking her MA in Guidance
and Counselling at Reading University, the subject of her dissertation being
symbolism and play therapy. She has published several papers on various
aspects of play therapy in relevant journals. Finding that social workers, nurses,
the staff of children's homes, teachers and other concerned carers were seeking
information ('What is play therapy? How can we use it?'), she responded by
giving an increasing number of short courses. These were based largely on her
own findings supplemented by hand-outs of appropriate theory. For source
material she had to rely mostly on American authors, ranging from the
invaluable early work of Frances Wickes and Virginia Axline (can anyone forget
Dibs?) to Carl Rogers and other sources listed in this book. We owe them so
much, especially for retaining a child-centred concern during the reactionary
period of more physiological, behaviourist and family-oriented theories and
practices.

A book by a British author is to be welcomed, especially at the present time
when, following Jung's 'way of the snake', the swing is turning once more to
psychodynamic insights, highlighting the great value of unstructured free play.
In contrast to the war conditions of the 1940s, the present main precipitating
factor is that of increasing recognition of child abuse. Social workers, doctors,
nurses, teachers, foster parents and many others ask how can they relate to and
try to heal these terrified, inarticulate young victims. We can briefly explain that
play therapy is a means of contact, of communication without words; what free
speech is to an adult, free play is to a child. But there is so much more to be
learned of the art – for it is an art – of the delicate skills, the intuitive perception,
recognition, interpretation and empathy combined with restraint, all of which
Janet has in plenty. This comprehensive yet readable book is not only timely
for the current need, but will be an essential source for use by students and
practitioners for many years to come.

Mary Swainson MA, DPhil
Leicester 1991

[Mary Swainson is a Jungian psychotherapist and author of five books,
including *The Spirit of Counsel* (Spearman, 1977). Based at Leicester University,
between 1948 and 1972 she pioneered one of the first psychological
counselling services for students.]

Preface

At work you might see me with a tray bearing fruit juice and biscuits in one hand, a battered toy tucked under one arm, entering a room bejewelled with toys. An hour later you could glimpse me with a mop and bucket, grappling with swamps of sand and water, having shooed the tame alligator back into the cellars. At the heart of this is a child who has come for play therapy. What is play? What is play therapy? The following chapters are designed to offer some of the answers; not all the answers, partly because I do not have every answer and cannot anticipate all your questions, and partly because you, the playworker, are an integral part of the proceedings and will take your unique gifts and characteristics into the playroom. I provide some scene-setting, and invite you, the reader, to be the impresario and to bring your own talents to the (often) productive and rewarding undertaking of play therapy.

I fell into play therapy by accident. In 1978 a colleague suggested we might 'do' some play therapy, which at that stage was an unknown concept to me as it was to most other professionals. However, I was interested, our agency backed us, and we were fortunate in having access to Dr Mary Swainson, who served as our consultant. The results of our first endeavours were encouraging, and the need was there in that referrals were over-subscribed. Thus, alongside a demanding full-time job, the play therapy project was born.

When preparing the first edition of this book I felt very much alone; play therapy was scarcely acknowledged in Britain. To my great joy, in 1992 I discovered other like-minded people in this country, and seized upon the play therapy books that miraculously had emerged. Since then play therapy has become increasingly recognized in the UK, and professional training courses in play therapy are available. The Association of Play Therapists has been formed in Great Britain. Importantly, professionals and carers are becoming increasingly aware of the preventative and therapeutic needs of abused children (Dartington Social Research Unit, 1995).

It is also interesting and instructive to look at developments in art therapy, dance movement therapy, drama therapy, music therapy, myth and story telling, puppetry, and expressive arts therapies, which share many commonalities with play therapy. Much hard work is required in what are, still, pioneer times, as we strive to learn how best to respond to the needs of the children whom we serve.

Although springing from a social work background because that is the area I know best, this book has relevance for other professionals such as occupational therapists, nursery and family centre staff, educational psychologists, special needs teachers and hospital personnel. Such professionals will need to frame what I am saying within their own context and make necessary adjustments and adaptations. I write from a white, western perspective, and modifications may be required to suit the rich tapestry of the multicultural society.

The children on whom we eavesdrop on the following pages are typical of a social worker's caseload. To preserve privacy and confidentiality, they are, however, fictional, being based on vivid encounters over many years. In extracts from sessions, children's remarks are in quotation marks, the play therapist's comments being within square brackets. Children known to social workers may be abused, grossly deprived, often on the brink of their own family, or living in foster or adoptive families, or children's homes. Many have disrupted and distorted early relationships, some are in urgent need of re-parenting, and some find the notion of a 'caring' parent quite difficult to assimilate. The word 'carer' is used in this book to define the adult who currently has a parenting role.

If children are to be accepted into play therapy, it is important that work is undertaken with the family, because it is not just the child who is 'the problem'. The understanding and support of schools, nurseries and allied professionals are also vital.

Child-centred play therapy is suitable for most multitroubled children (there are a few exceptions), and is one of the post-disclosure options when considering how to help abused children. In play therapy each child is different, cannily using the sessions to work on current difficulties and former tribulations. Sessions are the child's time, the child deciding what to do and how to do it. The play therapist is an informed, intuitive and interested adult, watching, waiting and responding. In the vast majority of cases there is improvement. Play therapy can be demanding, frustrating, tiring; it can also be a rewarding way of working with troubled children.

The Association of Play Therapists (UK) defines play therapy as follows:

> Play therapy is the dynamic process between child and play therapist in which the child explores, at his or her own pace and with his or her own agenda, those issues past and current, conscious and unconscious, that are affecting the child's life in the present. The child's inner resources are enabled by the therapeutic alliance to bring about growth and change. Plat therapy is child-centred, play being the primary medium and speech the secondary medium.

Janet West

Acknowledgements

I should like to thank Pam Donnellan, former colleague at Leicester Family Service Unit, and all the other people connected with the early days, for their active encouragement in rekindling play therapy. Subsequent colleagues and students have enriched the development of my practice, and I am grateful for their material and observations.

I am indebted to social workers, residential staff and nursery officers who have referred some of their troubled children; to carers and teachers who have been interested and supportive; to students who have listened, acted and challenged (not always in that order!); and to everyone who has given encouragement and validation.

Tribute is gladly offered to the children who have abundantly and generously taught me so much.

Most importantly, I am indebted to Dr Mary Swainson for sharing her expertise and knowledge, and for being objective as well as supportive in our invaluable and sometimes lengthy consultation sessions. Without her the play therapy project would never have got off the ground.

The editors of *Changes* (1984, 2(3), pp. 80–4) and the *Journal of Social Work Practice* (1984, **1**, pp. 49–65) have given me permission to rework an earlier article on termination entitled 'Ending or beginning?', and the editor of *Adoption and Fostering* (1990, **4**(4), pp. 31–7) has kindly allowed me to quote from 'Play work and play therapy: Distinctions and definitions'.

The following acknowledgements are offered to:

Gestalt Journal, Highland, New York, for permission to quote from p. 160 of *Windows to Our Children*, by Violet Oaklander (1978, Real People Press).

Charles C. Thomas, Springfield, Illinois, for permission to quote from p. 71 of a chapter by D. Lebo, 'The development of play as a form of therapy: From Rousseau to Rogers' in *Play Therapy: Dynamics of the Process of Counseling with Children*, edited by G. L. Landreth (1982).

Random Century Group, London, for permission to quote from p. 264 from *The Technique of Child Psychoanalysis: Discussions with Anna Freud* by J. Sandler, H. Kennedy and R. L. Tyson (1980, The Hogarth Press).

Methuen & Co., London, for permission to quote from p. 293 of *The Magic Years* by Selma H. Fraiberg (1968).

Octopus Publishing Group Library for permission to quote from pp. 20–23 of *The Prophet* by K. Gibran (William Heinemann Ltd, 1980).

PART ONE

Introductory

1   Toby

If we could only learn to respond effectively to children at the crisis point in their lives which brings them to us, and at subsequent crisis points which are part of growth, we might save many of them from becoming clients in one capacity or another for the rest of their lives.

(Winnicott, 1984, p. 19)

Using Toby as a case study, this chapter introduces the reader to

* The theory and practice of child-centred play therapy
* Criteria that are used when accepting a child for play therapy
* Preparations before the work begins
* The importance of the first session
* The main stages of Toby's play therapy
* Toby's art work
* Outcome

Exercise

* Write down three things that you know about play therapy, and three things you would like to know.
* Pretend you are a child coming to the playroom for your first play therapy session. What do you expect will happen? How do you feel?

'I'm here!' announced a smiling, fresh-complexioned face as it rounded the door, closely followed by a lithe-limbed track-suited body. I had been sitting in the playroom, clearing my mind of distractions, preparing myself for – I knew not what, for this was to be Toby's first session.

REFERRAL

* Information is required about the child's background, presenting problems and family situation.
* If play therapy is a suitable option, various preparations are necessary.
* See Chapter 4 for a more detailed discussion about referrals.

Several weeks ago a social worker had telephoned: 'I wonder if you could help? We don't know what to do with Toby.' From subsequent conversations with the social worker and school I gleaned information about Toby's background and his present situation.

Background

In brief, I learnt that nine-year-old Toby was the eldest of three children born to the same mother by two fathers. When he was a baby, his home was described as filthy, and Toby was often left in his own excreta. He was admitted to care at the age of six months following his mother's desertion, thereafter having several changes of address and/or carer, juggling between his mother (in various houses as Mrs Green struggled with accommodation problems), hospital (as a result of neglect), and foster parents. There were a couple of unsubstantiated incidents of possible physical abuse whilst Toby was living with his mother. Following a more stable period in Mrs Green's life, Toby had been at home for the past two-and-a-half years under a supervision order. The family had weathered some difficult times but was now almost at breaking point, with Mrs Green demanding that Toby be accommodated. Despite lack of coherent schooling, Toby was said to be quite bright.

Presenting problems

Problems in Toby's behaviour that precipitated referral included the following:

- Outbursts of extreme temper, recently holding a knife to his mother.
- Vicious fighting.
- Engaging in daredevil escapades.
- Trying to jump out of a window saying he wanted to die.
- Being involved in petty thieving (especially sweets).
- Being suspended from school for violent behaviour.
- Sometimes curling up like a baby.
- Calling himself 'bad', identifying with his second name Nicholas – Nick – Old Nick.

INDICATORS FOR PLAY THERAPY

There were several indicators that play therapy might be worth trying:

(a) Toby's behaviour was problematic in almost all aspects of his life.
(b) What was known of his history suggested he had suffered extreme deprivation at an early age, and bonding and attachment could be problem areas (Fahlberg, 1982).
(c) Toby vacillated between aggression and withdrawn, babyish behaviour.
(d) Toby was bright and seemed to have the capacity to respond to a safe, secure, child-centred environment that would not make demands on him, but would encourage him 'to be' whatever, or however, he needed to be within the session. Toby seemed to have sufficient grasp of reality to realize that there was a difference between the permissive ambience of the play-room and the norms he would be expected to adhere to elsewhere. Play therapy could give him the experience of being valued for what he was, warts and all, and he would have the opportunity to play out his concerns,

fears and anxieties. The theoretical base augured that once Toby had been accepted by someone such as the play therapist, he would be better able to accept himself, that his self-esteem and well-being would improve, and the various facets he was displaying would become more integrated and age-appropriate instead of split off and acted out.

(e) Although his mother had requested that Toby be accommodated, he was not imminently being ejected from the home and both Toby and his family were prepared to work on the problems.

PREPARATIONS

Having already talked to me and having engaged Toby and his mother in the notion of play therapy, the social worker took me to meet Toby and his family in their home. It was agreed that Toby and I would see each other for an hour each week during term-time in the playroom, where he would be brought by taxi and collected by a regular volunteer driver.

I told Toby that being in the playroom would be different from anything he might have experienced before, that this was a time for him to be, or say or do (more or less) what he wanted. At the back of my mind I knew there were limits – that he could not hurt himself or me, or wantonly destroy the play equipment, or wander round the building – limits that would be invoked if necessary. With the approval of Toby and his mother, I had also visited the school and had heard about the catalogue of problems that had led to his suspension, together with the plans that were being made for his return. The school was not sure whether play therapy would help, but was prepared to let Toby come for sessions in school time. So, here I was, at the beginning of my journey with Toby, wondering what would happen.

FIRST PLAY THERAPY SESSION

- The first session often holds the key to the work.
- Note the first thing a child does.
- The child shows you where the difficulties lie, and how they may be tackled.
- See also Chapter 5.

The initial session often indicates the work that is to follow (Chapter 5). The first thing Toby seized was Darth Vader,* 'I like this', followed by daggers and guns, 'my favourite toys'. He used the toy telephones to ring his mother, and fed a baby doll. Toby set up a garage, filling a yellow vehicle with petrol. Car play ensued, after which he continued to look round the room, making a fierce battle between Darth Vader and Action men. A tank shot Darth Vader, who remained unvanquished, kicking and thumping the tank until it fell over.

*Darth Vader is the chief villain in the Star Wars trilogy.

Darth Vader was strong, other tanks and vehicles retreating when he raised his arms. In the sandtray, with quiet absorption Toby set up a battleground in which big, angry forces defeated a ragged side. At the end of the session I commented that there had been a lot of power. Toby had not spoken much, but on leaving, he muttered deprecatingly that he hoped I had not been bored.

Toby had touched on several of the problem areas in his life including issues about power, strength and violence, his concern about his place in the family, his vulnerable baby-self, and his lack of self-esteem.

STAGES IN PLAY THERAPY

- A child's play therapy typically passes through various stages, which help us measure the child's progress. Briefly,

  1. All over the place.
  2. A focus begins to emerge.
  3. Ambivalence.
  4. More realistic approach to life.

- A fuller outline of the stages is given in Chapter 10.

Work in play therapy is rarely orderly as issues are often dealt with symbolically (*Chetwynd, 1982*), cropping up in snippets as and when the need arises. In the first phase of the work the child usually presents the 'problems' through play themes, often in a raw, even disjointed form. In the middle phase, play themes develop, with solutions and resolutions beginning to emerge often in a fragmented and patchy way. By this time, improvements are usually being reported in some aspects of the child's outer life, but the child may be vacillating in feelings and affections. The final phase shows constructive resolution of the play themes, the nature of the play and the child's relationship with the play therapist becoming more age-appropriate and the child's behaviour in the outer world reportedly being more realistic.

First stage

In the first phase of therapy Toby played a lot with Darth Vader, Action men and large and small tanks. I guessed from his interest in a film about the malevolent dealings of Old Nick, and from what Toby had said about himself and his forenames that he had identified himself to some extent with strong negative forces, and I considered it was no coincidence that he had chosen to work with Darth Vader and other powerful figures.

There was quite a bit of play about being unable to find his way, of not having anywhere to live, and of being given muddled directions.

In so far as sandtrays (Chapter 8) could be seen as a reflection of Toby's inner world, they were ambivalent. He made the first sandtray when his outer life was desperate – it was about fighting people, floods, battles and devastation. The following week he created a farm where wild and farm animals mingled and were labelled as 'not dangerous'. A couple of sessions later showed a sandtray of deep conflict with opposing armies, though they and a ferocious alligator became friendly and there was hope of reconciliation.

Second stage

A formative phase (of approximately ten sessions) emerged during which Toby played with a construction kit. (Note – construction, not destruction!) The Darth Vader/Action men/tank and gun battles continued but mellowed, and Darth Vader did not always vanquish. It was interesting to observe how, as the sandtrays progressed, Toby used smaller and smaller figures so that at the end of this sequence he had an almost equal-sided battle between small model soldiers.

I felt that Toby and I had developed a more reciprocal, sharing relationship, and he would initiate intriguing role plays in which, increasingly, I was a wise person, e.g. judge, sheriff and, more frequently, king, to whom Toby, the good knight, reported his deeds, being the bravest knight who asked to be 'christened' (I assumed he meant knighted). Toby was often the rescuer, with good prevailing; had he been intrinsically 'bad' we might have had a different scenario. Amongst other things I was asked to become a 'valuer', evaluating Toby's riches. This might have been a symbolic way of showing that he valued the sessions and, more importantly, that he might be feeling that he was worth valuing.

Toby's quest for accommodation and for a lost family continued, usually having a favourable, sometimes over-compensatory, outcome. He would script me or himself to be poor and homeless, and a benefactor came along, providing lavish accommodation, money and a job. Quite often I was playing several different roles more or less simultaneously, and occasionally roles were reversed if the scripting became particularly complicated. This suggested a close relationship, and Toby would anticipate my needs, for example, by giving me the appropriate hat or the telephone at the right time.

Toby undertook rigorous BMX- and tractor-driving proficiency tests, and successfully travelled in space where no one had gone before. There was imaginative and sensitive play about visiting other planets and communicating effectively with aliens in a strange language, this play probably being another reflection of Toby's inevitable question 'Who am I and where do I belong?'. It was as if Toby were equipping himself to 'travel well' on life's journey, even if it were strange and unpredictable at times, and elements of his play suggested that he had been on a big inner journey of reconstruction.

School play indicated that Toby wanted to succeed at school, and he directed several scenarios showing how difficult and puzzling school sometimes was, particularly when teachers gave mixed messages. By role reversal, I had to experience a bewildering first day at college, Toby kindly ensuring I had sufficient money and a helper to guide me.

In about half the sessions Toby mentioned his actual family, or played out family relationships, and I wondered whether he was beginning to view his own family situation more realistically.

During this phase Toby used the sandtray to create an army scene in which small-in-stature soldiers were victorious, no longer being pummelled by strong 'negative' forces.

An indication that the baby part of Toby was being provided for was explicit regression when he got into bed and asked me to feed him with a feeding bottle. This seemed to show that safety and nurture were available to him. (Some children play at being desperately angry, neglected, unfed babies.) In previous sessions there had been hints that he was concerned about his baby-self when he had been a good provider for a baby either he (or I) had.

As I got to know Toby better, I felt my hypothesis appeared to be confirmed that his most difficult behaviour was partly reactive to insecurity and to events that he considered unfair. In the play sessions Toby had shown that he could learn, that he could play, that he cared, and similar qualities were reported as emerging in his everyday life by his social worker, mother and school, where Toby was now doing well.

Final stage

Toby fell in love with the game Misfits,* which I considered was not entirely coincidental as he had indeed previously felt himself to be a misfit in his family. However, this did not now seem to be the case. In play therapy, board games of draughts became the main battleground. Some of the role plays were still a bit over-compensatory, with lavish gifts being showered by munificent benefactors. When play therapy was coming to an end I lent Toby games to take home for the family to play, giving him Misfits and draughts as presents to mark the end of his play therapy. By this stage, Toby and I were talking more overtly about the reasons he had come to the playroom, and what had happened there, and we concluded our work together with visits to a theme park and a steam railway.

ART WORK

- Art work is an optional activity.
- Drawings, paintings and sandtrays may offer an insight into the child's inner world.
- See Chapter 8.

Art work (and sandtrays) offer independent indicators about what is happening to children in their inner and outer worlds. Done spasmodically, when he chose, Toby's first painting was a house; his energies were around himself and his family. Several weeks later he prepared pictures of two properties for sale. The first was a castle protected by a deep moat and an electric current; the second was guarded by a swamp and sinking mud, though there was a special

---

*In the game Misfits, several cards (e.g. head, body, legs, arms) comprise a number of human figures. The object of the game is to assemble a whole, if jumbled, person.

entrance round the back. The castles might be seen as aspects of Toby, still defended, so some dangers remained, but there was a special way through, if it could be found.

Toby next painted a cryptic map that, if interpreted correctly, showed where treasures were buried. But, two weeks later: 'Scribble, scribble, scribble' as he swooshed paint in splodges and swirls. Children's progress in therapy is up and down, and a toddler bit was re-emerging. Later Toby painted an integrated pattern, a mandala (p. 207), the sort of thing that children sometimes produce at important turning points in the work.

A sequence of paintings was mostly of human figures with 'balloons' issuing from their mouths inscribed with messages, which I took to be a commentary on the play therapy and relationship with me. The first said 'Hello, Janet'; then in subsequent sessions 'I'm watching you everywhere', 'Having a nice time?', 'Mick Monster rules Not, OK', 'Thanks for the Tea, Janet', 'Hello', and, in his last session, he started to paint 'I am Toby and I will be gone soon', but he made a mistake and scribbled it out.

OUTCOME

To measure the child's progress, we look for

- A natural resolution of the themes played out in play therapy sessions.
- Improvements in the child's feelings and behaviour.
- Chapter 10 has a fuller discussion.

Evaluation and assessment are on-going, and the evaluation of Toby's work is explored more fully in Chapters 10 and 11. In brief, by the end of his play therapy (22 sessions) Toby was happier at home and Mrs Green was no longer demanding that he be removed. He had returned to school where his work and relationships had improved. In play sessions, Toby's play themes had come to a natural conclusion in that the battle scenes with the soldiers had dwindled, the role plays were still a bit 'high' at times, but Toby was able to talk more realistically and with understanding about what had happened to him. His relationship with me was balanced and age-appropriate.

OVERVIEW

It is not easy to offer a snapshot of a child in play therapy as it is difficult to transmit the richness, subtlety and minutiae of the work and of the relationship. However, I have presented some of the issues surrounding the initial referral and the preparations for taking a child into play therapy. In child-centred play therapy the play therapist is concerned with the 'whole' child (Crompton, 1990, p. 117), allows the child to determine how the sessions shall be used, and is open to what the youngster brings. As play therapy continues, themes become apparent which, if comprehended, might aid the play therapist's understanding; and predictions about the child's ability to cope in the future can be made. Evaluation is aided if the play therapist knows what changes are occurring in the child's outer life, and it helps if the play therapist periodically meets with the child's referrer and with other concerned professionals (in some cases with carers), to exchange impressions and information. Additionally, the play therapist would expect to participate in plans for the child's future.

The most important task is for the play therapist consistently to support the child through whatever happens in the sessions, accepting 'slipbacks' and 'slip ups' as the child grows towards wholeness. At times play therapy seems bewildering, and the play therapist welcomes the assistance of the consultant during difficult periods when feelings of chaos, confusion, hurt, anger and despair are around. Overall, there is faith that the process of play therapy 'works'.

POSTSCRIPT

Toby remained at home, thriving when a sensitive cohabitee joined the family, and he was greatly helped by careful life-story work organized by the social worker. When a teacher undermined Toby's confidence his school work temporarily deteriorated, but soon picked up when the problem was solved.

Summary

A snapshot of Toby's play therapy has introduced us to the principles and practices of child-centred play therapy. We learn that there are various criteria for a play therapy referral. One of the essential skills is to ensure that play therapy is the appropriate option for that particular child, and that adequate preparations are made to start the work properly. From all points of view, the first session is crucial, and often tells us about the areas that the child will choose to explore in future sessions. An analysis of the stages that children's therapy typically pass through helps us to evaluate the work, and to know when to terminate it. Children's art work and sandtrays are often a revealing commentary on the child's inner processes, and on the progress of the therapy.

Subsequent chapters in this Part examine play and play therapy in more detail, and the reader is invited to think about the child in the context of society's norms and expectations.

2 Play and play therapy

To 'play it out' is the most natural self-healing measure childhood affords.
(Erikson, 1977, p. 200)

This chapter

- Eavesdrops on one of Toby's play therapy sessions
- Introduces the reader to 'play', and different types of play work
- Defines child-centred play therapy
- Outlines the role of focused/structured work within play therapy
- Begins to examine the play therapist's role
- Points out some of the reasons why play therapy might fail
- Looks at the differences between
  - a fixed number of play therapy sessions
  - open-ended work
- Draws attention to the current lack of research findings
- Suggests that play therapy can be for adults too

Exercise

- How would you describe play? Demonstrate and act!
- Can play help children to feel better about themselves?
- When you last saw children playing, what did you feel? What did you think? What did you remember about yourself as a child?
- Play with, and observe, children of all ages and cultures, indoors and outdoors.
- How many ways can you think of for using play with children?
- How do you, as a grown up, play?

PLAY, PLAY WORK AND PLAY THERAPY

Toby pointed out a scratch under his left eye, saying the kitten had done it last night. We started to play with the soldiers on the floor but Toby transferred the game to the sandtray where an army base was created in one corner, emergency vehicles assembling in another. Toby's and my vehicles had a race (his won) and there were a few minor accidents, but nothing like the catastrophes we have previously experienced. Toby created a roundabout in the middle of the sandtray, and when his car broke down it was helped by the breakdown truck. When I saw vehicles ignoring the red traffic light, I was asked to call the police (who happened to be Toby), but was informed that it was OK for those particular vehicles to infringe the law.

The play became active as we found ourselves on an island warding off attackers. We took to the boats, spending a rough night at sea, Toby going in the life-raft to try to sort out the worst problems. We landed on the island – the home corner – and Toby became a toddler, asking for orange squash in the feeding bottle. We went to the fair, experiencing various rides, then returned home. I found I had two other children, Toby being the oldest, and all four of us went back to the fair, where Toby ran off and misbehaved. Once more we were back home, Toby escaping from his bedroom and, whilst I was again at the fair with the other children, he ransacked the house. Eventually the police brought him back and I had to be very cross with him.

I was instructed to talk to my friend whilst Toby did some drawing, and then several times I had to turn someone away from the door who wanted to remove my little boy. Toby became a puppy, whining and cowering when the dog catchers approached. I repelled the dog catchers and was advised to inform them that the puppy was well looked after and belonged to me. This play was repeated several times in various permutations, the puppy occasionally becoming the little boy.

The puppy smelt smoke coming from the kitchen and summoned the fire brigade. He was sensible about vacating the premises and, when the fire brigade had finished its job, we re-entered the kitchen, coughing, spluttering and finding our way amidst the blackened debris.

Why did the play therapist participate in this way? The play therapist's approach was neither random nor a whim of the moment but was drawing on proven theory and practice.

Play

- Play helps the child to

  - Develop physical skills.
  - Find out what is 'me' and 'not me'.
  - Understand relationships.
  - Experience and identify emotions.
  - Practise roles.
  - Explore situations.
  - Learn, relax, have fun.
  - Act out troublesome issues.
  - Achieve mastery.

- Play is symbolic communication.
- Play acts as a bridge between conscious awareness and emotional experiences.
- In play, children embrace the numinous, the luminous, and the practicalities of daily living.

It may be helpful to make explicit the following assumptions:

(a) in the majority of the white, western world play is to [most] children what language is to [most] adults *(Axline, 1969, p. 9)*;

(b) children usually express themselves more freely using play than in formal 'talking' interviews *(Bray, 1986, p. 19)*;
(c) children can reveal their troubles through play; and
(d) play can be a therapeutic tool *(Gavshon, 1989; Isaacs, 1948, pp. 49–50)*.

Hellendoorn (1988, p. 43) endorses that play helps to engage the child in a therapeutic relationship, allowing 'symbolic re-enactment of conflict-laden content and expression of repressed primitive wishes in "make believe" '.

Play allows opportunities for physical, emotional, cognitive and social growth, and is often pleasurable, spontaneous and creative. Play can reduce frightening and traumatic events; it may relieve anxiety and tension; it can aid relaxation, amusement, enjoyment. Through play, children learn about the world and relationships; it offers an opportunity for rehearsal, for reality testing, for exploring emotions and roles. Play enables children to express aggression and buried feelings, and can be a bridge between phantasy and reality *(Cohen, 1993; Lowenfeld, 1935; Moyles, 1994; Singer, 1973; Winnicott, 1971a; Yawkey and Pellegrini, 1984)*.

Nickerson (1973, pp. 1–6) sums up:

1. Play is a child's natural medium for self-expression, experimentation and learning.
2. Feeling at home in a play setting, the child can readily relate to toys and play out concerns with them.
3. A play medium facilitates a child's communication and expression.
4. A play medium also allows for a cathartic release of feelings, frustrations, and so on.
5. Play experiences can be renewing, wholesome and constructive in a child's life.
6. The adult can more naturally understand the child's world by observing him or her at play, and can more readily relate to the child via play activities than through an entirely verbal discussion.

And *Oaklander (1978, p. 160)* explains:

Playing is how children try out and learn about their world. Play is therefore essential for healthy development. For children, play is serious, purposeful business through which they develop mentally, physically, and socially. Play is the child's form of self-therapy through which confusions, anxieties and conflicts are often worked through. Through the safety of play children can try out their own new ways of being. Play performs a vital function for the child. It is far more than just the frivolous, lighthearted, pleasurable activity that adults usually make of it. Play also serves as a symbolic language ... Children experience much that they cannot as yet express in language, and so they use play to formulate and assimilate what they experience.

Irwin (1991, p. 617) observes that 'children's play is an intriguing mixture of phantasies, feelings and perceptions of real and not real reality, glued together with the spirit of pretend'.

Types of play work

- Spontaneous play.
- Guided play.
- Assessment play.
- Focused (structured) therapeutic play.
- Play therapy.

Play work can be divided into several categories, and it behoves us to think carefully about the type of work we intend to undertake (*Allen, 1947; Redgrave, 1987; West, 1990b*):

Spontaneous play occurs when children 'play' because they want to and for no other reason. The play is child-directed, adults often being superfluous. Spontaneous play is extremely valuable, should be encouraged and nurtured, and is considered to be part of normal childhood development in white, western society.

Guided play is worker-determined, for purposes such as giving the child permission and freedom to be a child and play (and indulge in spontaneous play), encouraging the child to relax and have fun. It can be a means of getting to know the child better, offering a non-threatening environment in which worker and child can be together. Guided play can be used to encourage carers to interact more favourably with and enjoy their children, and is employed in some forms of life-story work.

Assessment play (including disclosure and validation) is also worker-determined and usually time limited. What is this child like? Can play tell us what has happened? Can play help us judge what plans should be made in the future? Play-based methods can enable us to understand the child in ways that would not be possible if we relied on adult-type interviewing techniques.

Focused therapeutic play often results from assessment play or from detailed knowledge of the child, and usually attempts to deal with one or two previously identified issues. Similar to guided and assessment play, the aims and methods of therapeutic play tend to be worker-directed and time limited.

(Specific play ideas can be found in books such as *Aldgate et al., 1988; Cardiff Social Work Resource Centre (undated); Catholic Children's Society, 1983; Crompton, 1980; Dennison, 1989; Fitzgerald, 1983; Harmon, 1976; Jewett, 1984; Oaklander, 1978; Redgrave, 1987; Ryan and Walker, 1993; Striker and Kimmel, 1978; Waterhouse, 1987*).

Play therapy

In many dictionaries play therapy is, to my mind, inadequately defined (e.g. *Evans, 1978; Wolman, 1973*) being confused with the more directive and focused therapeutic play (*Goldenson, 1984*). Play therapy is more akin to psychotherapy. *Psyche*, from the Greek, means 'soul, spirit, mind: the principle of mental and emotional life, conscious and unconscious ...' (*Macdonald, 1973, p. 1085*). Therapy (from the Greek, *therapia*) means attending, caring, healing, serving, waiting on *(Liddell and Scott, 1940)*, which conveys something a bit different from the more active, focused values implicit in directive work. When we talk about play therapy, therefore, we imply a holistic approach, using play as a means of 'helping', in a non-invasive way, the physical, spiritual, emotional and cognitive aspects, both conscious and unconscious, taking account of the past, present and future of the 'whole' child. Play therapy is concerned with children's feelings, not just their behaviour *(Amster, 1964, pp. 11–19)*. The play therapist is largely 'waiting' and 'attending' upon the child, accepting and respecting the child and having implicit faith that the process of play therapy (the play therapy room, the therapeutic alliance and encounters between play therapist and child, and the overall concern that has led to the child being presented for play therapy) 'works' *(Moustakas, 1953)*.

Developed from the work of *Carl Rogers (1951)* by *Virginia Axline (1964f, 1969)*, play therapy draws from the humanistic school and is essentially child-centred (non-directive is a former, less accurate, term that is sometimes used), with the child, in a sense, acting as therapist. To play in the presence of a sympathetic and permissive adult can be healing *(Dorfman, 1951, p. 240; Newson, 1983; Winnicott, 1971a, p. 58)*.

The play therapist reflects the child's actions and feelings, participating in the play if so requested. In the early stages the play therapist does not structure the sessions but, having tried to help the child feel secure and to understand the rules of the playroom (pp. 175–9), waits to see what emerges. The agenda of the session is the child's; the play therapist taking responsibility for preventing danger, damage and impropriety *(Bray, 1984)*.

Play therapy is based upon the fact that play is the child's natural medium of self-expression. It is an opportunity which is given to the child to 'play out' his feelings and problems, just as in certain types of adult therapy, an individual 'talks' out his difficulties. *(Axline, 1969, p. 9)*

Child-centred play therapy

- Can be undertaken individually or in small groups.
- Is suitable for a range of troubled children.
- Has a humanist theoretical base.
- Can be evaluated.
- Requires play materials and a private room.

When a child is referred for play therapy an appointment is made, probably for an hour (perhaps less for younger children), usually weekly, at a regular time. The child comes into the playroom and looks round. All the play therapist does is to establish a permissive atmosphere. The play therapist may say 'You can do almost anything you like; and it's OK to say what you want and to feel and be however you are here.' Symbolically the play therapist is saying 'Within this room, this safe place, you are free to be as you want to be'. People sometimes ask 'What do you *do* with children? Do you *make* them play?'. The answer is 'Nothing. Leave children alone and in time most do play. It's their form of expression' (pp. 54, 157–8).

Children referred for play therapy exhibit behavioural and/or emotional problems. They may be 'acting out', difficult to control, withdrawn, under-functioning at school, failing to develop where there are no medical or physical problems. They may be finding it difficult to settle in a new foster home or children's home, they may have suffered abuse and/or deprivation, they may have had a traumatic experience or been subjected to unpleasant medical procedures. The list is endless, but the common factor is that the child's discomfort about what has happened is manifesting in the child's behaviour.

Since children's fears and anxieties have built up during their past experiences with persons close to them, children have little opportunity to explore and examine such feelings in either the home or school situation. Play therapy offers children a unique relationship with an objective and accepting adult, who is not usually involved in other aspects of the child's life. (In other forms of play work the play worker may have additional links with children and their carers.) The session should be viewed as the child's private time and children should not be expected to give an account of the events that occur in the playroom to anyone else, unless the child so wishes.

Child-centred play therapy and focused work

With severely abused or traumatized children, a combination of approaches, including child-centred play therapy, seems indicated, though with younger children play therapy alone may suffice (Gil, 1991, pp. 72–3, 181). If the child remains within the family where he or she was living when the traumatic incident(s) took place, family therapy could be seen as essential. Abused children may benefit from protection work (keeping safe, saying no, etc. – though research is equivocal) and sex education. Opinions vary about the advisability of encouraging youngsters to confront the traumatic event(s), and to share what happened and the feelings evoked by the incidents. If this is considered important and the child does not deal with the material spontaneously, a more structured approach may help (Friedrich, 1990, p. 71). Focused work may be undertaken by someone else but, if the play therapist is to be involved, both therapist and child need to be clear about the differences between focused and child-centred work. For instance

- there may be changed confidentiality. The therapist may pass on information to a carer, social worker, teacher, the police
- the therapist may challenge the child, especially when verbal or non-verbal discrepancies are noted
- exercises and special materials designed to elicit information or focus on specific topics may be introduced
- the therapist will be more directive.

Focused work can be undertaken within the overall framework of child-centred play therapy, provided that the above points are clear (Wilson et al., 1992, pp. 57–9).

> Focused work may be carefully introduced into play therapy sessions with badly abused and/or traumatized children, e.g. to help them to
>
> - Identify and express emotions appropriately.
> - Engage in anger work.
> - Undertake keeping safe and protection work.
> - Experience more positive parenting patterns and learn appropriate child roles.
> - Learn how babies and young children should be cared for.
> - Learn about socialization and peer group skills.
> - Undertake life-story work.
> - Work on issues surrounding loss and change.
> - Confront the traumatic events.

Play disruption

Play disruption occurs when, for no apparent reason, the child stops playing or talking, sometimes abruptly. *Erikson (1977, pp. 201, 206)* helped us to understand that this may happen when the child's feelings about, or in, the play become too overwhelming or threatening, or if the play therapist has moved in too quickly, either verbally or actively. The play therapist has to decide whether to call the child's attention to the disruption *(Haworth, 1990, pp. 207–8)* or whether to make a mental note and let the play continue.

PLAY THERAPY AND INITIAL APPRAISAL OF THE CHILD

The first crucial assessment is to determine whether the referral for play therapy is suitable and appropriate (Chapter 4). Once the child is accepted, the play therapist bears in mind that assessment and therapy overlap *(Barlow, Strother and Landreth, 1985, p. 355)*. The first few play sessions will enable the play therapist to confirm (or otherwise) hypotheses gained about the child's situation during the setting-up phase. In this context, assessment means weighing the presenting difficulties against what is known of the child's background and how he or she uses the sessions to explore and express inner conflicts and outer problems. A clearer picture will emerge about the child's inner and outer worlds, and the play therapist can then draw his or her own conclusions about what is troubling the child, which may confirm or deny what the referrer or carers have said. We must remember, however, that for some children, to 'play' in a strange room, with a strange adult present, is an uncommon experience that the child may not know how to handle *(Cohen, 1993, p. 150)*. In child-centred play therapy, a clinical initial assessment is not necessary, but a thorough, accurate account of the child's social history, and current problems, is. Information about the child will be added to and amended as play therapy continues.

Beginning play workers should avoid forming too rigid an assessment of the child's state of being until they are familiar with norms of play at different ages and stages. *Jackson and Todd (1964, p. 315)* offer some useful pointers:

Play may be studied both from the point of view of the choice of materials and from the nature and type of the play. Is it lively and freely expressed or oversolemn and inhibited? Is it at a level appropriate to the child's age, or is it immature and babyish, or perhaps oversophisticated and dominated by grown-up standards? One can decide from the type of play whether a child is comparatively normal or disturbed ... .

An inhibited, over-anxious child may sit, or stand, in the playroom, unable to indulge in any activity. Children without boundaries and respect for themselves may wreak havoc and destruction. Immature children may play in a relatively 'babyish' way. There is the child who needs to take control and has to have everything just so, ordered in neat lines and who is scared by free-flowing and messy substances such as paints, clay, sand and water. Or children may indulge in scatterbrain play, handling more or less everything in sight in the first ten minutes. Gradually these children find their own norms, will 'level out', and the bulk of their disruptive behaviour or overwhelming emotions will disappear.

THE THERAPEUTIC ROLE

When Toby started play therapy the play therapist accepted him however he was, in whatever mood. She tried neither to lead, direct nor distract him, respecting his pace, working with his spontaneous feelings and interacting with him if requested, for it is the child who largely controls the session, and person-centred therapy does not rely on diagnostic labelling with preconceived ideas of what will happen. Toby could choose what to do. He was not criticized or questioned, apart from the play therapist occasionally trying to draw out what was happening in the playroom. He could do what he wished in any way, provided the playroom rules were kept (*Axline, 1969, p. 16*), and he had freedom of speech. The ambience of the therapy setting was geared towards his safety and inner growth (*Carkhuff and Berenson, 1967, pp. 65–6*). The play therapist may be seen not so much as an expert evaluating the play and unravelling the child's trauma, but more an enabler and co-explorer, trying to follow the child's lead rather than to control the play or alter the child. The child-centred approach offers children the opportunity to establish their own ways of communicating, and they receive feedback when the play therapist reflects to them the affect and content of what is happening.

The therapist

- Accepts the child, the child's play and behaviour.
- Reflects back non-judgementally to the child what he or she is saying and doing in sessions.
- Maintains safety and therapeutic boundaries.
- Is responsible for obtaining a safe, private, child-friendly play space.
- Liaises with relevant people in the child's environment.
- Is professionally accountable, maintains confidentiality and seeks adequate supervision.

Gender of play therapist

Provided they have suitable personal qualities, technical knowledge and the intuitive ability to be alongside suffering children, men and women can be equally effective in the play therapy role *(Doyle, 1990, p. 35)*. *Jones (1986)* found that on the whole the gender of the therapist was not particularly important. However, some children relate better to people of a specific gender, and selecting an appropriate play therapist may be crucial for a few abused or abandoned children *(Hall and Lloyd, 1989, pp. 28–35)*. Children may prefer one-to-one sessions with someone of the opposite gender to their abuser(s). Other children, because of the material they need to explore, may prefer a play therapist of their own gender. Others do not have a particular preference.

In a strange way, the play therapist can be genderless in play sessions *(Lush, 1977, p. 78)*, though the importance of a thorough, unambiguous acceptance of one's sexuality cannot be overstressed. It is probably this grounding in one's own gender identity that enables some children to view the play therapist as asexual and as one onto whom they can project all sorts of phantasies to do with male and female figures in their lives.

TIMESCALES

Time-limited play therapy

Time-limited play therapy is often brought about partly through lack of resources, and partly because there is a school of thought that children can accomplish a reasonable amount of work in eight to ten sessions. This timescale is ample for many children, though not for those with very troubled backgrounds. Towards the end of the set number of sessions, a review may be undertaken and some children may have the opportunity of continuing in therapy.

Open-ended play sessions

The younger the child, and the less complicated the child's background, the quicker the child's response to play therapy (see Table 2.1).

Table 2.1 Response rates of the 'average' child referred for play therapy

Age	Some improvement expected within	Significant improvement expected within
Up to 6 years	4 weeks	2–4 months
6–8 years	4–6 weeks	3–6 months
8–10 years	4–8 weeks	4–12 months
10–12 years	4–8 weeks	4–15 months

There are the following provisos:

– Severely traumatized children may take longer.
– Children 'in limbo'* may reach a certain point, but go no further until their future is secure. 'In limbo' children can even deteriorate.
– Grossly abused children may progress in fits and starts, some of the 'down' periods appearing retrogressive and chaotic.

If there has not been improvement within six to eight weeks, the case should be examined critically to see whether play therapy is appropriate.

PLAY THERAPY THAT 'FAILS'

> • The referral may have been inappropriate.
> • Sessions are sometimes sabotaged.
> • The child may still be being molested.
> • The child may find the sessions difficult and uncongenial.
> • Play is repeated yet fails to be resolved or to provide relief.
> • The play therapist is ineffective.
> • The child is preoccupied with some other life task.

Not all referrals are successful. Some children are unsuitable for play therapy. Sometimes play therapy is 'sabotaged' by a carer (or teacher, or social worker) who does not *really* believe that the child needs play therapy, or does not want anything to change, so the child may be prevented from attending sessions and, in severe cases, prejudiced against the play therapist. Occasionally carers are jealous, wanting attention themselves, and if they cannot have it they deprive their child. A few carers may be unable to accept the phase of worse behaviour, which some children experience as part of the therapeutic process (pp. 100–3). Such problems, not in themselves uncommon, should be overcome if sufficient time is spent in the initial stages on setting up the work properly (Chapter 4) and appropriate help offered to the family to unblock the difficulty. If not resolved, this type of problem can jeopardize play therapy, and the play therapist may decide against working with the child.

Occasionally children may find sessions painful and react by not wanting to come. In these cases gentle encouragement may help the youngster continue. Inadequate play therapists, or play therapists who lack skill in certain areas, can mangle sessions so that the child's best interests are not served, and such children may indicate that they do not wish to continue. Some 'in limbo' children may be having to deal with other major life problems. For a few children, play therapy may be found to be inappropriate, and referral elsewhere indicated.

In the case of 'failed' play therapy, carefully try to terminate the work so that the child is not made to feel a failure. The play therapist would endeavour to

*Without a permanent home or in a state of unknowing.

assure children of his or her interest in their well-being, and would want to avoid giving the impression that it is the child's 'fault' for not 'succeeding'. Even in 'failed' work, it is more than likely that something will have been gained from the sessions.

PLAY THERAPY AND RESEARCH

> • There is not much research available.
> • The main finding so far emphasizes the importance of the qualities that play therapists bring to their work.

Formal research findings are limited and equivocal *(Barrett, Hampe and Miller, 1978; Ginott, 1961, pp. 143–7; Heincke and Strassmann, 1975; Phillips, 1985; Wright, Moelis and Pollack, 1976)*. Some studies have been hindered by questionable research methodology, by a failure to distinguish between therapeutic play and play therapy, and the importance of the whole child has been overlooked *(Faust and Burns, 1991)*. *Payne (1993)* explores the problems of research within the expressive arts therapies. Valente and Fontana have a relevant chapter in Payne's book outlining research they undertook in dramatherapy *(Valente and Fontana, 1993, pp. 56–67)*. Mary Boston has considerably improved the research profile on behalf of child psychotherapists *(Boston, 1989, 1991; Boston and Lush, 1993, 1994)*. In her thought-provoking article, *Boston* discusses the difficulty of assessing inner change and symptom removal, and argues that acknowledgement is needed for the scientific status of intuitive observation *(1991, pp. 320, 321)*. *Van der Kooij and Hellendoorn (1986)* have gathered together some research chapters on play therapy which make interesting reading.

Does play therapy 'work'? The pragmatic answer is 'yes', but what is meant by 'work'? Out of approximately 130 children worked with or supervised by the author, improvement during play therapy was shown by all except five. With hindsight, two were 'in limbo', at the mercy of the courts and did not know where they would be living or what would be happening to them. They withdrew from play therapy, and would not now be accepted into the play therapy programme until their circumstances were more certain. Two other multi-abused children withdrew after a few sessions and, again with hindsight, it was felt that the choice of one-to-one play therapy was inappropriate for them at that stage (pp. 42–3). The fifth child had learning difficulties, and it was decided that focused therapeutic play would be more appropriate.

As a result of play therapy, many children who had been considered 'un-fosterable' or 'unadoptable' have moved into appropriate families quicker than had been expected. Children have been enabled to remain within their own homes. Children in foster home breakdown have either stayed put, or have been able to make a more positive move than had been anticipated. In the majority of cases, carers, teachers and others have described considerable improvements, and usually most of the presenting problems have disappeared or abated. Long-term follow-up studies are required.

Lack of facilities has precluded the author from undertaking a scientific research study on the above claims, but the children themselves, parents and the above-mentioned professionals have reported improvements. Changes are probably due to a combination of play therapy and the therapeutic process, the attention that the child is getting, and the attention given to the family and child's key carers. This is not to claim that the children have become paragons, or are miraculously freed from problems for the rest of their days, because of course they remain subject to life's vicissitudes. But the children have had a springboard from which to bounce to the future, and seem better able to cope with adverse circumstances.

PLAY THERAPY WITH ADULTS

Adults already participate in art, dance movement, drama, music, puppetry and sandtray therapies; the principles of child-centred play therapy can also be applied to grown-ups (*Cattanach, 1994, pp. 15, 141–58; Cohen, 1993, pp. 168–86; McMahon, 1992, pp. 24–5*). Some adults may have problems arising from a wounded inner child, e.g. early abandonment, neglect, abuse, family dysfunction, disease and disability, that have not been therapeutically resolved. These are issues in their own right which can easily be compounded when the adult becomes a parent and carer. Play therapy has helped carers whose own trauma in childhood prevented them from playing and who, in turn, were having problems interacting positively with their children. It is important for parents who have been abused as children to find, and relate to, their inner child, and to be able to play. Play is sometimes helpful for adults who have a multiple personality disorder, and with adults and adolescents who have repressed much of their early lives as a result of severe abuse and/or trauma. People who want, or need, to regress, and who wish to succour their wounded inner child, may respond to play therapy, and play therapy should be a 'must' for intending play therapists.

Playing with toys can be evocative and, if not always, the memories often trigger feelings, attitudes and physical gestures from childhood (*Jennings and Minde, 1993, p. 145*). As *McMahon* writes (*1992, p. 24*) 'Play is not just a filling of time before real work and learning begin but an essential element of growing and being fully human'. Using a psychodynamic and strategic paradigm, *Ariel* has developed a model of family play therapy: 'play seemed to reflect thoughts, feelings and covert transactions which would probably never have emerged if direct communications were to be employed' (*1992, p. xii*).

A relatively new area, play therapy with adults might

- Help get in touch with one's (wounded) inner child.
- Give an opportunity to learn about, or re-experience, play.
- Assist carer–child and family relationships.
- Be useful for people who have had traumatic childhoods, especially those who have cut themselves off from bad childhood memories.
- Be advisable for intending play therapists so that they experience being a play therapy client.

Summary

It is important to understand the value that is put on play in white, western society. Having outlined four types of play work, we have defined child-centred play therapy in more detail, and argued the appropriateness, at a later stage in the work in some cases, of introducing focused work within the child-centred paradigm. We have also considered play disruption – what is happening when a child suddenly stops, or changes, activities. Professional considerations of the therapist such as accepting referrals, the therapeutic role, and gender of the play therapist, are explored, and we examine average timescales for children in therapy. The reasons why play therapy fails are postulated, and the lack of research into play therapy is deplored. Play therapy with adults is an emerging field. Finally, all intending play therapists should be play therapy clients.

Before embarking on a more detailed study of play therapy, readers are invited to consider the needs and place of children within society.

3 Children in society

Yet there are vast numbers of children of all ages silently calling out for help.
(Holgate, 1972, p. xi)

In this chapter, we are challenged to understand that

* The concept of childhood varies from culture to culture, and within cultures
* Children have rights and needs
* The word 'children' embraces a range of ages, developmental stages and conditions, from infancy to adolescence

Exercise

* Can you define what childhood means to you?
* Describe what the concept of childhood means in your family, to grandparents, parents, adolescents, younger children.
* What do you know about childhood in other cultures?
* In what types of family do children live?

SOCIETY AND CHILDHOOD

Beliefs influence behaviour, so it behoves playworkers intending to use a child-centred approach to examine their attitudes towards children, as well as their understanding of the role of children within society *(Fox, 1982)*, and to be aware that there are variations in attitudes towards children, both within one culture over a period of time *(Ariès, 1986; De Mause, 1974; Humphries et al., 1988; Pollock, 1983)* and contemporaneously between strata of society and different cultures.

What is a child? Children and childhood are viewed differently throughout the world *(James and Prout, 1990, p. 2)*. Do you believe children are primarily good, worthy of respect, and entitled to a non-invasive life experience that facilitates the development and integration of the physical, emotional, spiritual and cognitive components of their being (e.g. *Froebel, 1974*)? Should children be given a nurturing environment and allowed to be self-directive *(Rousseau, 1925)*, with their own rights? Or are they inherently bad, the property of their parents and the state, needing correction and control so that they conform to social and educational expectations, and will provide for the society in which they live *(Crompton, 1980, pp. 8–13; La Fontaine, 1990)*? It is most important for intending play therapists to know where they stand on this issue, and what their approach is to children and children's rights *(United Nations, 1989)*.

From books about the history of childhood *(Hoyles, 1989; Schorsch, 1979)*, we learn that

1. Childhood is socially construed. Notions of 'the family' vary, as do laws and welfare services. Some societies and cultures value children and define the purpose of childhood; others have seen children only in economic terms as potential wage earners.
2. Childhood can be experienced differently, according to gender, class and race.
3. There is a shifting definition of childhood.

In 'Constructions and reconstructions of British childhood: An interpretive survey, 1800 to the Present', *Hendrick (1990)* traces what he sees as the major stages in the development of the notion of 'childhood'. The area that he posits British society is now working on is whether the child is a 'family child' or a 'public child'. Are children their carers' possessions? In what situations does the child become public property? The growth of agencies such as the Children's Rights Development Unit (235 Shaftesbury Avenue, London WC2H 8EL), and the advent of the Children Act 1989 are, one hopes, beginning to give *children* more rights and powers *(Woodhead, 1990, p. 60)* though, at the present time, children's views are rarely sought and children are not often included in statistical documents *(Qvortrup, 1990, pp. 81, 83)*. Moreover, many adults within British society still have problems in recognizing the intrinsic rights of children to safety, protection and adequate care *(Donovan and McIntyre, 1990, pp. 162–5)*.

Adults' views about children

- They need a lot of correction and control.
- What was good enough for me when I was little is good enough for my child.
- They are my children and I can hit, frighten, deprive them of food, have sex with them if I want to.
- The social services will take them if I don't want them.
- Children do what I say, not what they want.
- Children are never satisfied.
- It's their fault I'm like this.
- Children are hard work and cost a lot of money.
- I need children to increase my own status and self-esteem.
- Children are great.
- Each child is unique and should be encouraged to grow up with his or her own interests.
- Good, caring conditions help children to achieve their potential.
- Children need families.

What are *your* views about children?

Children's rights and needs

Exercise

- What do adults consider children's needs to be?
- What do children feel that children need?
- What does the state consider to be the needs and rights of children?
- What is the difference between needs, rights and wants?

The UN Convention on the Rights of the Child *(United Nations, 1989)*, ratified by the UK government in 1991 and now signed by the majority of countries, has been described as a 'turning point in the international movement on behalf of children's rights … giving the child the right to voice opinions and to participate in decisions concerning his or her person'. Children are not totally the property and sole responsibility of parents *(Flekkøy, 1991, p. 216)*, though in practice their direct access to rights is still restricted.

The UN Convention has four broad areas of rights for children

- survival
- developmental
- protection
- participation.

Until the late nineteenth century, English common law gave the father sole rights over his child. Under the Children Act 1989 children now have a *right* to have their welfare treated as the paramount consideration in decisions made about their upbringing, and they have limited rights to self-expression and self-determination *(Stainton Rogers and Roche, 1994, p. 222)*. There is room for improvement!

Defining 'needs' in a multiracial society is complex *(Woodhead, 1990, pp. 65, 72)*. In white, western culture it is considered that children have basic biological and emotional needs that have to be met if the child is to prosper. 'Children's physical, emotional, social and intellectual needs must all be met if they are to enjoy life, develop their full potential and grow into participating, contributing adults' *(Pringle, 1980, p. 15)*. *Maslow (1954)* formulated a hierarchy of needs (Fig. 3.1). They are all important, but primary needs – those at the bottom of the pyramid – have to be attained before the needs of the stage above can be realistically met. Thus physiological requirements are the vital underpinning; if these are adequately met then the next most important needs are for physical and emotional security, and so on towards the pinnacle of self-actualization, self-fulfilment and adequate self-expression to which people strive. (Maslow acknowledged that there are occasional exceptions when, for instance, disturbed children may jeopardize their safety at the expense of seeking esteem.) *Pringle (1980, pp. 33–58)* identifies children as needing love and security, new experiences, praise and recognition, with the opportunity to take reasonable responsibility. Almost by definition, most of the children referred for play therapy have suffered deprivation of varying extent *(Gath, 1985)*, and play therapy can be one of the ways of freeing them towards self-actualization.

Play therapy should, therefore, be seen within the context of the child's daily experiences, and is most successful when the child's basic needs are being adequately met and there is experience of 'good enough' parenting *(Winnicott, 1986)*. Children whose basic needs, including those of security and dependency, are not being met, will understandably have less emotional energy for the

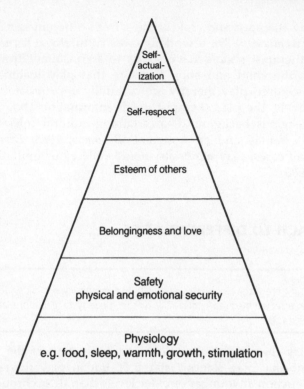

Figure 3.1 Maslow's hierarchy of needs.

therapeutic process. Limited work is likely to be achieved with the child who has recently been uprooted and is being temporarily accommodated with unfamiliar people before being moved elsewhere, or the child subjected to continuing erratic and abusive parenting. The child who is cold, hungry or is still being abused will also have little emotional or physical energy for the therapeutic process.

Cross-cultural considerations

Exercise

- You are a white worker, and a black child is referred. Are there any special considerations, or do you carry on as usual?
- You are a black child in a playroom with an old white person, and some toys you don't feel comfortable with. What can, or do, you do?

Child-centred play therapy, in which children are encouraged to be self-expressive and to take the lead in interacting with the play therapist, may not be indicated for children who are culturally expected to be subservient to adults and to suppress feeling (O'Connor, 1991, p. 53). Good professional practice indicates that child and play therapist share the same racial background. If this is not feasible, careful consideration has to be given to the pros and cons of the play therapist and child coming from different racial groupings *(D'Ardenne and Mahtani, 1989)*. If working cross-culturally, it is recommended that the play therapist should have access to a consultant from the same background as the child and should ensure that play materials and the tenets of child-centred play therapy are culturally appropriate. In order to respond sensitively, the play therapist needs information about the child's cultural and religious background, ascertaining cultural roles and norms with the child's family and environment *(Brummer, 1988; Dwivedi, 1993b; Lau, 1984)*. In all cases, play materials should reflect our multiracial society *(Ahmed et al., 1986)*.

THE APPROACH TO DIFFERENT AGES

Exercise

- Write down the different developmental stages between infancy and older adolescence.
- How are children affected by disease, disability, gender, poverty, race, culture, abuse, and loss, in each of these stages?

It helps the play therapist's assessment and evaluation of the work to be familiar with normal play stages (Table 3.1), but in play therapy children may partially function at younger or older levels than their chronological age owing to the need for regression or because of their pseudosophistication. Children may identify with several ages, ranging from babyhood to grand-parents, and toys and materials suitable for all developmental stages should be available *(Hellersberg, 1964, p. 169)*. Polly (p. 69) had worked through the major part of her therapeutic regression and was beginning to assess herself at her rightful age: 'I'm seven. Well, I'm a bit seven, a bit eight, and a bit six.' The play therapist confirmed that people are often a bit of several ages, sometimes having a bit of baby too, but that's all right.

On the rare occasion the play therapist might suggest the play, it is wise to start the child on age-appropriate activity. Left free with an accepting play therapist children will soon find their own level.

For example, take play with sand. Two-year-olds tend to use sand as a sensory medium, something to learn about and enjoy by feeling and letting it pour through their hands – lovely! Five-year-olds will probably use it as a medium for phantasy play, such as Dick who buried himself and the play therapist in it. Older children may make the sand firm with water, constructing and carving realistic buildings or irrigation works. However, in play therapy there was a 12-year-old girl who poured so much water into the tray that it looked like a soupy mess, and she spent the whole session wallowing in it. Several children, some as old as 11, who were unable to make positive relationships with their mothers created a game, which continued for weeks, of 'hide-the-fingers' wherein they and their female play therapists searched for and caught each other's fingers underneath very wet sand. So the level of play might be a factor in assessing the child's needs.

Table 3.1 Friendship and play stages

Years	Play	Friendship
0	Solitary, incidental interest in other children	Momentary physical playmate
1	Spectator (children watch each other)	
2	Parallel (children play near each other)	One-way relationships
3	Association (children appear to be playing together)	Note: it is normal for children to have an imaginary friend
4	Co-operative, sociodramatic, imitative	Co-operative
5	Aggressive, physical fighting, competing	
6	Intimate (mutual sharing)	Often same-sex friends
7		
8	Autonomous	Interdependence
9		Sharing interests, meeting needs, greater emphasis on friends' desirable personal qualities
10		Gangs, cliques, individual friendship, pairings
12		Longer-lasting friendships relating to matters of inner importance

(Adapted from *Cass, 1971; Hurlock, 1978; Millar, 1968* and *Sandström, 1979, pp. 189–96*)

'NORMAL' AND 'TROUBLED' CHILDREN

Sometimes workers ask 'What is the difference between 'normal' and 'troubled' children in the play therapy setting?'. Obviously each child varies, but most 'normal' children given a playroom and an attentive play therapist spontaneously explore the room and their relationship with the worker, use play materials in a free and sometimes novel way, play alone or involve the adult, are often happy and positive, make decisions and express appropriate negative and positive feelings. Such children may spontaneously tell other people about the session, just as they might communicate to a friend or parent about a visit to the park.

Troubled children may not have had the opportunity of satisfying play needs and may have missed out a stage which, in a therapeutic setting, they have another opportunity to experience. When left completely free, troubled children often regress and revert to play from an earlier developmental level, perhaps indicating where the trouble spots were. Behaviour may be extreme or polarized, over-active or withdrawn. A few children may not be able to play, or may play in a stilted way. Some troubled children may abuse or block the play therapist; others will be lacking in spontaneous joy and energy, and may be cowed and afraid *(Ginott, 1961, pp. 38–42; Moustakas, 1953, pp. 17–18, 59–60; Moustakas, 1959, pp. 48–9, 99–100)*. Most tend not to disclose much, if anything, to other people about their session.

Summary

'Children' and 'childhood' are generic terms covering young people in a range of developmental stages, and about whom various attitudes may be held depending on culture, class, political and sociological viewpoints. Play therapists need to know what to expect from children at different developmental levels. The UN Convention supports that children have rights and needs. What are play therapists' views and values towards children, childhood and child-rearing practices? It is imperative that we adapt flexibly to the multicultural society.

All these are important underpinnings for actually putting play therapy into practice.

PART TWO

Play therapy in practice

4 Referrals and the referral process

Nobody in the child's environment recognised the distress signals, and often the children were considered naughty or rebellious.

(Winnicott, 1984, p. 20)

In this chapter we gain background knowledge about
- Four children referred for play therapy
- Suitable age ranges
- Situations and behaviours that bring a child to play therapy
- Children for whom play therapy may be unsuitable
- Play therapy and the abused child
- Play therapy and the legal process
- Starting play therapy
  - accountability and confidentiality
  - preliminary meeting with child and family

CHILDREN IN PLAY THERAPY

Gemma's mother had neglected and abused her, and following her mother's death in a road accident, and after a couple of foster home breakdowns, eight-year-old Gemma was in a long-stay foster home. Gemma was a bright child and wanted to be adopted, but learning problems at school plus periods of babyish and violent behaviour militated against this. Much of Gemma's early life had been spent in local authority accommodation because of her mother's vagrant lifestyle. Gemma had been in hospital a few times for a mysterious digestive complaint.

A potentially able boy, seven-year-old Andrew was at home but his parents were saying they could not cope with him. He lied, had school phobia and stole. He exhibited several psychosomatic complaints and had periods of almost complete withdrawal. Andrew's young life had been disrupted because of his mother's difficulty in settling down and her chronic, at times severe, illness, which meant that Andrew had previously had several short-term admissions to foster homes. His stepfather was said to be unduly strict.

Six-year-old Polly, a dynamo of a child, was in a foster home awaiting an adoptive placement. As a baby she had been neglected and abandoned by her young parents, eventually being returned to her mother and new stepfather. Polly was re-admitted to care following an aggressive attack against her for which her mother was prosecuted. There were suspicions, but it could not be proved, that her stepfather had sexually assaulted Polly. Polly had strongly mixed feelings about her mother, hated her stepfather, and experienced volatile relationships with peers and adults. Psychosomatic complaints included an occasional virulent rash, and what Polly described as 'heartache'. She was unpredictable with young children, vacillating between being spiteful or competent and caring.

Six-year-old Peter was in residential care, having had an impoverished early life with a drug-riddled mother. He had been sexually abused by one of his mother's partners and by an older boy in his second foster home. Peter was outraged by yet another move. He was in jeopardy of being suspended from his new school, was smearing, wetting and destroying the children's home, and had eating problems.

AGES OF CHILDREN REFERRED FOR PLAY THERAPY

There are no hard and fast rules, but children in play therapy would normally be between the ages of four or five to ten or 11, though the author has worked with children as young as two-and-a-half and as old as 12½ at the time of referral. Very young children may have separation problems and those who are in a day nursery may be better helped within that setting (if the facilities and staffing are adequate); several nurseries are now instituting 'special play' for selected children. Undertaking play therapy within any institution means that child and worker have to be free to behave in ways that might not habitually be expected or allowed, and for some children (and staff) this can be confusing.

Sophisticated older children would doubtless wrinkle their noses at the prospect of spending time with a *play* therapist in a playroom. In view of the therapeutic need for many older distressed children to regress, to play, and to re-experience missed childhood stages, the play therapist may begin the sessions on an age-appropriate level, for example by encouraging the child to draw, paint or model, devise dramatic role plays or puppet shows, or through some form of life-story work or counselling. If this takes place within a playroom (or near a playroom), when the time is right the child will drop his or her defences and will play. As a last resort, a bright 12-year-old boy was referred who made it clear that he did not wish to be associated with the playroom. When painting in the waiting room became too messy he volunteered to move to the painting area attached to the playroom. From then onwards he was hooked and violent, angry acting out and regression ensued using the playroom and play equipment in a child-centred way.

SITUATIONS AND BEHAVIOURS THAT PRECIPITATE REFERRAL

Exercise

• How many 'problems' you can think of that children might have when referred for play therapy.

Referrals are typically received:

1. In a crisis when the child's behaviour is such that the parent (or carer) is requesting the child's removal from home or residential placement.
2. As part of the process to prepare a child for an eventual change, such as moving to a permanent family after a disrupted life with several changes of address and carer.
3. When it is recognized that multitroubled children might benefit from therapeutic help in their own right.

Such children are usually manifesting a cluster of 'problems' from the following (cf. Connell, 1985, p. 46):

– immature behaviour, and/or pseudomaturity
– attachment difficulties
– 'failure to thrive'
– physically or sexually abusing other children or animals
– masturbating, or inserting things into their genitals or anus
– suffering from psychosomatic problems
– eating disorders
– sleeping disorders
– wetting, soiling, smearing
– telling lies
– inappropriate emotional responses
– elective mutism
– undue withdrawal, temper tantrums, violent outbursts
– extreme mood swings
– lack of affection, difficulties with relationships
– chaotic and messy, or unnaturally pernickety
– self-harm, hurting animals or smaller children
– under-functioning for no apparent reason
– learning disorders and problems about attending school, in particular school refusal (i.e. children who stay at home or at some other place; not truants who go to school then leave).

The children may have suffered significant trauma such as:

• sexual, physical, emotional or organized abuse
• severe illness or accident
• the death of a significant person
• exceptional loss(es)
• emotional pain
• inadequate parenting
• a disrupted and/or impoverished lifestyle
• exposure to drugs or alcohol.

It is interesting, and sometimes instructive, to ask 'Why is the child being referred now?'. In chronic situations it may be an end-of-tether syndrome; the adults are at their wits' end and the referral may be a last resort. Alternatively, an understanding adult might at last have recognized that perhaps something can be attempted to try to improve the child's lot. A frequent precipitant for referral is when a 'crisis', usually a critical change in a child's life often involving loss of some sort, compounds severe or long-term behavioural problems *(Wolff, 1981, p. 11)* and the child either explodes or becomes withdrawn. It would be better, of course, if the child could be referred for play therapy *before* the crisis, and if the need for therapeutic help could be routinely addressed at all reviews and planning meetings when the well-being of children is discussed.

Cautionary notes

- Children exhibiting only one or two 'problems' might more appropriately receive an alternative intervention such as family work, behavioural case-work or focused therapeutic play.
- Chaotic young children with very poor early parenting, including those who have perhaps suffered extreme forms of abuse, may initially have a greater need for re-education and re-parenting *(Fahlberg, 1988)*.
- Children subjected to gross abuse require special consideration (pp. 42–3).
- There are some other children who may not be appropriately referred for play therapy (see pp. 39–40).
- Other professionals working with the child should be approached to ascertain their views on the appropriateness of play therapy.

Dockar-Drysdale (1990, 1993) has some useful thoughts about what she calls integrated and unintegrated children. Unintegrated children are said to have had a difficult start in life which, although not intellectually remembered, is probably recalled through feelings. Children who are pushed into premature independence may become rebellious, angry and anti-social. These children have problems in making relationships or accepting guilt, and find symbolization difficult. Unintegrated children need, claims Dockar-Drysdale, to fill in their gaps in experience, which may involve regression. Integrated children are more able to respond to verbal communication and reflection of feelings.

> • If the child is to have play therapy, the family should also accept therapeutic help.

Play therapy should not be seen as a 'dumping job' with the play therapist 'sorting the child out' and heroically solving all the family's problems. Play therapists need to be aware that children are sometimes brought for 'help' because of parental difficulties projected onto the child *(Erickson and Hogan, 1972; Will and Wrate, 1985, p. 26)*, or because the carer really wants attention him or herself but dare not, or cannot, ask directly. Needy, immature carers may feel neglected or jealous of the special attention being given to the child in play therapy *(Adcock et al., 1988, p. 35)*, and when accepting a child for play therapy it is important that the social worker, or someone else, should work actively with the carers or family. The focus is then taken off the child as 'the problem',

and parents are offered attention in their own right. Children are not intrinsically bad, and their behaviour can often be seen as reasonable once the pressures
generated by their family and early life are understood. To a large extent the
child is a product of his or her background so, if the child is to change, the
family also has to alter. However, using the theoretical assumption that children
have the ability to heal themselves *(Axline, 1969, p. 66)*, and that change in one
part of a system can affect the whole system, play therapy can be feasible and
partial results obtained without family involvement. Such results may be less
long lived if the family is unwilling to change, but the gains made in play
therapy cannot be completely undone for the child.

PRELIMINARY INFORMATION

The following information is required

- Personal details about the child.
- The child's present circumstances.
- Reasons for referral.
- Child's background history.
- Is the child involved in court or child-protection procedures?

Obtaining adequate information and suitable referrals from professionals
unfamiliar with play therapy can sometimes be tricky, and an initial information sheet to referrers can be beneficial. Potential referrers may need educating!
 The following information is helpful:

(a) *Child's name,* age, date of birth, gender, ethnic origin, present address and
    school, and current family situation.
(b) *Reasons for referral and presenting problems* as seen by the referrer, family,
    school, child.
(c) *Social history* giving details of the child's family of origin and of subsequent
    moves, changes and losses.
(d) *Personal details* about the child including developmental and medical history,
    plus treatment and medication.
(e) *Future plans* for the child. This is particularly relevant if a change of address
    or school is imminent.
(f) *Is the child on a court order, on the child protection register, or subject to an abuse
    enquiry or court proceedings?*

 In Toby's case (Chapter 1), in assessing whether it was a suitable referral,
the play therapist had phone calls and meetings with the social worker,
former teacher and Toby's mother, during which impressions of Toby's circumstances and present predicament were shared. The social worker provided a
written chronological synopsis of Toby's history, including moves and reasons
for them. The play therapist checked that future plans did not indicate any
immediate moves for Toby and that he would soon be re-entering school. (She
would have accepted him had he continued to be excluded.) Everyone involved

seemed committed to supporting what was seen as a last-ditch attempt to 'help' him. The social worker and Mrs Green spoke to Toby about the possibility of play sessions, which he accepted with interest, and this was followed up by the play therapist and social worker making an introductory visit to him at home.

Early questions

Various questions need to be asked to screen out unsuitable play therapy referrals and to check that child and family are receiving appropriate help:

(a) *If 'reasons for referral' include a physical problem, recent marked dramatic changes in behaviour, serious mood swings, unusual withdrawal or acting-out behaviour,* has the child been medically examined recently? Such an investigation should be asked for to exclude psychiatric or physical irregularity, including auditory or visual difficulties.

(b) *Is the child suffering from autism, hyperkinetic syndrome (consistent short attention span and distractibility) or from a childhood psychosis?* If so, play therapy is not recommended and further specialist advice should be sought.

(c) *If educational or learning problems are mentioned,* has the child seen an educational psychologist? Such a referral would screen for cognitive and developmental difficulties that might impede learning. A recent medical examination as in point (a) above may also be appropriate.

(d) *Does the child have severe learning difficulties?* Play therapy may be of limited value and, unless the work is time-limited, beginning play therapists are advised against this type of referral.

(e) *If speech impediments are noted,* has the child been assessed by a speech therapist?

(f) *Do the child's problems significantly involve the family or social situation?* Are there indications that family members, the school, or other involved adults might undermine individual play therapy *(Reisman, 1973, p. 237)*? What are the needs of the child's carers *(Molin, 1988, pp. 241–50)*? Is family therapy, counselling for the parent or adult couple, or work with the school more appropriate? Would alleviation of external environmental stress (e.g. housing, financial problems) help? Sometimes someone or something other than the troubled child can more appropriately be the target of intervention *(Pincus and Minahan, 1973).*

(g) *Is the child's lifestyle reasonably secure?* Before therapeutic work can be undertaken, there has to be an assurance that the child's basic needs and the love of a regular parent-figure, or parent-figures, are being provided *(Adcock et al., 1988, p. 22; Branthwaite and Rogers, 1985, p. 5; Pringle, 1980, p. 81).* Children living in temporary accommodation, or where an imminent court case may affect their future, are 'in limbo' and may only partially respond to play therapy *(Boston, 1987; Dyke, 1987; West, 1990a)* because their energies will understandably be focused on 'Who am I?'

and on where, when, and if they will be moving rather than on the therapeutic process. There may be an argument for offering play therapy to a child who might be moving 'some time'; but an alternative form of play work may be more appropriate for a child whose move is imminent as it is advisable for the child's accommodation to be reasonably secure and for there to be a reliable, trusted adult figure available before play therapy commences *(Wolff, 1981, p. 218).*

(h) *What were the child's early experiences?* If early parenting was grossly inadequate, young children may be so chaotic, unintegrated and without the usual internal controls that education and socialization may be necessary before play therapy can be effective.

CONTRA-INDICATORS

Play therapy may not be appropriate if

- The child
  - has severe learning difficulty
  - cannot differentiate between phantasy and reality
  - suffers from autism, hyperkinetic syndrome, personality disorder, childhood psychosis
    is living in short-term accommodation and/or is about to undergo a major change
  - is antagonistic towards play therapy.
- The family
  - is not prepared to co-operate
  - will not accept help, despite its dysfunctionality affecting the child.
- The authorities
  - ask for disclosure work
  - are not prepared to support the play therapist.
- The play therapist
  - has insufficient time
  - is without supervision and adequate support.

Unless they have specific knowledge, experience and supervision, beginning play therapists are advised against working with the following referrals:

1. *Children with severe learning difficulty.* They may respond more effectively to an alternative form of play work.
2. *Children who have problems in differentiating phantasy from reality, and with disorders such as autism, childhood psychoses, hyperkinetic syndrome and personality disorder (Daws and Boston, 1981; Escalona, 1964; Tustin, 1981).* Work with such children should only be undertaken by qualified, experienced therapists. Psychiatric advice should be sought if there is any doubt.

3. *Children with learnt maladaptive behaviours resulting from family dysfunction.* Family therapy or family work are preferable, occasionally with individual work running alongside.
4. *Children on the verge of some major life change.* Wait until their future is more stable. Focused therapeutic play or guided play may be helpful.
5. *Play therapy is not disclosure work* (assessment play and focused therapeutic play would be more suitable). It would be inappropriate for children to start play therapy during an investigation, because this blurs boundaries for child and play therapist. However, inevitably there are times when the child makes a fresh disclosure during the course of play therapy (p. 132).
6. *Children who are too young or too old,* unless there are special reasons and the child's level of maturity is sufficient for play therapy.
7. *Children whose safety and protection are not assured, and whose basic needs are patently not being met.* The child's circumstances need to be improved before play therapy can be considered.

CHILDREN WHO HAVE BEEN ABUSED

Types of abuse

- Neglect.
- Physical abuse: children may be maltreated, deprived of food, administered noxious substances, tied up, locked away.
- Emotional abuse: verbal abuse, children treated inappropriately, taunted, threatened, deprived, ignored.
- Sexual abuse: being touched or made to touch sexually; encouraged to participate in non-age-appropriate sexual activities; being filmed in sexual acts, being sexually involved with individuals or groups, related or strangers.
- Paedophile rings.
- Prostitution rackets.
- Organized and intergenerational abuse.
- Many children suffer from several forms of abuse.

Children can be abused emotionally (*Iwaniec, 1995*), physically, sexually and during ritual or organized abuse (e.g. paedophilia, sex rings, pornography, intergenerational abuse and satanism). It is usually the distressed, acting-out child in the post-disclosure stage who is referred for play therapy, though withdrawn children should not be overlooked. Children who have been seriously abused are likely to exhibit a cluster of problems, including emotional and behavioural disturbances, psychosomatic and interpersonal difficulties and, in the case of sexually abused children, psychosexual problems (*Lusk and Waterman, 1986; Vargo et al., 1988, Zimrin, 1986*). Particularly acute may be the 'damaged goods syndrome', low self-esteem, lack of trust and expectation of trickery (*Salo, 1990, p. 80*), impermanence, repressed anger, blurred role boundaries, pseudomaturity and/or regressive behaviour, and retarded development (*Sgroi, 1982, pp. 40–7*). These characteristics are not just the province of abused children, but apply to most badly damaged youngsters.

> Problem areas that may be exhibited by abused and troubled children:
>
> - Emotional and behavioural disturbances, including behaving older or younger than the child's chronological age.
> - Psychosomatic and psychosexual disorders.
> - Interpersonal difficulties.
> - Trust issues.
> - Knowing what is appropriate behaviour.
> - Poor self-esteem.
> - The child may find it difficult to distinguish and express appropriate emotions.

Some severely abused children may exhibit post-traumatic stress disorder (flashbacks, acute anxiety, depression, memory impairment) *(American Psychiatric Association, 1980; Bannister, 1989, p. 91; Bentovim and Boston, 1988, pp. 26–31; Deblinger et al., 1989; Haugaard and Reppucci, 1988, pp. 94–6; Kilgore, 1988; Webb, 1991, pp. 20–2).* Additionally they may show signs of victimization – also known as the Stockholm syndrome – by their support for the perpetrator(s) and hostility towards 'rescuers', denial that anything had happened, or repeated recapitulation of the experience. Other problems may include residual guilt, generalized fear of strangers and situations, fear of the play therapist as a potential persecutor, and inability to cope with anger and depression. Anger about what happened usually emerges later *(Doyle, 1990, pp. 4–17; Goddard and Carew, 1988; Jones et al., 1987, pp. 260–2; Saphira, 1985).*

Knowledge about appropriate post-disclosure treatment for abused children is still emerging *(Federation, 1986; James, 1989; Long, 1986)* and, at the time of writing, further recommendations from research studies about therapeutic work with abused children are awaited. It seems clear that a multifaceted approach is probably necessary, with facilities for direct, focused work with the child that will give scope for re-growth, re-parenting and re-education in the broadest sense. Groupwork and family work may also have a part to play.

It is becoming increasingly recognized that many abused children need one-to-one therapy *(Doyle, 1990, p. 36; Driver and Droisen, 1989; Walker and Bolkovatz, 1988, pp. 249–69),* and play therapy may be useful for children who fall within the usual criteria for play therapy referrals. In child-centred play therapy, the child has the opportunity to take control and learn to exert power; play therapy encourages expression of genuine feelings; and offers an opportunity to develop a trusting consistent relationship with an adult. It challenges the depersonalization and stereotype of collusive adults that the child may have experienced, and the play therapist is listening to and supporting the child, not just interpreting and controlling as in disclosure sessions *(Wells, 1989, p. 45).*

In setting up the work, sensitivity is required to ensure that the child does not view play therapy as a continuation of the investigation, or a replica of the one-to-one circumstances of the abuse *(Jones, 1986, p. 378).* Sexually abused children may have more difficulty in boundary-keeping (after all, their own personal boundaries have been invaded) and, once given permission to be and to feel, exaggerated, lopsided responses may emerge for a time as the child learns to 'balance up'. Inappropriate sexual behaviour in sessions is also possible in some cases (pp. 130–1).

Grossly abused children

Severely abused children may

- Have been multi-abused – a combination of physical, emotional and sexual abuse on one or more occasions.
- Have been made to abuse children and/or animals.
- Suffer from post-traumatic stress disorder (PTSD), or dissociation.
- Have particular problems with relationships if subjected to intergenerational abuse, and if their parents have been abusers.
- Have undergone 'system abuse', e.g. in protracted, adversarial court cases; by being placed in unsuitable and/or rapidly changing substitute family care; by being given inappropriate treatment.
- Need a combination of treatment modalities, e.g.
  - individual therapy
  - group therapy
  - sibling group work
  - family work
  - protection work
  - re-education, re-parenting
  - sex education
  - life-story work
  - work around anger and loss.

Social workers and others will be familiar with a continuum of abuse ranging from the relatively minor (though all abuse is an unacceptable infringement against the integrity of the child's burgeoning personage) to the grotesque, unbelievable organized abuse that has been uncovered amidst bitter dispute. We are in the early stages of learning about children who have been tortured as part of physical, sexual and emotional abuse inflicted on them by groups of men, women, other children and animals. Some children have been subjected to mind control techniques. We are slowly realizing that children are being horrendously abused in the name of pornography. Another emerging trauma is children suffering from AIDS and drug-related conditions. In addition, we are trying to come to grips with children who, when removed from home, have suffered secondary abuse from the system that should protect them. Some children have had unacceptable experiences in care caused by too many changes of carer, by sometimes living in unsuitable substitute families or children's homes, and by being re-abused whilst in a supposedly safe environment. On the other hand, there are a few cases of children being left by the authorities with abusive parents or carers, and the trauma this creates when the child is eventually removed.

Therapeutic work with severely traumatized children *(James, 1989; Johnson, 1989)* is an emergent area, current knowledge suggesting that several types of therapeutic input are necessary. Good, reliable parenting (and re-parenting) is vital, possibly with focused work such as life-story, or social skills, or peer relationships. Some deeply traumatized children have a consistent facade that hints at, but denies, deep-down issues. They can gain some benefit from child-centred play therapy but, if constantly engaged in denial of the painful events, may respond to a more structured approach such as *Friedrich's* 'traumatic events interview' *(1990, p. 71)*. Small groupwork may have a part to play and sympathetic psychiatric assessment may be desirable. If offered too early, one-to-one child-centred play therapy can be too scary for some children. With its apparent lack of boundaries and direction, severely abused children may be afraid of 'letting go', via play, into their imagination and unconscious. Also, there may be something about the full attention of an adult that, in the child's mind, replicates the abusing situation.

Severely traumatized children deserve the best help that can be offered by carers, and professionals with appropriate training and expertise. In the interests of all concerned, workers new to play therapy are advised to start with less troubled children.

PLAY THERAPY AND THE LEGAL PROCESS

- Is there any legal impediment to the child having play therapy?
- If there is a legal impediment
  - Have the judge and court officials approved that the child should have play therapy?
  - Could your records be seized by the court?
  - Is there any way that help can be offered to the child?

Traditionally, play therapy has not been considered appropriate by the legal system for children who are to appear as witnesses in an abuse case even if, on therapeutic grounds, remedial help is indicated. However, certain elements of the judiciary are becoming more aware of, and sympathetic towards, the needs of child victims, particularly as there is often a regrettably long delay before a case comes to court. In some circumstances, a qualified and experienced play therapist, with the permission of the court, may be able to undertake play therapy under specific conditions. The play therapist should ensure that he or she has received clear directions about how to conduct the sessions, and whether transcripts and video recordings are to be made available to the court.

Sometimes play therapists find themselves unwittingly involved in the legal process, especially if children with whom they are working make disclosures during the course of play therapy (p. 132). Play therapists in that predicament need careful advice about whether to continue with the play therapy pending an investigation. They should not fall into the trap of becoming a quasi-agent for the court or statutory department, as there can sometimes be pressure to get, or refute, 'evidence' *(Friedrich, 1990, pp. 271, 274)*. Play therapists may also be asked to appear in court for contested custody, care or supervision orders.

Wilson et al. (1992, pp. 218–24) helpfully discuss the presentation of therapeutic work in the court setting, amongst other things advising play therapists in this situation to be wary of the way in which informal contact with the child could be construed, and to make sure that the case is handled properly, with case notes being reliably written.

ACCOUNTABILITY AND CONFIDENTIALITY

Smooth flow of the work is aided if accountability and confidentiality are agreed between play therapist, referrer and/or other professionals, carer(s) and child, so that boundaries are clear and confusion and manipulation avoided. 'When cooperation and mutuality exist among these significant persons, it is rare that the child does not begin to move in a positive direction' *(Moustakas, 1959, pp. 325–6)*.

Exercise

- To whom is the play therapist accountable?
- Can you work out what should and should not be considered confidential between the
  - child
  - family of origin
  - foster family, children's home, hospital
  - social worker/referrer
  - school
  - other professionals
  - play therapist.
- Pretend you are a child. What does the word 'confidential' mean? Do you feel you have much control over what grown-ups say to each other about you?

If referrers understand the principles of play therapy, they are normally co-operative and a productive working relationship can be expected. It is usually best if the play therapist maintains confidentiality about the detail of sessions, unless of course further abuse or other criminal activity or matter of concern is disclosed. With the child's knowledge, it may be appropriate for the play therapist to meet occasionally with the social worker or referrer, carer and teacher, and to attend case reviews so that feedback can be given, progress discussed and concerns shared.

Occasionally, confidentiality may be modified. There may be times, for example with children in residential care, when the play therapist would share the gist of the sessions with the child's keyworker, in the hope that the keyworker could support the work and the child's interests within the staff group and the establishment in general. The other main area of shared confidentiality is when it is suspected (but there is as yet no hard evidence) that a child has been (severely) abused. We are in the early stages of trying to help children who have been subjected to mind control, and/or who have repressed conscious awareness of dreadful things that have happened to them, but their play throws up snippets of the child's experiences, some of which may not make too much sense to the play therapist. It is helpful if the social worker, or someone well acquainted with the child's background, can see the case notes and put the material in context.

The play therapist relies on feedback, usually from the referrer, so that the child's reported behaviour in everyday life can be matched with what is experienced in the playroom. Such information should not be used judge-

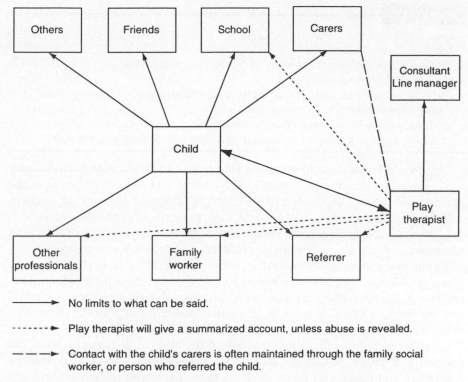

Figure 4.1 Confidentiality about the content of play therapy sessions.

mentally against the child ('Your teacher said you were awful in class today'), but helps to weigh the effectiveness of playroom sessions.

In Toby's case, the play therapist had periodic talks with the social worker, home tutor and teacher (though, when a social worker changed, this was difficult for a time). When a review was imminent the play therapist asked Toby what he wished her to tell the review, and he was also encouraged to say what he wanted to review members.

PRELIMINARY MEETING WITH CHILD AND FAMILY

If it seems that the offer of a play therapy vacancy, and issues of accountability and confidentiality can be satisfactorily worked out, the next stage is to start the child's (and family's) introduction to the playroom. Most play therapists meet the child and carers beforehand, preferably in a setting familiar to the boy or girl (usually at home), in the hope that the child will at least recognize the play therapist on the first session in the playroom and will begin to get the feel of what the sessions and the worker are like, and so that carers can be more involved in the process.

Exercise

- How would you feel, as a play therapist, when seeing a child and family for the first time?
- How would you structure the meeting? When and where will it take place?
- By the end of the meeting
  - what would you have hoped to convey to the child and carers?
  - what information would you have hoped to obtain?
- What will you say to the child? What are the last things you will say to him or her?
- As a child, what do you expect will happen when you first meet the play therapist?

The play therapist would normally be introduced by the referrer (who may have given an information sheet to the carers) and tries to respond to the queries and feelings of adults and child. Paying attention to the child, perhaps getting on the floor at eye level and maybe expressing an interest in toys or activities, is often sufficient to break the ice, provided the play therapist does not move in too quickly. For young children, a special toy in one's pocket can sometimes be a useful point of contact. A chirping bird that set itself accidentally was a great icebreaker when the ten-year-old boy, who was a prospective client, his foster parents and therapist were hunting the sitting room high and low for the bird (there were a lot of plants), only to find it in the therapist's pocket!

Usually the referrer has already involved the child in discussions about the playroom. Younger children are attracted by the notion of 'special play', though with abused children care has sometimes to be taken over the use of the word 'special'. Older children can be given the opportunity to say why they think they are coming to the playroom. It can be suggested that quite a lot of children find it helpful to be in the playroom with the play therapist for an hour each week, during which time they can do more or less what they like. Photographs of the building and playroom can be shown, the children perhaps displaying them to their parents.

Dietary restrictions (if refreshments are being offered) and, for younger children, their way of asking to go to the lavatory, should be ascertained. With sexually abused children, the child's terms for body parts and sexual acts may be useful knowledge. Some play therapists check that it will be acceptable to discuss sexual matters if raised by the child in the session. Carers should be encouraged to dress the child in play clothes.

The play therapist and referrer need to explain confidentiality in terms that are understood by adults and child. If appropriate, agreement will be reached about the use of video- and audiotapes, and information given about written records and what might be shared in the play therapist's consultation/supervision sessions. As a general rule, carers do not observe play therapy sessions, nor do they have access to records, video- or audiotapes, as play therapy is to help the child and not to assist the parental figures in analysing the child's behaviour (Moustakas, 1959, p. 254).

It may prove helpful, and is honest, to say that play therapy is often beneficial, but its 'success' cannot be guaranteed. Bearing in mind the stages of play therapy (Chapter 10), the play therapist may explain that carers might feel that the child is getting worse for a while, but, if so, this is normal, and anxieties can be shared with the professionals. Parents, and the referrer, should be made aware that children usually do not volunteer much information about what goes on in the playroom, and the adults are requested to respect this and not to pry and ask questions.

All parties need to confirm the practical details about when and where the sessions will take place, what transport and escort arrangements will be made, the circumstances under which sessions may be cancelled, and how cancellations can be made. The play therapist may follow up the visit to see the family with a letter confirming the practical details.

On occasion, as part of the preparatory process, the play therapist may wish to observe the child in the school setting as this gives an opportunity to see how the child functions in such an environment. If not considered unethical, there are advantages in observing the child *before* the play therapist has been identified to him or her.

At the preliminary meeting with child and family

- Begin to make a therapeutic relationship with the child.
- Clarify
  - the child's and family's queries about play therapy
  - confidentiality
  - the line of communication between carer(s) and play therapist
  - practical details about the sessions: place, time, dates, how the child will get there, and who will take the child, what happens if the child, escort or play therapist has to cancel a session.
- Encourage the child to be dressed in play clothes.
- Try and convey to the child that play therapy is a different experience.
- Obtain further information for diagnostic and assessment purposes.

Summary

The chapter began with a synopsis of the reasons why four children were referred for play therapy. The majority of such children are between the ages of four and 11 years, but play therapy can be suitable at other ages. Situations that bring children into play therapy are outlined in more detail, and the reader is urged to think about a number of things that need to be considered. We recognize that play therapy is not suitable for all children; sometimes a different form of play work is more appropriate, and children with certain difficulties, such as autism, should be referred elsewhere. Abused children often warrant special consideration, as may children subjected to the legal process. Accountability and confidentiality have to be clarified between play therapist, child, family, referrer, etc. Guidelines are offered for the play therapist's preliminary meeting with the child and family.

When the initial stages of the referral has been satisfactorily accomplished, the first session is the next important stage.

REFERRAL CHECKLIST

Play therapy is a useful way of helping quite a number of children so play therapists and their managers may have to work out their own priorities, particularly if there is a waiting list.

1. Bearing in mind developmental norms and the child's situation, is there a problem? Whose problem is it? How can the problem best be tackled and is it likely to be amenable to play therapy? Are the family carers also receiving help?
2. Is some other form of play work appropriate?
3. Is co-operation from school, carers and relevant others forthcoming? Can the child attend play sessions in school time?
4. Is the child receiving treatment from, for example, a psychiatrist, family therapist, behavioural psychologist, speech therapist and, if so, is play therapy compatible?
5. Do the professionals agree that play therapy is worth trying, and are they prepared to co-operate?
6. Do carers feel that play therapy is worth trying, and are they prepared to co-operate?
7. Can you negotiate confidentiality so that you can get the information you require but the detail of the child's work can remain private?
8. Is anyone likely to sabotage the work?
9. When, where, what time and what date can you begin work with the child?
10. Would you like to observe the child in the school or residential setting?
11. Is it necessary to have a prior meeting with the child and carers? If so, the following are some of the things you might want to include, enquire about or give information on:
    (a) photographs of the building and playroom
    (b) a simple explanation about what will happen in the playroom
    (c) any dietary restrictions?
    (d) how does the child indicate she or he wants to go to the lavatory?
    (e) suggest that the child wears play clothes
    (f) confidentiality between play therapist and child; the play therapist will not normally talk to parents about the sessions, and will usually discourage direct communication between them and the therapist, apart from practical arrangements. The referrer tends to be the intermediary
    (g) perhaps a statement that play therapy does not always work but is worth trying and that, if it is successful, children sometimes get worse before they get better
    (h) use of video- and audiotapes, case records, consultation
    (i) carers should be told that often children do not talk much about what happens in the playroom, and they should be asked to respect this
    (j) check escort arrangements for the child.
12. How will you know when play therapy can be terminated (Chapters 10 and 11)?
13. What will you do if the child reveals signs of further abuse (p. 132)?

The first session

Every child is a new experience.

(Reisman, 1973, p. 121)

In this chapter we study

- The importance of the first session, especially the first things the child does
- The relevance of the first session for future sessions
- Underlying theoretical and practical issues

GEMMA'S FIRST SESSION

Gemma was looking too smart for the playroom, and was perhaps slightly nervous as she came in, but seemed pleased to see me. (See p. 33 for background information.) She picked up a doll. I reminded her she could do more or less as she likes, and that this place isn't like being at home, being at school or in hospital. Gemma takes the doll to the shop, which she tidies. 'Come on, baby, let's put you in your chair. Shush.' She answers the phone 'No, no, I mostly have to stay here now. Sorry. Bye. Thanks.' Referring to puppets, she tells me 'Oh, these are things my friend's got in school. What's he? Got some legs, this one has. Let's tidy the toys up.' Gemma sings and talks. 'I'm sorry, the shop's closing now.'

Gemma hits the punchball hesitantly, exaggeratedly claiming that it nearly knocked her out.

Looking at some toy rabbits 'I thought they were real'. There are two carrots, which she gives to her first and second favourites. 'This is nice' and she puts flowers into the rabbits' cage.

'Uugh!' touching the paints. Gemma quickly rummages through the musical instruments.

Going into the home corner 'This place is messy'. [You keep your toys tidy] – the play therapist knew this, having visited her at home. 'I've tidied up my shop, and now I'm tidying where I live. Ready for cup of teas – for all my babies. I've got three babies, two of my best dresses.' She puts one potty in the home corner and one in the shop. Discovering the first baby in the shop, Gemma says 'Did I leave you in my shop, baby? Come on'. She asks where her escort is, and I factually reply.

'I bought my little cat – he smells lovely' she says, pointing to a material cat on her belt, which she hangs on the fire extinguisher. 'Mary (the escort) says she'd been here to see you before.'

'Two cots for my two lovely babies.' Gemma collects the big playroom broom. 'Taking this to my house to sweep up. The other baby can walk.' [She's a bit bigger.] To the doll Gemma says 'I'll come with you because you can't walk that good, can you? There are lots of ants round here.'

'Just going to phone mum up. "Hello. Yes. Yeh. Yeh. That will be nice. Bye. Thanks." ' Pretend-pours drinks out. To the babies 'Get your dinners ready as well'. Gemma asked where the Hoover was, having thought she remembered it on the photos, but we didn't have a Hoover. I fetched the photos, and she couldn't spot it. Gemma explored a cupboard.

'Better go back inside my house. Just going to make your beds.' she puts the small baby in a high chair. 'I might have to go back in my shop. You (baby) can come with me. You'll be all right here? I'm sure you will. I've got to do some ironing as well, you know.' Gemma gave food to the babies, plus bowls and spoons. 'I think the house is just about tidy. Phew! Kettle's ready for all of you to have a drink.' Gemma makes tea. 'I don't take sugar. Sometimes I do – depends what drink it is. That was delicious. Come on, eat up, what's wrong with you? You must have been hungry, eating a big fish like that. Good girls.'

I realized I'd forgotten to put out the feeding bottles and dummies, which I fetch, reminding her that she can do things here that she might not be able to do elsewhere, and she can say what she likes. I also mention that she can help herself to refreshments. Gemma comments that the playroom is 'better than I thought'.

'All got your bottles and dummies now, so shush. You've got to go to bed before I go back to my shop. I've got to get more food.' She tidies away the babies' clothes that she had removed when they went to bed, making sure the children were securely tucked up. They were given a dummy and a full bottle of squash. 'My little pushiboo. You can put your lovely dress on in the morning. There. Phew! Now they're asleep I'll wash up and have to go. The house is quite tidy. Just need to do the ironing.'

Gemma looks at a stuffed dog. 'He's lovely. What's he meant to be?' I say it can be what she likes here. 'He could be my horse. I've always wanted a horse.'

Gemma looks at the dressing up clothes. 'Lovely. This could be the room where I put on my nice smart clothes.' She puts on a gold jacket, a cowgirl skirt and a red felt hat and looks at herself in the mirror. 'Wet sandtray', she observes.

'I better go to my shop now. Good boy, horse, you be good, I'll have to go to sleep now. People will be saying 'Why isn't the shop open? No other shops open round here' . She irons her hat. 'I'm going now, children, and be good. The house is just about clean. I'm in a rush now. Yes, I've got to go now. Mummy will be back later – she's always back later. Bye.'

'Shop's open. No, I just have to do something. Shop's coming open. Hooray, isn't it? I'm awfully sorry for the delay. My children have been pestering me a bit. What would you like? 40p. I'm awfully sorry, I've run out of that. I'll look in the store room. I think we've run out. Oh, lucky, one package left. Here's the tin. Be careful with it. Bye. Take this inside. Someone might steal it. Getting to be quite dark. Have to go home now. That's me done for today.'

Gemma collects cuddly toys. 'They're all ever so nice.' She gives one to each baby and has one herself. 'It's home time now', and she takes off her dressing-up clothes.

'Quite a hard day. Lots of crowds. Hallo (to horse), come on, get up.' She checks the rabbits 'All all right'. Gemma tells me she hates guns. 'Goodbye' patting the horse. In the home corner. 'I wonder what time it is? Bed time' The phone rings. 'Hallo. I'll come round tomorrow with them. Bye. Time for me to get into bed'. Gemma climbs into bed and snores. 'Five o'clock in the morning. The horse needs some food, I can hear him neighing. Ooh. Better get some carrots for the bunnies.' To one of the babies 'I'll get you some drink in the bottle. You've woken your big sister. You naughty little girl. I'll get you some. Now come on, both of you get to sleep. Mummy's been up nearly all night. Not morning yet, you know. Teddy's asleep, and my bear's asleep too.'

Gemma looks at the dolls' house. 'Mess here as well'. Returning from the toilet 'Uugh, horrible!' as she briefly touches the wet sand.

Gemma made two feeding bottles of squash, pouring herself a mug of squash. She took two biscuits, but did not eat them. She gave the bottles to the babies. 'Back to bed now. All the children done. I'm awfully tired. It's been quite a hard day today' and she gets into bed. 'Children, go to sleep. Your bottle's full, now shush. Nine o'clock. Oh no. The children are asleep. Better than normal – they were awake last night. Rabbits are all right.'

Gemma paints a person with a bright outside but a jumble of squally colours inside. She puts on some different dressing-up clothes.

'Oh, the children still aren't awake. I'll have to go to my shop soon, even if they aren't awake. My horse will come and tell me if they need anything, I'm sure he will. He did last time.' She requests that the painting be put up in the home corner, saying the children did it.

Gemma asks the horse to tell her if the children wake up, and she goes to the shop, putting on different dressing-up clothes. 'Quite early this morning. I could stay at home but I decided ...'. Phone: 'Hallo. Children's shop. Can I help you? Would you like me to save it? Some coffee. OK, I'll save the last pack for you. OK. Bye.' She draws the curtains back so that the people know the shop is open.

'The children are awake. I'll have to come out of my shop. The biggest is always awake. It should be the youngest, I used to hear.' To the 'older child', 'I'll let you sit in my nice chair and if I hear anything I'll be very angry with you. You can walk now – you're getting cleverer and cleverer each day. When your little sister wakes up you better come and tell me. If you don't I'll be quite angry. I've warned you, so there you are.'

Back in the shop there's some confusion as the customer comes for the thing she had ordered, but Gemma thinks it is a new customer, so refuses initially to serve her until the problem is sorted out. The shop closes.

I told Gemma that we would have to finish the session in about five minutes.

She was back in the home corner. 'Hasn't she woken up? A lady's been to my shop today. She asked me if I'd like to go on holiday with her. I'll be going in quite a while, but not yet. I'll have to go soon. I'll find someone to look after you, but I'll have to go soon. Time for you to go to bed. Don't be upset about it.' She puts the big doll to bed. 'If your sister cries, tell her not to be upset about it. I have to go on holiday. I have to have a break from you some time. I've finally found a time to have it. Don't cry. I'll be staying tonight. I'll go to bed but in the morning you might have found that I've gone.'

The telephone rings. 'Hallo, yes. I've told my children I'll be coming on holiday with you. My children are a bit upset. I've put a sign on the shop saying I'll be going and the shop will be closed for a bit. Bye, see you in the morning.' To the children 'Go to bed now. When I wake up it'll probably be morning.'

Gemma takes off the dressing-up clothes and gets ready to leave the playroom. I tell her that I'll see her at the same time next week, that the same play things will be there though a few of them might be in different places. Going through the door, Gemma observes 'It's quite cold out.' She forgets her fragrant cat, which I give her.

The play therapist's written observations after the first session

1. The first thing Gemma picked on was the baby, so this may be where the work lies.
2. Great emphasis on tidying up the mess. This may verge on the compulsive: a defence against her inner chaos?
3. Gemma protested against guns, wet sand and paints. This, again, is perhaps where the work lies. Is part of her denying the chaotic bit inside which, according to the referral, bursts out sometimes?
4. Inner chaos is possibly exemplified in her painting, which fits her neat and assuming *persona*, a neat outside but a jumbly inside.
5. Although a bit old for her years in some ways, Gemma appears to be an excellent carer. Her conversation with her children is mostly sweet-toned, kindly.
6. I suspect that she is over-compensating, and that she needs a lot of care herself.
7. I was struck by how she handled the termination phase of the session, actually playing out the ending for her 'children' by going into the holiday phantasy. She must have had so many endings in her life. I felt she did it quite caringly, though I am struck by the magnitude of this part of the play.
8. Her final comment was that it was 'quite cold out'.
9. Gemma played by herself, creating several roles, but I felt included, if at a distance. I also felt extremely inadequate as she pointed out the deficiencies of the playroom!

Exercise

- What do you feel about this first session?
- Has the groundwork for this referral been adequately prepared?
- What sort of greeting is appropriate for the child, and how will you set the scene?
- What are the most important things for you to do and remember?
- How will you record the session?
- How soon after the first session can you discuss it with your consultant/supervisor?
- What will you do if you feel distressed and puzzled by what happened?
- When embarking on a new referral, write a motto
  - for yourself
  - for the child.
- Pretend that you are six years old and are going for your first play therapy session
  - how do you feel?
  - what are you expecting?
  - what are you thinking about?
  - what would help you feel OK about going to the playroom?
  - what would *your* motto be?

THEORETICAL AND PRACTICAL POINTS ABOUT FIRST SESSIONS

The first session is crucial *(Allen, 1964, pp. 101–5)*, setting the scene for what is to follow *(Ginott, 1982a; cf. Axline, 1964f, p. 22)*, and should be recorded as fully as possible and discussed with the consultant *(Despert, 1964, pp. 110–14)*. It is important that conditions are right and that preparation has been thorough (Chapter 4). The first session often reveals the work that the child needs to do, and points to the way that the work will be achieved *(Howarth, 1990, pp. 39, 41–2)*. Note the initial thing a child does as, in retrospect, this often holds the key.

If photographs of the building and playroom have already been shown, the child probably experiences a sense of some familiarity as the building is approached. The play therapist is available so that there is no need to wait, and, if they have previously met, it is helpful if the play therapist's appearance has not altered too drastically. A few children, particularly those who have been in hospital or in institutions, may express a desire to look round the building at some stage. This seems permissible, provided it does not happen every week, so that the child can see that the playroom is not a children's home or hospital in disguise, and a look round may set the child's mind at rest, particularly if previous adults in their lives have lured them into a false sense of security.

On arrival, the play therapist gives full attention to the child, in the escort's presence confirming what will happen to the accompanying adult during the session, and reiterating that the child will be collected at the end of the session. It is important, particularly for young children who do not have a developed concept of time, to stress that they *will* be returning home or back to school, and to link this with something in the child's daily routine, such as getting back in time for a meal, or playtime. Six-year-old Angela had been in care but was now at home with her single-parent mother, who had brought her for play therapy. The play therapist might say 'Mummy is going to do some shopping now, but she will come back for you in an hour and then you will go home together for dinner'. A clock on the playroom wall can show children how long they have in the room.

Take a child's-eye view of the playroom. Try to make it look inviting, without too much clutter and stimulation, so that there is space in which the child can decide what to do. It is neutral territory on which children can impose *their* phantasies and needs. To value children and to allow them autonomy in this way are probably puzzling experiences, and it can help put the play setting in perspective if the play therapist clarifies that the playroom is not like being at school, nor home (nor at a youth club, hospital, children's home, or wherever else the child knows), but that it is a place that is theirs for a regular time each week where they can do (almost) what they want.

Axline's eight basic principles (p. 154) are useful; begin where the child is, accepting her or him as she (or he) is. Do not praise, cajole or, perish the thought, threaten. Reflect what the child may be feeling. 'Perhaps you feel excited, seeing all these things, and you don't know what to do first.' 'I wonder whether it feels scary in here with me and you're not sure what's going to happen.' The child's words, gestures and feelings are important, and the play therapist's task is to understand the child's signals and endeavour to help the child feel safe.

Children approach the first session in, broadly, one of three ways. Some plunge into activity and are soon engrossed in play, maybe involving the play therapist, maybe not, perhaps checking whether it is all right to do such and such a thing. Other children feel uncertain and a little lost. Provided the play therapist has done his or her best to ease the child's entry into the playroom, the therapeutic role is not to rescue an inactive child nor to become directive or crowd the child. The play therapist can empathically verbalize what the child might be feeling, saying things like 'I wonder if it feels strange here and you're not sure what to do or what is expected', 'Perhaps it's hard because a part of you wants to look at the toys, but a part of you is scared.' It is better if the play therapist can sit out the child's resistance or difficulty, but this is not easy, especially for new therapists. If the atmosphere seems too uncomfortable with a 'stuck' child, the play therapist could invite the child to look round, offer to explore the playroom together, or perhaps give the child a choice of two or three activities. If the child appears shy, reserved and uncertain as to what to do, the worker might say 'Here we do what we like', setting an example by, for instance, playing with some cars, keeping an eye on the child who may then find his or her own way of relating to the playroom and play therapist.

Some children, especially those deprived of toys and the opportunity to play, might be so overwhelmed by a well-stocked playroom that they just *look* at toys, or rush from one to another and, on rare occasions, the play therapist might consider restricting the range of material for the first few sessions. A few children might boisterously ransack the room in the first ten minutes!

Playroom limits are discussed on pp. 175–9. Some children feel overwhelmed by total permissiveness and freedom, so the play therapist may indicate some of the boundaries fairly early in the first session. With other children, boundaries are fed in as the need arises. Parameters about which rooms the child can use are important. Show the child where the toilet is and, if refreshments are offered, what the play therapist's expectations are about this. The play therapist may need to explain audiovisual equipment, show children if an observation screen is being used, and let them know if the session is being recorded.

At some point it may be wise to get the child's perceptions of who you (the play therapist) are, your name, what the child thinks is the purpose of coming to the playroom *(Winnicott, 1984, p. 21)*, and at the end it is often useful to recapitulate when the next contact will be, and ask how the child is feeling.

Play therapists who take notes during the session may want to say why they are writing. The explanation varies according to the child's age, but phrases like 'I'm writing about our time in the playroom', or 'It helps me remember the things we do' are usually acceptable. The majority of children do not appear to be bothered by note-taking, but it should be made clear that the child is more important than the writing. Sometimes obliging children do not want to interrupt the play therapist's 'work'. Other children will check whether certain things have been recorded. Yet others will 'help' write the notes. Children who do not like notes taken, or who may on occasion feel that the writing gets in the way, will usually tell the play therapist in no uncertain fashion!

During the course of the session, the play therapist may clarify that the child will not be expected to tidy up (if that is the case), and confirm that the child will be coming for the next few weeks. Young children usually have a grasp of the concept of school terms, or holidays, or religious occasions or birthdays, so saying something like 'You can come here every Tuesday afternoon until Christmas' is probably sufficient at the beginning, bearing in mind that play therapy may continue beyond that time and that 'extending beyond Christmas' will be discussed with the child at an appropriate stage.

Throughout the session the play therapist concentrates on letting the child lead the way and on reflecting something about what the child may be doing or feeling. The play therapist is confirming the child's *being*, giving space to the child to *become*. This may be a new experience for some children as well as workers, not all of whom (workers or children) find it comfortable at first. It helps if the play therapist endeavours to relax and enjoy the session, with detached awareness that enables both involvement in, and observation of, the process, without being too self-conscious. The working relationship between child and play therapist, the therapeutic alliance, which is made up of the play therapist's sense of self, technical knowledge and intuitive understanding of troubled children and of the therapeutic process, is one of the important factors in the overall success of play therapy as it activates the healing potential in the human psyche *(Jung, 1966, quoted in Allan, 1988b, p. 99)* and, without it, play therapy may founder *(Fordham, 1978, p. 91)*.

Remember that you convey information by your attitude and approach, as well as your words.

'I'm called Janet. What do you like to be called?'

'I'm someone who plays/spends time with children when they feel all upset and muddled inside. I'm not a social worker, or a police lady, or a …'.

'It seems that some days you feel a bit unhappy/sad/angry (or whatever). Coming to the playroom sometimes helps children feel better/make sense of what has happened.' (You, or the child, may want to be more specific.)

'You're not coming as a punishment because you've been naughty.'

'Your mum and teacher know that you're coming to see me, and it's OK by them.'

'Coming to the playroom isn't like being at school, or Cubs, or hospital … It's the sort of place where you can choose what to do, and I'll make sure we all keep safe.'

'Sexy touching's not allowed, and we won't hurt each other.'

'I'll be here, or play with you if you ask me.'

'You don't have to do anything if you don't want to.'

'So-and-so will bring you to the playroom (details about how this will happen) on Mondays, the day you go back to school after the weekend. So-and-so will bring you at morning break, and you will be back at school in time for dinner.'

'We'll see each other every Monday until the holidays. We can carry on afterwards, if you want to, but we'll talk about that a bit later.'

'Your mum will let me know if you can't come because you're ill. If I'm ill I'll make sure someone tells you when I'll be able to see you again.'

'You can tell anybody you want to about what happens in the playroom. I'll have a chat with (the person who referred the child) now and again, but I'll tell you and we can decide what you would like me to say. Also I'll go to your reviews; I'll tell you about it, and ask you what you would like me to say to the people. I won't usually see your mum.'

'If you told me someone had hurt you, or had been sexy with you or another child, then we would have to think together whom we should tell.'

'This is your time, to use as you like.'

'I'll tell you a few minutes before we finish and it's time to go back to school.'

'We can have a drink and some biscuits/fruit. What sort do you like?'

'The toilet's there.'

'Shall we find out how this works?' (video, audio system, one-way screen).

'This is what we could do about tidying up …'.

ANDREW'S FIRST SESSION

Andrew looked round the room, took off his coat and dug in the sand. (See p. 33 for background information.) He unpacked a box of cars, picking out a helicopter 'I had one of these and I broke it'. He shot me from across the room, then, apparently randomly, shot out of the window. He went into the home corner. Back to vehicles in the sandtray. Further exploration of the room, communicating with me through his eyes. He asked about the building we were in, then returned to the sandtray. The play flitted between the home corner and sand. There was further exploration of the play equipment.

Andrew carefully selected a lorry, crashing it through other cars. He connected some wagons together, playing with a tank with great gusto. He seemed to get excited and packed cars into the garage, crashing some off the roof.

More quiet home corner play. In another part of the room he sat down, looking round. Lots of messy water and sand play.

A look of disappointment as the session neared its end. He had a drink, put the cars back into the box and tipped more water into the sand. He asked if he could take a tank home, but was told that playroom toys had to stay in the playroom.

The play therapist's thoughts on Andrew's first session.

1. I was impressed with Andrew's quiet inner confidence. Much of the time he was absorbed, talking quietly under his breath. He didn't appear to 'need' me actively.
2. The main themes seemed to be:
   (a) Cars into and on top of the garage – a sequence of crashing the cars, five in all. Are these part of his family? Or bits of himself that he wants to crash?
   (b) The gun. He shot me at the beginning. At the end of the session I found the gun buried in the sand. Aggression (or fear, or whatever the gun stands for) can be contained? Or needs burying?
   (c) A lot of sand play – he really *used* it, soaking it. Very engrossing for him, putting the two elements together.
   (d) Although he had seen the refreshments, he did not bother until the end of the session, when he took a biscuit (and wanted to take a tank) home.

POLLY'S FIRST SESSION

Polly bounced round the room. (See pp. 33–4 for background information.) She asked to see the building and to come back and finish playing. I agreed so that she could check that it was not a children's home or hospital in disguise. Polly wanted to take a doll with her on her tour of the building, and wrapped it up. 'Can I take the bag with me? She might not like it on her own. And a blue pen, so I can write where we're going. Ah, bastard!' as she dropped an armful of bedding. We inspected the premises. 'The baby likes it.' Back in the playroom Polly put the baby in the crib, 'It were nice, wasn't it?'.

'Don't be a baby, we've got one', she ordered, picking up a doll. She selected *Tootles the Taxi* to read to me later. Clutching a teddy, Polly told me she was the mummy, asking me, her big sister, to find her purse. Then she became the shopkeeper.

In the home corner Polly told me it would soon be dinner time. Then she asks for writing materials. 'What would you like me to write?' she enquires. 'Go to bed, and Santa will come at three o'clock. I'll cover you up when I've done this writing.' She is angry with me (the baby), threatening to leave home if I don't behave. She sorts out the dinner, telling someone on the phone about Santa. More food play. She brings a baby in the cot to where I am, plus food for all of us. It's night time and we go to bed.

The play therapist's thoughts on Polly's first session

1. After checking out the building, Polly was amazingly quick into the 'work'.
2. It seems that Polly will be working on her baby self, partly directly and partly at a distance, by turning me into the baby; and on her experiences of being mothered.
3. At times she needed to assert power and control over her environment.
4. I suspect she will be playing out a lot of her early experiences.

PETER'S FIRST SESSION

Peter donned a police hat and suggested fighting, but the latter did not immediately happen. (See p. 34 for background information.) He took pretend photos of me then created a big slope and we had to swoosh a car up. Then we scooted the car along the floor to each other. This was followed by intense fighting with swords and guns, and we hurled cushions at each other.

Peter found five vehicles, putting them in the sandtray. I had to make a road. He identified the smallest vehicle as the little boy; the 'little boy' and some other cars were stuck and we had to help them. 'Pretend the little boy is buried.' Peter identified two breakdown trucks, one a 'helper' for himself and I had one as a 'helper'. The buried vehicles were rescued, but were re-buried and this time the helper lined up the vehicles safely. 'Finished that.' He created big splashes designed to reach me. 'Get on you? Good.'

Peter slipped, knocking his knee, crying vigorously like a toddler and complaining he had grazed himself. I seriously first-aided the afflicted place, realizing that I was working with earlier grime and an old scar! He played with the garage.

The play therapist's thoughts on Peter's first session

Peter used the session effectively. The main impressions I had were:

1. Anger, kept within bounds, but he needs to be able to ventilate it and, maybe, eventually to name with what, or whom, he is angry.
2. It seemed that in the sandtray Peter had outlined his predicament. He had

identified with the little car that was in danger of being swamped, buried, overtaken. With a helper, and some help from himself, he could get out. Earlier in the session he had made the cars try to drive up impossibly steep slopes – but at least they could move and had not broken down.

3. There was a regressive element, and a very hurt bit of him that needs care. He also plays age-appropriately.
4. He used me directly, and will probably work out a lot of his anger and pain on me.

Comfort for the play therapist

- Is the playroom warm, clean and inviting? Take a child's eye view.
- Are there appropriate play materials? Have you remembered to put out special items?
- Is the audiovisual equipment working? Are pen and paper to hand?
- What about the refreshments?
- Organize yourself so that you are ready on time. Welcome the child and escort. Check that the escort knows what to do and, in the child's presence, go over what time the escort will collect the child, and where the child will be returned.
- Invite the child into the playroom, keeping the welcoming comments to the minimum after the first session. If not involved in the play, seat yourself where you have a good overall view of the playroom.
- If appropriate, in the early stages you could emphasize to the child that this might feel a bit strange and scary, but it's OK if the child wants to look round.
- The child doesn't have to do anything.
- If providing refreshments, you might let the child know what your expectations are, whether he or she can help himself or herself, or whether they are to be had at a fixed time
- Warn the child that the session will be ending. Five minutes is usually considered adequate.
- Let the child know whether he or she is expected to tidy up.
- At the end of the session you could ask the child how he or she is feeling now.
- Remind the child about the next session. Accompany the child to find the escort.
- Return to the playroom and reflect on what has happened.
  - what was the process?
  - what was the content?
  - did you manage to be child-centred?
  - what about your counselling skills?
- Write up your notes, and tidy up.

Summary

In this chapter we have shared the case notes of the first sessions of the children whom we have already met, and read the therapist's post-session reflections. We learn that children use their sessions differently, and that the first thing a child does can indicate the key issues that will be worked on in therapy. Theoretical and practical aspects of first sessions have also been explored.

One of the things we discover in the first session is something about the play idioms through which the child communicates, and these are discussed more fully in the next four chapters.

FIRST SESSION CHECKLIST

1. Was the preparatory work effective?
   (a) Does it seem that carers, referrer, escort and school (and any other professionals) are clear about their respective roles as far as the play therapy sessions are concerned?
   (b) Does everybody know about the following: dates of sessions times of sessions transport arrangements to and from sessions?
   (c) What should happen if any of the people essential to a play session is ill, has to cancel or is on holiday?
2. Has the child been adequately prepared?
3. What are the rules for confidentiality? Is the child aware that there may, rarely, be things the play therapist might have to tell another grown-up?
4. Have you booked the playroom, and are the waiting facilities adequate?
5. If using audio- or videotapes, or a one-way screen, is the equipment set up and have the appropriate consent forms been signed?
6. If you have previously seen the child, is your appearance similar to when you first met?
7. Record the first session as fully as possible, including what you and the child say, feel and do. Note, in particular, the *first* thing a child does on entering the playroom. Are a pad and pen to hand? Have you set time aside to record?
8. On the rare occasion a parent or other adult is in the playroom (p. 181), ensure they are comfortably seated and indicate that they should not take any initiative, unless you ask them to, advising them that the child's attempt to engage them should be deflected to the play therapist or the toys.
9. Remind, or inform, the child of practical details:
   (a) when the session will end and who will take her or him home or back to school
   (b) where the lavatory is
   (c) what arrangements (if any) there are for refreshments
   (d) whether the child will be expected to tidy up.
10. Decide what the appropriate limits are likely to be (p. 175–9).
    (a) When will you inform the child about the limits?
    (b) What will you do if the child infringes the limits? *Warn, remind, action* are useful key words.
    (c) What is your ultimate sanction?
11. Prepare yourself for this vital first session. Focus your thoughts on the child. Do your best to feel into and empathize with the child.
12. Tidy up (if that is your lot!), and write your notes.
13. Afterwards, how did you feel in a client-centred play therapy setting? Were the methodological and theoretical frameworks clear?
14. Detailed consultation after a first session should help clarify what has happened. If the play therapist can understand and *accept* the child and the play (or lack of it), that understanding and acceptance should free the child to use the time in the most appropriate way for that individual.
15. What have you learnt about yourself from this session?

6 Relating through roles, relationships and words

It is mostly of no avail to treat ... arrested [psychic] development with reason alone. We must try to understand the symbolic language with which the many-sided psyche expresses itself in images.

(Kalff, 1980, p. 165)

- Some children relate mostly verbally, through roles and relationships
- Words, tone of voice, gestures and emotional content are important
- Children may act out scenarios in dramatic role play, sometimes casting the play therapist as co-actor
- Puppets are another means of exploring life events
- Some children, perhaps inviting the play therapist to participate, like telling or making up stories
- Many children enjoy being read to. Books, myths and fairytales that resonate to the child's experiences might be available
- Writing letters, stories and 'workbooks' are other methods of verbal communication
- Children who have experienced early deprivation may spontaneously enter a therapeutic regression
- Other aspects of early carer/baby play include hide-and-seek and hunt-the-object

Some children express themselves more through toys and art materials (Chapters 7 and 8); others relate predominantly through words, roles and relationships; others employ hybrid play (Chapter 9), a mix of the two, the emphasis sometimes shifting as play therapy progresses. Speech is direct communication with another person, quite a daring thing, and many children are more articulate with their fingers or through their actions than with words. Children who have problems in using language often experience a hold-up in human relationships so the play therapist waits until there is sufficient trust for the child to speak freely. Sometimes children play alone, sometimes they involve the play therapist, the child projecting his or her own needs into the (phantasy) role plays. The child can impose many roles on the play therapist, who at times may be actively involved and scripted by the child. Many children spontaneously re-create the baby or toddler state so that this time they can re-experience it differently.

Toby (see pp. 3–4)

'You don't know I've got many disguises, policeman and bus driver, motorbike man and doctor.' The scenario became complicated as I was, rapidly, the baddy, a girl called Helen whom the baddy was assaulting, and Helen's mother. I was told to murder someone and throw him off a wall, for which I was clapped into prison. Then it was Helen who had murdered, and I the mother to whom the police (Toby) broke the news, asking me (the mother) to go to the police station to see Helen, who had killed previously and was to be imprisoned.

In court I was the judge, Helen the defendant, and Toby variously the policeman, a witness and Helen's social worker. Toby gave evidence as the policeman. The charge was that Helen kills people by stabbing – sometimes provoked and sometimes unprovoked. The social worker (Toby), told the judge about Helen's background, advising that the only hope for Helen was to go to prison for life. Toby organized a funeral service, setting out chairs for the hearse, and resting the coffin on two chairs at the rear. We were so engrossed and had not realized time was up. I asked the escort to wait a few minutes, as it was important to finish this play. The coffin was lowered into the grave while we stood by reverentially.

I made links between the stabbing play and the assaults Toby had made with a knife. He said he sometimes got angry when provoked, and sometimes when not provoked.

Exercise

- What words, concepts and sentence structures do you use with the average five-year-old? The average eight-year-old? The average 12-year-old?
- How do you know whether the child is functioning at his or her chronological age?
- What listening skills do you use?
- How do you check whether you have understood the child?
- Do you encourage children to tell their own stories?
- What is a story? What props would you have available?
- Do you barge in to tell *your* story, or the story belonging to other children?
- Do you correct a child to tell the *right* story?
- If you were a child, how would you tell *your* story? Do this – in imagination, then actively.

DRAMATIC ROLE PLAY

- Spontaneous 'acting' is natural for many children.
- Grown-ups may feel self-conscious.
- Children select events relating to their inner and outer experiences. Themes from television and videos have an 'as if' quality, and are conveying messages about the child.
- Scenarios and roles can change quickly.
- When playing in role, ensure that your inner ears, eyes, thoughts, feelings and intuition are maintaining therapeutic awareness.
- You may be asked to dress up. What would be the most useful dressing up items?

Many children spontaneously enter into dramatic role play when they ascribe roles to themselves (and the play therapist). Children are often acute observers and have a detailed 'feel' for the roles they want, so the play therapist can be meticulously scripted and directed by the child in order to create the required effect. Toby and some of the other children we have met have already provided some examples of role play. Dramatic play includes all variations from mime to improvized acting, role play, or a set play. Gemma performed a wonderful parody of a slapstick seaside show, liberally insulting her play therapist audience. Smaller children are 'acting out' when they let the dolls take roles representing themselves and their parent-images. Some children dress up and project themselves into another character from which a phantasy develops *(Bettelheim, 1976; Gondor, 1964; Irwin, 1983, p. 166)* and through which they express inner needs and urges. Other children enact dramas around a current problem in their everyday life. For instance Toby set up some scenes in which he was bullied, subsequently becoming the bully, then the policeman who prevented bullying. Twelve-year-old Keith scornfully berated the teacher (play therapist), himself becoming the teacher and demonstrating how much better a job he could do.

In role plays, relationships between the two 'protagonists' can become very 'real' as experiences are shared *(Fine, 1979; Moreno, 1946, 1959, 1969)*. The play therapist felt awful when Toby angrily shouted at and ridiculed her, speculating that she was perhaps experiencing how he felt when his mother and stepfather gave him confusing commands and belittled him.

PUPPETS

Exercise

- Make yourself some puppets. Which would be most useful? Try out various types.
- Relax and let the puppets tell a story.
- Which puppets do you identify with, and why?
- Could you use puppets in other areas of your life?
- Be a child and make puppets from paper bags, cardboard, etc. Use them, and have fun!

Puppets are popular with some children *(Hawkey, 1979, p. 360)*, are a rich source of symbolic play and can be a helpful therapeutic aid *(Irwin, 1983, pp. 159–64)*. Shy children sometimes speak more fluently 'behind' the puppet, which says and does things the child might find too difficult to express overtly, and for which he or she does not feel so responsible *(Currant, 1985, pp. 55–60; Oaklander, 1978, p. 104)*. There may be occasions when, if involved by the child, the play therapist might encourage the child to elaborate on certain aspects, or provide alternative scenarios *(Marcus, 1979, pp. 375–6)*.

Six-year-old Peter played with the family puppets (see p. 34). The mother puppet was dreadfully rough with the little boy puppet; then the little boy and wolf attacked the mother, getting the better of her and putting her in the rubbish bin. On this occasion the play therapist accepted what Peter had acted out, saying that sometimes it is hard for little boys when they don't like what the mother does to them, and they feel angry and want to get rid of the mother. Toby put on several puppet shows, the themes varying. Sometimes the bold animals would go in search of a timid rabbit, the rabbit being overjoyed to be found and to discover that the big animals were taking an interest in it. When playing with family puppets, there tended to be mayhem, though as play therapy continued puppet family scenes became more constructive.

Puppet collections vary. Since children's problems usually centre round the home situation, a cluster of characters is important *(Woltmann, 1964, pp. 395–9)*. Some selections include happy and unhappy parental figures and assorted children. Other play therapists prefer the archetypal king and queen, prince and princess, a crying and a smiling baby, the wicked witch and wizard. Yet other collections are a 'family' of animals, with additional friendly and wild creatures. Stereotyped interaction between puppets seen on television may be less useful, but there are exceptions.

Twelve-year-old Martin was sometimes outgoing with his play therapist and sometimes withdrawn, perhaps mirroring the ambivalence he felt towards his mother but was unable to express freely (see p. 92):

> He picked up one of two emu puppets. 'What's this? Oh, an emu' and he manipulated its face into a fearsome expression, attacking me. I fought it off. It attacked me more ferociously, pinning me down by the back of my neck. Martin's expression was hard and determined.

A few weeks later:

'Let's have a fight' and our emus fought violently. He was very strong, but didn't quite hurt me. He caught my emu's legs between his own legs, and I screamed and wailed, hoping that he would shout to get rid of the tension that I sensed was bottled up inside him. He responded, but fairly mutely. He commanded my emu to be dead, and I made it twitch so Martin angrily attacked it, finally beating it with his emu's legs. They died.

STORIES AND WORD GAMES

Some children tell stories, often 'about a boy' or 'about a girl', or a person or animal with whom the child identifies *(Mitchell, 1981; Wood, 1988)*. An extension of this is the 'mutual storytelling technique' *(Durfee, 1979, pp. 406–8; Gardner, 1979, pp. 313–21)*. When the child tells a story the play therapist tries to ascertain its (sometimes hidden, symbolic) meaning, and may relate another story based on the same theme(s) but with alternative adaptations and resolutions of the conflicts that were thrown up by the child's tale.

It was possible that the surgery ten-year-old Pam had undergone had affected her brain, and she introduced a sequence of memory games. She and the play therapist took turns to buy and play musical instruments, adding a new item to their list each time it was their turn. Because Pam had been 'living in her head' and the play therapist wanted to encourage her to 'live more in her body', the play therapist suggested that they could mime, or dance, to the music as well. A bit later:

She makes up a game about instruments being broken and we start with eight, working down to one, having to remember which ones we'd discarded, and why. She has a final fling when the instruments are all mended. She got the large xylophone refuelled, and the instruments that were 'broken' ended in full vigour.

The next week Pam said that they would play a game about visiting a cake-shop. Similar to the musical game, a different cake was added each time. She reverted to the musical instruments, play therapist and child selecting an instrument with which they made appropriate actions, so there was a drum for marching, a mouth organ for a jolly dance, a triangle for a clock dance, a tambourine for a Spanish dance. There were variants on the musical instrument game: on how many instruments could each person play three notes in 30 seconds? How many instruments could be played at the same time? Kim's game taxed the memory too! A sequence of sand games was invented, the play therapist having to guess what Pam was making in the sand. In her last session Pam and the play therapist mimed using an instrument in an unorthodox way, having to guess what the instrument was. The mimes became more open-ended, the most imaginative of Pam's being an orchestral conductor whose tambourine player arrived late.

Peter made up a game whereby the play therapist had to close her eyes whilst he clambered on the furniture, and she had to guess how he had got to wherever it was. This seemed to express Peter's puzzlement about what had happened to him in the past and the almost magical way he had been transposed from one placement to another. The 'game' persisted until Peter began to feel more secure.

Exercise

- What stories can you remember having an impact on you as a child?
- What would your own collection of playroom books contain?
- Can you enable children to tell *their* stories and not impose your own, e.g. if taking turns in storytelling?
- Sometimes pictures and photos, sounds and smells, evoke stories.
- Be prepared to work with the child's phantasies and not to dismiss them as 'It wasn't quite like that …'. Perhaps say 'Tell me more about …'.
- Enjoy reading children's books and comics, and watching children's television and videos.

THE WRITTEN WORD

- If the child asks, help with spelling but otherwise do not teach the child or control what is written.
- Burning up writing (and drawings), especially if about nasty things, can be therapeutic. Beware smoke alarms!

'For children under some kind of stress written communication may be of considerable significance' *(Crompton, 1980, p. 116)*. Eleven-year-old Jean was a paradox of a girl and was both young and old for her years. In a low stream at school and overwhelmingly attention seeking, Jean took a responsible attitude towards her brother, who lived elsewhere, and towards life in general. Much of her play therapy was about communication, relationships and regression. Initially she brought photographs to her sessions, explaining about and puzzling over family relationships, and making greetings cards for all and sundry. Then letter-writing took over. At Jean's instigation she and the play therapist took it in turns to sit in the home corner and receive their respective letters through the letter box. For example:

> Dear Tabitha
> I hope you are keeping well after this letter I will paint some pichers [*sic*] for you to put in your house and I will make some for Margaret and Diana. See you soon.
> Lots of love,
> Jean
> X

(Margaret and Diana were secretaries.)

The play therapist sent a letter to Jean when she missed a session because of measles, and Jean replied (Figs 6.1 and 6.2).

Towards the end of play therapy it became appropriate to move Jean from weekly to fortnightly sessions. This was discussed with her, then confirmed in a letter which the play therapist wrote, Diana typed and Margaret illustrated (see Fig. 6.3).

Seven-year-old Wendy loved writing, created her own book about being in the playroom, and set her play therapist word puzzles. She was a bright child, but had dislocated herself from her feelings, so gradually the play therapist encouraged her to dance some of the things about which she was writing. This, coupled with 'feelings' games and a supportive foster home, seemed to help, and Wendy became more spontaneous, alive and less 'in her head'.

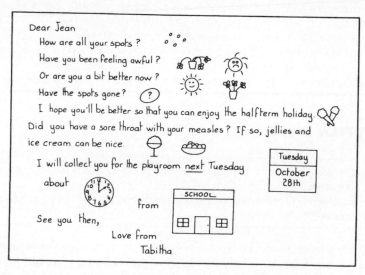

Figure 6.1

Dear Tabitha Diana and Margaret

Thank you very much for the get well card that you sent to me.
you will be pleased to know that my measles is much Better now
and Im able to play out It is halfterm tomorrow and Im going to
spend it with my Foster Mum once again thanks a lot

       Lots of Love

       Jean

    XXXXXXXXX
    XXXXXXXXX
    XXXXXXXXX
    XXX XXXXX

Figure 6.2

Dear Jean,
I said I would write you a letter and here it is!   I'll bring
you to the Playroom on

      Tuesday - 7 February

      and Tuesday 14th February

On Tuesday - 21 February the man from London is coming to see me, so
I'll send you a letter   that week.

Then it will be

      Playroom - Tuesday - 28 February

      Letter - Tuesday - 6 March

      Playroom - Tuesday - 13 March

      Letter - Tuesday - 20 March

      Playroom - Tuesday - 27 March

      Letter - Tuesday - 3 April

      Playroom - Tuesday - 10 April

Then it's the Easter holidays. We'll work out the summer term a
bit later.
      with love
      from
      Tabitha

Jean kept the letter and coloured the drawings.

Figure 6.3

Exercise

- Try writing with your non-dominant hand (i.e. if you are left-handed, use your right hand, and vice versa) on lined paper.
- Take off your adult head, spell phonetically, and 'forget' rules of grammar, layout and punctuation.
- Use children's words and sentence structure.
- Look at children's written work.

THERAPEUTIC REGRESSION

- Children may revert spontaneously to an earlier age, maybe to a point where their needs were inadequately met.
- There is a qualitative difference between children who are experiencing their own regression, and those who are undertaking ordinary 'baby' play.
- Some children systematically go back through the developmental stages to baby-hood and then regrow.
- Other children go fairly directly to infancy, and regrow.
- A few children replicate their birth.
- Typically the regression happens in bits and pieces – a bit here, another bit there – amongst other play themes.
- The play therapist plays parental and other roles assigned by the child unless, usually at a later stage, the therapist decides to model alternative parenting.
- The therapist should be careful that the touching involved in baby play is not interpreted sexually, nor should it become sexual.
- Only very rarely does the regression slip out of the playroom with the child. Carers and/or the school should inform the play therapist if this happens.

Therapeutic regression is normal *(Harter, 1983, p. 121)*, is often considered valuable *(Fordham, 1978, pp. 136–7)* and is a term used when children revert to earlier ways of behaving; a six-year-old may act like a toddler, a ten-year-old as a baby. Some children regress when the pressures are too great or when they have sustained a traumatic event or loss *(Gumaer, 1984, p. 8; Jewett, 1984, p. 34)*, returning in behaviour and attitudes to a period when they felt safer and less was demanded. Others regress because of a need to re-experience a developmental phase that was not suitably handled at the time. Regression in play therapy

> … may be expressed not only in the materials used but in the type of play –
> the child in phantasy takes over the role of others and constitutes herself the
> mother, the teacher, or the baby in scenes in which for the moment she lives,
> disclosing, as she plays, her individual conflict. *(Jackson and Todd, 1964, p. 318)*

After various phantasy adventures, Toby (p. 4) said he wanted to play the 'naughty baby's game' and he looked for the feeding bottle and dummy. As a baby, and then a squalling toddler, Toby tipped up most of the play boxes, running off and ransacking the house. In the session a fortnight later Toby, as a combination of little boy, baby and puppy, threw the baby doll from the crib, into which he clambered, asking for feeding bottle and dummy, and he re-grew himself in a calmer environment.

In Polly's early life there had been inconsistent, erratic, sometimes inadequate parenting, and from being a baby she had had to fend for herself and had shown an independent, unbiddable streak (p. 33–4). Polly was a striking example of how a child spontaneously initiated regression. *She* knew the work she needed to do in her play therapy. In her first session she took control, ordering the play therapist to be the baby and Polly was the angry mother who left home threatening not to return. Polly fed the therapist/baby and herself with feeding bottles and sent the therapist/baby to bed (*Guerney, 1983a, p. 48*). Towards the end of the fifth session:

> She wants to become the baby and snuggles into my arms and I cuddle her, rock her, feed her with the bottle and stroke her, saying what a nice baby I've got. She asks for a bed and removes her shoes. Then she's a bigger baby, making ga-ga noises, and I respond likewise.

A week or so later Polly gave the play therapist some dinner (fish and potato), enquiring whether she could manage to eat it with a spoon whilst Polly fed the babies. The next session, having said she would be the baby and the play therapist the mummy, Polly made a bed and after a short time she asked the play therapist to hold and feed her. Then Polly 'fell downstairs', crying as she lay on the floor, but not expecting to be picked up. She also played at being dropped. Sometimes she lay on a cushion, sucking a bottle, making increasingly angry kicks. During regressive episodes, Polly used baby talk and ga-ga noises. She sat on the play therapist's knee looking at *Baby's First Book*, gradually picking more advanced books and jigsaws corresponding with her 'growth'. At a certain stage she crawled. 'Pretend I get bigger and bigger … pretend I'm smaller again.'

Several months later:

> 'Pretend I've brought you a present' and Polly wraps the baby doll. I unwrap it and am delighted to find the baby. 'She's very special for you.' This play is repeated. 'You can have her in your bedroom. Pretend you're excited and it's Christmas day.' Then it's my (the play therapist's) birthday and I'm nine. 'Pretend you drop the baby', which I do. 'You're not really sad, are you?' [I would be if I dropped a real baby.] 'Pretend you're 20 and you want to pick her up. You're the baby's mother.' I do as she asks, holding the baby carefully, stroking her. Polly sat on my knee and I cuddled her. She then wriggled to the floor between my legs. 'Pretend I want to go in the cot' and she squeezed herself into the doll's crib. 'You can lift me up' and I cuddle her as I had the doll.

The play therapist felt that Polly had created a rebirthing experience. After this episode, the intensity of angry mother/baby play disappeared.

Twice Peter (p. 34) fell in the playroom, on both occasions sobbing desperately and exaggeratedly for about 20 minutes, and he had to be cuddled and treated like a baby. From other things he said and did, it seemed that he was crying for himself and for the loss of and confusion about his real mother. Another sign of his regression was the extremely swampy play in the sandtray;

playing in this way may also have helped his soiling and wetting problems. Later, his messy play pushed the boundaries until the play therapist imposed limits, and he played out being a whimpering baby. In dolls' house play, the scared baby had to look after itself, being largely ignored by the parent figures. Sometimes the play therapist was the baby, and Peter the cruel, angry and inconsistent father.

Seven-year-old Rebecca declared that she needed to re-experience being a baby and, in several focused sessions, she went through the developmental processes from being a newborn baby to a two-year-old, at that stage saying that she was now all right, and had no further need for regression work.

To a greater or lesser extent many children spontaneously enter into therapeutic regression *(Irwin, 1983, pp. 150–1)*, knowing to which stage they need to return *(Dockar-Drysdale, 1990, p. 42)*. The play therapist helps by accepting, and responding to, what is happening, and by realizing that the child is reworking and re-experiencing something that was not satisfactorily accomplished at an earlier stage. Regression is usually short-lived and keeps within reasonable bounds, though if it impinges into the child's outer world, concerned adults may need reassurance. For instance, at a younger age, seven-year-old Wendy, whose foster placement was being jeopardized, had endured poor parenting and she went through a regressive phase in the playroom as she played out her negative experiences, but this time asking the play therapist to be a more adequate mother figure. Whilst this was going on, Wendy became unusually babyish at home. However, her schooling and peer relationships remained normal, and the foster parents were reassured that the immature behaviour would pass.

In 41 out of 47 sessions Martin (p. 92) spent much time reading, tucked away in a den. It could be argued that he was regressing to a safe, uninterrupted place. After initiating extensive hide-and-seek he attacked the play therapist, and what she stood for, with emu fights, snowballs and a sword.

> He goes to the water. 'What are these for?' indicating two boats and two containers. [For people to mess about with.] 'Are those (the containers) for sinking the boats?' [They can be what you want them to be.]' He swamps the boats, then says 'I'll play with the sand now. Make a sandcastle – the sand's not wet enough.' I ask what he can do about that. 'Put water in.' He moves to the Jack Straws game, and thrusts me dead with a small plastic sword. Martin's head emerges from his 'corner', 'I'm dead.' Comes to life. Pushes his body out. 'Head banging' as he knocks his head against the side. [Head banging] I echo. Clambers inside. 'Gone home. ET's gone home.' [ET's gone home] I say, reflectively. 'ET – ET hungry.' [ET hungry] I repeat softly. Martin shows me a biscuit. 'ET got some food,' to which I respond [ET's home and he's got some food]. 'Good' said Martin. [Good] said I.

Martin's speech and behaviour were uncharacteristically childish and there was an atmosphere of rebirth. ET was 'at home' in the corner-womb, and had food. *Wickes (1963, pp. 14, 20)* comments: 'The time [for dying] is when one phase of life has reached completion and is outgrown, and the germ of new being is ready for birth within the psyche', and ' … life is a process of deaths and rebirths. We must die to become'.

Exercise

- Find out as much as you can about your early life. Look at photos, revisit people and places, feel the feelings.
- Imagine yourself at various ages. What were the traumas in your life?
- Could *you* undertake a regression with your therapist?
- Can you see some of the frustrations and tensions in the lives of your own children?
- Observe and interact with children of all ages and from different backgrounds.
- What do you know about the lives of children from other cultures, and of children with disabilities?
- Improve your knowledge of normal and abnormal child development.

HIDE-AND-SEEK AND ALLIED GAMES

Children of all ages, in therapeutic regression, seem to delight in these games in which they are working on early trust and basic parent/infant relationships. The baby is partly pleased to find itself a separate entity, and partly afraid (*Alvarez, 1988*).

The play therapist wondered in Martin's case whether hide-and-seek indicated ambivalence about the sessions as well as regression and an urge, at some level, to be discovered.

> On arrival, Martin put his hand round the door. 'Come and find me' and thus ensued extensive hide-and-seek. We took turns, and he hooted if he felt one of us was getting stuck.
>
> Whilst I was hiding I was experiencing feelings of fright and pleasure. Do I/don't I want to be found? Pleasure when the tension was over and I *was* found. I wonder whether this is how he feels about fostering. Will he, or won't he, be found by a family? Is he, or isn't he, finding himself?

Kalff (1980, p. 47) suggests that in hide-and-seek children are showing that they are ready to have some of their 'secrets' or hidden selves uncovered, that they want to be searched for, and 'found'.

> Jean initiates a game of hide-and-seek and I remind her that we must remain within the playroom complex. She hides first. I pretend not to know where she is and eventually discover her under a cushion. When I hide for my second time, she adopts my way of commenting 'I wonder where she is? Is she in the ho ne corner? No. Is she behind the door? No. I wonder where she is?' The third time she hides she makes an excellent job of covering herself in blankets behind a long curtain. Each time she is found she squeals with delight.

The game of hide-and-seek was replaced when Jean asked for biscuits to be hidden, searching for them becoming a weekly ritual.

Other children initiate allied games of peep-bo, finding and linking fingers and hands in the sand, and of hunting for hidden objects. All these relate to 'am I?/aren't I?' 'will I/won't I be found (by the play therapist-parent)?'

- Think about the games that are typically played by carers and young children.
- Many of these games have a role in child development, especially in working on
  - 'who am I?'
  - loss versus continuity
  - 'am I findable?'
  - 'are you dependable?'.

Summary

Children in play therapy do not always use age-appropriate language to express themselves. Some create compelling role plays, their dialogue and ideas often bringing inner conflicts into the light of day. Others find it easier to project their scenarios on to puppets and dolls. A few children find satisfaction in telling stories or writing letters. Many children spontaneously enter into therapeutic regression, regrowing bits of themselves that were damaged the first time round, with some of the hide-and-seek games being reminiscent of early baby play.

Having looked at some of the ways children communicate through roles, relationships and words, the next chapter examines how children express themselves, often symbolically, using toys and play-based activities.

7 Relating through toys and play-based activities

Inside each child there is a story that needs to be told – a story that no-one else has yet had time to listen to.

(Winnicott, 1984, p. 21)

- There is overlap in all categories of play
- Some children play predominantly with toys and playroom materials
- Communication through roles and relationships may be secondary
- The play therapist may be actively involved, or a spectator and commentator
- Supporting and accepting the child's play is important
- Understanding something of the symbolism of the play may help us make sense of what is happening

---

Some children express themselves more easily using toys and play-based activities rather than speech and personal interaction. Playroom toys should lend themselves to imaginative, symbolic play and allow the revelation of feelings *(Boston, 1983b, p. 6; Ginott, 1961, pp. 240–5)*. Some play therapists select toys and other play materials that they think might evoke relevant play. For example, two dolls' houses and family dolls might be provided for children subjected to family breakdown; baby materials might be available for a child who might regress, or who might need to express feelings about a new baby in the family. Other play therapists have a wide range of equipment, but may focus on specific items if tackling a particular issue. Toys have the potential to act as transforming symbols and to tell a story. Of course, the play therapist cannot be exactly sure of the meaning of the play, and rarely would interpretations be conveyed to the child. Readers may find alternative explanations for the play material, but it is hoped that something about the language of symbolism will be conveyed.

Exercise

- Write, or draw, a list of play materials you think would be suitable for the playroom.
  - Why have you made this choice?
  - Have you taken into account the multicultural society?
- Pretend you are five years old. What would you like to find in the playroom?
- Do a similar exercise for the ages of eight, ten and 12.

HOME CORNER

Exercise ———————————————————————————————

- As a play therapist, then as a child, draw your ideal home corner.
- How does it reflect the multicultural society?

_____

The home corner is usually a play house, or the corner of a room. In the home corner children often portray what they have experienced at home, what they have witnessed, or what they phantasize about. The child may 'be' various ages, ranging from babyhood to old age, experimenting with roles and relationships. Some children who feel insecure bolt doors and windows; others throw things around; others are meticulous.

Gemma often used the home corner, carefully tidying, cleaning, making it more attractive, and looking after her 'children'. 'Having kids is very difficult', she observed. She telephoned the play therapist, inviting her to visit, serving some food she was trying out for the first time that had been recommended by the shopkeeper. In the play, Gemma talked about how much she had to do at home and what hard work it was, but she resisted offers from the play therapist friend to babysit so that Gemma could go out. Gemma observed 'Mummy (her birth mother) knew how to be a mummy, but she wouldn't be a mummy'.

Peter (p. 134) is somewhat different:

> He was telling the baby that the baby could not have any biscuits. 'Go away, you just woke the baby up. Silly woman' he hollers to me. 'You go down the cop's house', and he cooked the baby's dinner. He shrieked 'Someone keeps shouting at me to go away'. For no apparent reason, Peter threw the kettle, kicked a bowl and broke a brush. Fetching dry sand, he mixed it with water in the kettle, puddling it round the home corner, in the process tipping over his mug of drink.

On another occasion Peter ordered his play therapist into the home corner, made her clean it up, tied her hands behind her back, attaching her to an upturned basket where she remained for some time. Eventually she was freed, her 'father' deliberately placing her hands on the hot hob, and she was then hacked to bits before being turned into stew!

In these extracts the children are perhaps somewhat starkly illustrating some of their individual associations with 'home' and the sticky problems revolving round their early relationships (or lack of relationships) with their prime carers. When this play is accepted and worked through, energies may be transferred to other more mature types of play, with the home corner assuming age-appropriate status.

FOOD

The use the child makes of play food or actual refreshments can be informative. With some children, their play reflects that food is not a problem because, if it crops up at all, the food is sufficient, to the child's liking, and the play therapist is often invited, in whatever role, to partake of pretend delicacies in the home corner, or biscuits at the table. Other children, however, present a gloomier picture. In the play they may be denied food (either there is none, or it is withheld), or they may be tricked (they are told it is something they enjoy, but it turns out to be nasty), or they are deliberately fed poison and substances such as dog faeces.

Food is a basic essential that symbolically conveys valuing and caring, as well as having practical nutritional aspects, and children who have experienced problems with food tend either to binge on playroom biscuits, or to hoard them 'for later'. A few children will resolutely ignore refreshments until they feel cared for enough to relax, trust and take the playroom food. Children less traumatized at the early feeding stages respond more 'normally' to the availability of biscuits and a drink, partaking if they feel the need.

DOLLS' HOUSE AND DOLLS

Exercise

- Commercial dolls' houses are rarely exactly right. Design your own. Talk to other play therapists and discover what they find useful.
- Find the child-within, and discover what his or her ideal small house would be.

Some children choose never to play with the dolls' house; others do so occasionally.

'I'll make a house, shall I? It's a nice house, look. Two beds, so his brother can go to sleep as well. It's a nice house, ain't it? Nice, isn't it? Nice little house I've made. Will you make the downstairs? You might make it good. Where's the baby? Here's the lion to watch the house. Can the cot go downstairs? I'll put it upstairs with the mother and that, because that's where I used to sleep when I was a baby. Good, this house. Cooker to go downstairs' ...

This sequence occurred in one of Tim's sessions around the time he was making a den for the Incredible Hulk and himself (pp. 97–8) and was coming to terms with some of the turmoil in his home life. There was space for the baby in the new Tim's world (in his real life he, as a baby, had probably been considered something of a nuisance), and there was a cooker to provide nourishment.

Having spent some time playing with the doll's house, Toby (p. 4) pushed a lorry alongside the house and filled it with furniture. The lorry drove away, later returning the furniture to the dolls' house. The upstairs was well furnished, the downstairs sparse.

This could have represented a number of things. Toby was unsure whether he belonged in his own house, so figuratively moved out, but returned to reclaim possession. However, the furnished upstairs and bare downstairs *might* suggest that he felt better on his own than with the family, or that his foundations, ground floor, were a bit skimpy?

The next week Toby set out the dolls' house conventionally and, a few sessions later, additional furniture was added to the downstairs and Toby said 'This family's getting rich'. Around this time his relationships with his own family were becoming enriched.

Dolls' house play can be quite revealing. For instance, nine-year-old Brian made an explicit bedroom scene with a man lying on top of a woman and, from the way he described what was happening, which included some unusual observations, it seemed likely that he had first-hand knowledge. Eleven-year-old Jean had clearly identified with the children's home in which she lived, and set up a television lounge, a dining room with lots of tables and chairs, and strings of bedrooms.

Two dolls' houses can be useful. One child played out neighbours' quarrels with venom and foul language; another worked on her present and her future home.

Dolls fulfil a number of roles. Children may play realistically, putting dolls to bed, feeding them, taking them for a walk, and so on. In some instances, children may use the baby doll to express the baby part of themselves. What the child does to the baby (doll) is either what was done to the child when a baby, and/or is what the child has seen someone else do to a baby, or is wish fulfilment, and often over-compensates about what the child would have liked to have happened to the baby part of him- or herself. In an early session, Andrew had thrown a yellow car (probably symbolizing his father, pp. 79–80) at a baby doll in a crib, but five sessions later he was caring for the doll. This altered behaviour with the doll occurred around the time that Andrew was coming to terms with his stepfather.

For quite a while, Polly (pp. 33–4) was extremely angry with the naughty baby, eventually loving and caring for it. Another little girl constantly hurled the baby around the playroom until, at long last, she was able to tolerate her jealousy towards her small sister. Dolls have been stabbed, strangled, had their limbs cut off and put in the garbage pail; or they have been loved and nurtured. They have represented a congregation, a class at school, family members or residents in a children's home. They may be brought in as substitute characters in complicated role plays. The dolls get into all sorts of tangles and go through loving, as well as desperate, experiences.

Anatomical dolls favoured in some forms of disclosure work are probably not standard equipment in most play therapy rooms, but this is one of the areas where knowledge and experience are still evolving. Children who have used them for disclosure purposes may have particular views about anatomical dolls, either liking or loathing them. If such dolls are part of the playroom resource, the child may be wary and may welcome clarification about the difference between disclosure and therapy sessions.

CONSTRUCTION TOYS AND JIGSAWS

On several occasions eight-year-old Ann constructed imaginative scenes with Lego, the play therapist commenting that sometimes people feel in bits and pieces, but the pieces can be put together to make something. In using construction toys, children may be expressing how they have felt (even pre-verbally) about being 'broken up', a 'discarded piece' or 'joining together', 'making something new' as they move into substitute families or their own circumstances improve. Demolishing creations made from construction toys can be a vivid expression of feeling. Building and creating can be positive and satisfying, and may show that the child is in a forward-looking frame of mind. Philip (12), considered a duffer at school, made advanced Lego models in the playroom showing a good understanding of construction and 'mechanics'. He had high standards, and would break up items that were not exactly right. (Destroying work was one of his problems at school.) Having accomplished things to his satisfaction in the playroom, he became more self-confident, and agreed that his play therapist could talk to his teachers. From thenceforth he had an improving profile at school, and life at home also became much better.

Jigsaws may have an integrative function, and many children turn to them at times when they are literally puzzling over or are confused about something, when they are trying to make sense of what is happening, or are in the process of integrating some hitherto split-off part of themselves.

WEAPONS

Exercise

* You are a seven-year-old child.
  - what fighting weapons would you like to have in the playroom?
  - what weapons would you invent, if none were available?
  - why do you think grown-ups are sometimes upset about weapons?

Fighting is an inherent part of human nature, and many children want to act out using weapons. If none are available, weapons are likely to be invented, so great is the child's need to 'fight' in controlled conditions.

> Six-year-old Peter attacked me with sword and gun. When I fired back he deflected the bullets so they entered me. Having spanked the baby, Peter shot me in the genitals and mouth, rendering me dead/asleep. He tied me up, verbally humiliated me, and threatened me with a dagger. On another occasion Peter stabbed his reflection in the mirror, saying 'I don't care about me'.

In play therapy, weapons are used to defend the frightened, defenceless, immature parts of the personality and to attack outer threats. They can also be the means of getting rid of the old to make way for the new. Aggression does not necessarily indicate viciousness, is a healthy part of normal development, and children are constantly 'fighting' to overcome and become. Those who feel insecure are more likely to fight, unless they have been so overpowered and intimidated that the fight has gone out of them. Those who have been cruelly molested may be sadistic, wreaking on others what has happened to them, and acting out what they would like to do to their attacker if they were big or strong enough. Attacks on the play therapist tend not to be personal, but are more likely to be directed against what the therapist represents in the child's psyche.

> Twelve-year-old Martin shoots me several times and I play dead, coming alive and he shoots me again. Then he gave me a gun and instructed that we had to shoot each other. I stalked round the room and we fired at each other. Martin informed me when I was dead, taking my gun and removing the bullets, then making me alive again. Once when I was dead he barricaded himself with cushions, remarking 'Your bullets cannot harm me' and he was some superhero figure. I threw a woollen ball at him, saying that this might defeat him, but it didn't. He was invincible, but also gave me the power to come back to life. Then he rushed around with his gun, and I pretend-chased him with mine. After a quick scurry he was lying in wait behind some cushions and we had a further shoot-out. Then he ran off again and I chased him, varying our route.

This occurred around the time that Martin was trying to find himself in relation to the play therapist, about whom he had some ambivalence, and led into a more positive relationship.

Occasionally Andrew would shoot randomly, only later daring to shoot at his play therapist. Gemma and Polly were not much concerned with guns, though sometimes Gemma would ward off potential attackers and she indulged in some intensive sword skirmishes. Sword fighting can be energetic and taxing, the child usually telling the play therapist what to do. The majority of children are aware of the dangers of sword fighting, which they normally keep within reasonable limits.

TABLE AND OTHER GAMES

Not all play therapists approve of table games in the playroom, but games can have their uses *(Schaefer and Reid, 1986)*. If, when playing games, the child-centred approach is followed through and the child can do what he or she likes, the play therapist could comment that it is all right to cheat, or 'play like that' in the playroom, but that in other settings the child will need to adhere to normal rules. Some children let their imagination run riot and make up all sorts of extraordinary rules. With other children, games are more serious, children play earnestly, and the game can often represent some life situation. *Nickerson and O'Laughlin (1983, p. 184)* argue that, as in life, games have constraints and rules, thus offering 'an opportunity to tangle with and master (life's) complexities and vagaries in a telescoped and therapeutically focused manner'.

About halfway through his play therapy, table games replaced army warfare in Toby's sessions (p. 4). The game Misfits was one of his favourites, with draughts taking over and becoming the main battleground:

> During the session it occurred to the play therapist that the games were perhaps a different trial of strength from the Darth Vader/tank/Action men

episodes, and Toby confirmed this by volunteering that he imagined the game was a war.

The play therapist allowed Toby to take a game home between sessions, hoping that it would be a family activity, and table games for himself and the family were given as parting presents.

How the child feels when playing games, and the role in which the play therapist is cast, can be revealing. Is the child out to win at all costs? Is the child placating towards the adult? Is the play therapist urged to be powerful and vindictive? How does the child's approach replicate experiences in the child's outer and inner worlds?

CARS, ANIMALS AND VILLAGE TOYS

Andrew's play with these items is discussed as an example of how he chose to play out some of his problems with specific toys. Other children may select different artefacts to tell their story. Andrew (p. 33) had adequate language and seemed at ease with his play therapist, but did not verbalize much. By careful, quiet observation, being available when required, and scribbling detailed notes, the play therapist was able to watch his play and hypothesize what was happening. Although cars, animals and village toys are written about separately, they could be seen as facets of a core problem, his relationship with his stepfather.

The themes of his play therapy concerned issues of power (himself versus his big angry stepfather), played out symbolically with cars and wild animals; and integration and partnership, demonstrated by the way he used cars, animals and village toys.

Cars

Cars can symbolize the ego (*Swainson, 1978, p. 184*) and, as his play progressed, Andrew's use of a yellow and of a red/cream car became increasingly interesting. In the first session he played with cars in the sand and a garage (a car's house). Crashing off the garage roof became a feature, and the play therapist wondered whether he might have felt that his house was crashing about his ears. In the second session he selected a yellow car, which was subsequently thought to represent his stepfather's yellow car. The yellow car explored the playroom and, in particular, the dolls' house, often crashing through piles of furniture.

A red/cream car appeared in the fourth session and, like the yellow car, charged through the dolls' house furniture. It was surmised that the red/cream car could symbolize Andrew, who would like to emulate his stepfather. In the next session Andrew shot the yellow car, and the red/cream car freely rushed round, charging through a heap of animals. Both cars were brought together in the garage, though the yellow car was soon to hang over a big drop. The yellow car then ran over village houses.

A week later the red/cream car drove *between* the village toys and farm animals, the yellow car also driving round things, and both cars travelled alongside. There was no longer such urgency to clash and crash, to dominate or be dominated; the cars drove carefully and harmoniously.

Session 9 portrayed the cars alongside, but this time the red/cream car bashed the yellow car. (Hypothetically, Andrew could now withstand his stepfather to some extent.) Then the red/cream car was freed to drive over some farm animals and encountered wild animals. It went to the garage, paying a quick visit to the tipped-over yellow car.

The following week the red/cream car was in the garage and, later, Andrew made a road in the sand for the yellow car; he was prepared to help the yellow car progress in his world.

Session 11 featured Andrew shooting the red/cream car. The two cars drove alongside, were attached to a tractor, and drove together again. Other aspects of his play suggested that Andrew was internalizing the symbolism of the cars, so did not have so much use for them in his play. Finally, the red/cream car mounted the yellow car, pushing it out of the way. The two vehicles drove alongside, and separate roads were made for each car. They were garaged, people being placed in the yellow car.

Within a few play sessions Andrew's school attendance had improved, and complaints from home diminished.

Animals

According to *Cirlot (1971, pp. 10–13)*, animals are 'of the utmost importance in symbolism', reflecting a hierarchy of instincts and unconscious areas ranging from big, savage wild animals (which could be likened to strong, animal-like instincts) to the commercially useful placid cow, to the (usually) tamed, often obedient instincts of the domestic dog which contrast with the more independent cat. *Cooper (1978, p. 12)* talks about animals representing different aspects of a person's nature, or instinctive and intuitive forces as distinct from intellect, will and reason.

Andrew first used animals in the fourth session. Once the yellow car crystallized to represent his stepfather Andrew had, importantly, to contend with less tangible feelings (not just actions) of oppression, powerlessness, and a striving for equilibrium, which seemed to be represented in his animal play.

Animal play centred around the snake and powerful wild animals. 'Dead' he pronounced as a big elephant stamped on the snake. Later, the snake assumed much of the role of the yellow car as it too explored the playroom and, in session 6, Andrew attached it to and tried to integrate it with, the yellow car.

In the seventh session the red/cream car was energized by a gorilla being placed on its roof and a *family* of ducks was put inside the car.

In the ninth session:

Andrew stands up an elephant, stag, gorilla. He drives the red/cream car through them without knocking them over. The gorilla chases the red/cream car. The elephant and gorilla stand in front of the red/cream car which is surrounded by an elephant, stag, hippo, lion and leopard. Growling noises. The red/cream car tries to get out. The lion stops it. Growling/hissing noises. The gorilla is wedged on the elephant's trunk. The elephant pushes the red/cream car and lion. The snarling lion catches the car. Andrew is absorbed. He sets up a similar scenario with more wild animals. He stands a windmill in front of the car within a circle of animals. The snake slides its head into the circle between the lion and gorilla. The red/cream car moves gently and is re-surrounded. The animals walk away, leaving the windmill. The elephant moves in front of the car, the gorilla behind, the windmill alongside and something on the bonnet. Other animals surround it. The snake slides out beneath the elephant. Hissing, prowling noises. The snake lies round the outside half of the circle of wild animals. The elephant is placed firmly in front of car, mounting it. All are taken away.

Next week the animals and snake were piled into the breakdown truck. The panther (who symbolically saves the dragon from the evil one; *Cooper, 1978, p. 126*) was placed on the winch, then the cabin. Perhaps the worst was over.

In session 12 the snake ran round the village toys and into the breakdown truck, its work done. Andrew erected the gorilla, and a big and small elephant stood trunk-to-trunk. 'One is big and one is little' he observed, showing them to the play therapist. She assumed this could indicate reconciliation, a meeting of opposites, of stepfather with stepson. Andrew placed the wild animals in the breakdown truck, moving them to the garage where he stood them on the roof, winding the snake carefully through them. There was no need to fight or fall off. All were safe.

The final session showed Andrew trying to balance the hen and chickens, the duck and ducklings, on the windmill. Equilibrium and balance of the family seemed to be his concern.

Village toys

Village toys featured in ten of Andrew's 15 sessions, but the events in sessions 12 and 13 are perhaps the most interesting.

A house can be a sheltering, enclosing self-symbol *(Swainson, 1978, p. 184)*; a village is many-faceted. Andrew patiently erected the buildings in an oval, placing roads, trees, animals and people randomly inside forming the roads into a square. Big and little gorillas were inserted, the snake curled round part of the outside, every space filled with wild, then farm, animals. Reflecting on these different aspects of his psyche, the therapist commented: [All these things living together. Are they happy or fighting?] 'It's Christmas day', he responded. [Oh, a special day.]

The following week Andrew surrounded the red/cream and yellow cars with the village toys, and the cars broke out. After travelling different roads, the cars herded the village toys so that once again he made an oval/square/circle configuration, which the cars subsequently collapsed. His psyche had produced these mandala shapes (pp. 207–8) which could be understood as another demonstration that Andrew was integrating internal and external warring factors and was creating within himself a new, inner, stronger being.

Many children play with the snake. Snakes inhabit all sorts of terrain and have many symbolic meanings *(Cooper, 1978, pp. 146–51)*. They can be strong, gentle, companionable, or slimy, dangerous, frightening creatures. They may symbolize the life force of inner energy, and a Freudian may see phallic connotations. Snakes are also paradoxical, like the medical symbol of the caduceus where the snake is both healing and poisonous.

Ten-year-old Pam was knowledgeable:

'The snake, I think it's my favourite thing', she said a bit ambivalently. 'I've got an excellent idea. You know you get snakes in the desert – horrible ones. I thought of putting it in here (sandtray). I'll make it desert-like; they usually have big hills sometimes. See if you (snake) like it. This can be a side-winder. It could be an adder, but you get them in Britain. Grass snakes in the grass. He could be a cobra. He's made pretty patterns in the sand.'

Summary

In this chapter we have explored some of the ways children express themselves using play materials in an object-related way. The home corner enables all sorts of personal and domestic dramas to be enacted. Pretend-food may reflect the child's early and current experiences of being (badly) cared for and fed. Dolls and the dolls' house fulfil a similar function, dolls coming in for much punishment and maltreatment. Construction toys and jigsaws are often used positively, suggesting rebuilding and growth, though they can portray destruction and confusion. Weapons, too, are multifaceted, being used in healthy achievement or depressing violence. Table and other games sometimes have a part to play and may reveal something of the child's feelings. An example is given of how a child, using vehicles, animals and village toys, expressed, and found resolution to, his inner conflicts. The following chapter encourages us to peep into the more fluid forms of expression afforded by painting and drawing, clay, sand and water.

8 Relating through the plastic arts

The greatest reassurance we can give to children is the feeling that they are understood and accepted right down to the painful sad bit in the middle. If we do not deny this painful bit of themselves, they need not do so, and their natural resilience can then take them on into life again.

(Winnicott, 1984, p. 20)

Plastic materials give children the opportunity to express the inexpressible through

- Paintings and drawings
- Clay and modelling
- Sand and water

Exercise

- Some grown-ups feel inept and clumsy with paints, crayons, clay, etc., but play therapists need to contact the child within who enjoys 'creating', without adult censure.
- Can you recall your experiences with paints, clay and so on when you were a young child?
- Recapture the satisfaction of using these materials. With your non-dominant hand, paint and draw feelings, phantasies (allow the pen or brush to take over), incidents from your childhood, dreams.
- Find some sand and water, and have a great time!
- Look at paintings, drawings and sculptures done by a range of children.
- Watch children at the seaside, by a stream – join in!

Piaget and Inhelder (1969, p. 54) argue that 'Drawings and play have a special place in the linking of internal and external domains'. As a mirror of the child's inner world, materials such as painting, drawings, claywork, sand and water are invaluable. They do not require spoken language, and yield to the child's inner creative urges. Plastic materials afford a satisfying form of expression for children who communicate more easily through form and colour rather than verbally *(Gardener, 1980; Gillespie, 1986, p. 19)* and also enable ventilation of preverbal confusion. The child's creations should be kept safely and displayed in each session.

PAINTINGS AND DRAWINGS

Art therapy requires specialized training and is a therapeutic method in its own right *(Dalley, 1984; Dalley et al., 1987)* but 'art' is a wonderful and satisfying form of self-expression *(Gumaer, 1984, pp. 94–121; Naitove, 1982)*, and paintings and drawings are very useful in the playroom *(Gardener, 1980; Nader and Pynoos, 1991)*. It is sufficient for the play therapist to accept and receive the child's art work, but a deeper appreciation of the creative efforts can aid the play therapist's understanding of the therapeutic process *(Thomas and Silk, 1990)*. Important points to remember are that a painting should be viewed as a partial representation of the child's world, and needs to be assessed in conjunction with what is known about the child and other aspects of the play *(Fordham, 1994, pp. 51–67; Furth, 1982; Kalff, 1980, pp. 74–5)*. Look at what is missing and inferred, as well as what is represented. Be prepared to find the unexpected, and sometimes the unwelcome *(Cardiff Social Work Resource Centre, undated, p. 13)*. Viewing a chronological series of a child's paintings or drawings over a period of time can give helpful insights; the meaning of images sometimes changes *(Allan, 1988b, pp. 99–103; Jung, 1959)*.

The child-centred play therapist neither criticizes, evaluates, nor 'teaches' children how to draw, but offers freedom to express whatever needs to come out, accepting that whatever the child does is valuable. A useful medium for some children, if they are not too repressed to try it, is finger painting. Here is direct contact with a messy substance, accepted by the play therapist *(Arlow and Kadis, 1979)*. Colours, of course, are important and can have a symbolic language of their own. If a large number of colours is available, or if children can mix their own, it is interesting to see what they choose. Drawing and painting are not necessarily normal practice in all cultures. We need to be aware that topics may not always have the same importance and relevance, and can be portrayed differently. This is especially true as far as the human figure is concerned *(Cox, 1993, pp. 108–10)*.

Andrew

Paintings produced during a child's play therapy can assist assessment and evaluation. An initial painting might set the scene. For instance, Andrew's first painting (Fig. 8.1) could be seen as representing a jumbled up child, which in many ways he was (p. 33). His final painting (Fig. 8.2) might suggest that he

Figure 8.1   Figure 8.2

had firmly established his identity, was balanced, mobile and in control. The latter painting confirmed the play therapist's opinion, based on the content of the play sessions and feedback from the school, that play therapy was 'succeeding' and that sufficient progress had been made to consider termination.

Polly

Polly (pp. 33–4) had her ups and downs during play therapy, and at one stage there was a deterioration in her coping mechanisms and she was quite depressed. The social worker was wondering about referral to a child psychiatrist, but her paintings suggested to the play therapist that Polly was making her way through the difficulties, which would probably be short-lived. This turned out to be the case and referral was unnecessary. (However, untrained play therapists are warned against making this sort of prediction.)

Figures 8.3–8.8 were among those dashed off by Polly. Figure 8.3 was done early in play therapy. 'It's a very cross thing' she said, as she painted her initial in black. Then she made a blue blob to the left: 'You've got a picture in there. Cross, cross, cross' as she added more black crosses. 'Put a little door over there' – a green shape. Polly was, indeed, a 'very cross thing' but the painting persuaded the play therapist that there was hope – the green door could be seen as an opening, and the blue picture seemed quite positive and forward-looking.

A later painting (Fig. 8.4) showed two suns. The top right yellow one, she said, was the play therapist and the bottom left blue one herself. Polly explained that the jumble of colours in the bottom right corner was a rainbow. The play therapist privately wondered whether the jumble of colours also represented the tangles on which Polly still had to work. Polly spattered the painting with rain, a fertilizing, cleansing agent. She painted two rainbows in following sessions.

Figure 8.3   Figure 8.4

Figure 8.5   **Figure 8.6**

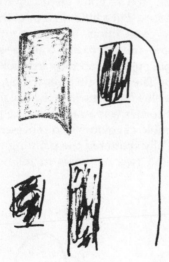

Figure 8.7   **Figure 8.8**

For Polly, houses were a constant theme. Distressed about the impending summer holidays, and wondering whether she would ever have a permanent home to go to, Polly painted three sides of a house without windows, doors or foundations, so her 'house' was somewhat flimsy (Fig. 8.5).

A traumatic event in Polly's life had been when her mother was involved in a fight in which she (the mother) was badly injured on the stairs. Figure 8.6 was, perhaps, expressing this incident. The four small windows were blue, whereas the oblong shape in the middle (the stairs?) was an energetic red. In Figs 8.7 and 8.8, done on separate occasions, the left-hand upper window was in red. In Fig. 8.7 the other windows and doors were in blue, whereas in Fig. 8.8 they were outlined in blue, the upper left window being filled with red, the lower left window was black, and the two right hand windows had yellow middles, the upper with a brown surround and the lower with a green surround. The bedroom window in Fig. 8.7 was red and disproportionate in size. An evocative representation of a prostitute's house? In Fig. 8.8 the red window is smaller and the other windows filled in, more complete, light being central in two, though there was still some downstairs gloom to illumine.

Towards the end of her play therapy Polly painted two mandalas (Figs 8.9 and 8.10), symbols of wholeness (pp. 207–8).

Six-year-old Peter (p. 34) painted occasionally. His first painting was of three lines, not firmly joined together but suggesting a box (house?) without foundation, reinforcing the feeling that he was baseless. His second painting was of a headless person taking a dog's head for a walk on a lead. When more co-ordinated, Peter drew vehicles, reverting to a few desolate streaks when life was not so good. His final painting (Fig. 8.11) was of a rich, filled-in concentric pattern, a mandala.

Eight-year-old Gemma (p. 33) first painted a person with blobs of black and brown inside, suggesting a neat persona (outer appearance), but with some out-of-place things (feelings) inside. The next few paintings were done by her baby and little girl selves, indicating that these were the areas that were being worked on in play therapy. The first of these paintings had a black G. her initial, scribbled over, with other-colour splodges underneath. She wrote 'To M u y'. The next was a lollipop, again with unexpected colours in the middle, and the third was a drawing of a little girl. Later, Gemma freed up to do some splattery, swooshy paintings, and then painted SuperGirl, not objecting to messing her hands in the paint – a far cry from the perfectionist child at the beginning of play therapy. Subsequent paintings were more age-appropriate, exploring relationships and her environment.

Working with children's art forms

- Observe the creative process, noting the child's mood whilst doing the painting, or other art form.
- How do you feel about what the child is doing?
- Some children give a commentary so you know what is happening.
- It is in order to enquire
  – can you tell me about this?'
  – 'I wonder what the story is?'
  – 'what would happen if ... ?'
  – 'you seem to feel glad/angry/pleased ... about what you have done.'
- 'That doesn't look like a camel, camels aren't green' is not an appropriate therapeutic remark! Do not criticize or teach.
- Date, name and keep paintings, drawings and models, displaying them in the child's session. Don't leave them for other children to see.
- Sandtrays can be recorded by photographs, sketches, notes and videos. Water play is more elusive!
- If you look back over a sequence of paintings, models, sandtrays, etc., you may notice that a 'theme' or 'story' emerges which may offer an insight into the child's world.
- Do not make premature, unnecessary or 'clever' interpretations.

Figure 8.9

Figure 8.10

Figure 8.11

Figure 8.12

INTERPRETATION OF PAINTINGS, DRAWINGS AND MODELS

Based on the principles that conscious analysis and interpretation are not necessary, and that 'glib' interpretation is irresponsible *(Braithwaite, 1986, p. 16)*, most child-centred play therapists would not offer the child overt interpretation of the pictures. Symbols and colours can have many meanings, so in any event private interpretations should be tentative. Occasionally it may be appropriate to ask children what they feel is happening in the painting, and why, or invite them to tell the story of the picture; though not all children can, or will, respond.

A feature to look out for is the haptic phenomenon, a term used to describe an object or part-object (or objects), often disproportionate in size, that may be linked to the child's bodily sensations and/or subjective experiences in which the child feels emotionally involved *(Lowenfeld and Brittain, 1964, p. 258)*. Andrew was anxious about his own aggression, which could get a bit out of hand at times when he would lash out at people, and he was often chastized by his burly stepfather. Andrew's self-portrait (Fig. 8.12) revealed outsize arms and hands. He might have felt that his arms were 'outsize', and he could have been portraying his stepfather's strong arms? Or could they be his arms that feel big and energized when he wants to hit out with them? Or are they the arms he would like to have? Whatever the cause, the arms in his painting were undeniably oversized. There is another example (Fig. 8.7) where the upstairs window is out of proportion. Objects that are so distorted in size may indicate that they are particularly significant to the child, even if at an unconscious level *(Thomas and Silk, 1990, p. 126)*. The play therapist can comment on the 'big' or 'little' thing, and get the problem out into the open, or can watch and wait, observing if and how the troublesome item becomes integrated. See how the windows are more of an equal size in Fig. 8.8?

CLAY AND MODELLING

Exercise

- Handle clay, noting what it feels like and its texture.
- How does it make you feel?
- Use it to model
  - your family
  - television characters
  - animals
  - monsters
  - feelings
  - a baby.

Clay has a basic, elemental quality and can be used for messy play as well as sophisticated symbolic expression. It allows three-dimensional work that can be moulded and altered, thus having more flexibility, sometimes more reality, than painting or drawing. Children can change their minds as they go along, so often their hands, rather than their head, lead the way. 'Mistakes' are easily rectified or in themselves become the trigger for inner expression.

Brian's father was in prison. Nine-year-old Brian lived with his mother, his younger brother residing elsewhere. Brian was referred for play therapy because of allegations that he lied, stole and was disobedient. There was a suspicion of sexual abuse, but nothing was proved.

Brian's play therapy was like a journey of inner exploration and clarification in which he was finding his values. Most of the work was accomplished symbolically, some with a sexual connotation, and with a strong archetypal component. In the early stages, secrets were important, being superseded by archetypal figures, in particular mother-related ones. On one level, his models may seem random; but on another level they reveal a story when the possible symbolic language of the items is uncovered.

In the first session Brian made halves of a shell, then a prehistoric monster. Shells reveal and conceal, and this summed up his therapy. Towards the end of the session he looked at the den: 'I'll make a base' which he did, creating a secret doorway.

In the fourth session, Brian formed a teapot house, explaining there was only one person in the house. That person was dead, Brian said, and liked being on his own. He could keep secrets, was watching television and was having a drink of tea. Brian made a window in the house, saying that Mr Teapot Man lived alone and did not have any friends because of not sharing his secrets. Brian made a car and a big-mouth garage that opened and closed its door. The play therapist said [He's living in a teapot and he won't share secrets. Can he share a little secret?] 'No, he doesn't deserve friends.' [I wonder why he can't share secrets?] 'Because of his plans to get out of the teapot. He's locked himself in. The only way is to get the lid off.' Brian told the play therapist that Mr Teapot Man's latest plan was how to get out of the teapot. He modelled a garden in the teapot, but rats and mice (symbols of decay, turbulence and darkness *(Cooper, 1978, p. 137)*, maybe of an overwhelming nature as their number increased) entered the spout and (presumably) spoilt his creative growth. He painted the inside of the house black, the outside yellow and green, with a brown door.

Four sessions later Brian modelled a butterfly, a potent transformation symbol suggesting change and rebirth *(Cooper, 1978, pp. 27–8)*, followed by a bomber plane! The potential for change was there, but might be dangerous or devastating.

Animals became a major theme. There was an elephant and a snail, a slow animal reflecting the basics of earth, with a spiral shell suggesting movement and change *(Cooper, 1978, p. 154)*. As it was Easter, he made a rabbit, an Easter egg and box, symbols of rebirth and resurrection.

Another clay butterfly heralded basic renewal, leading into the last four sessions in which Brian modelled 17 items, starting with a house which changed into a dice – as though his house (which could be interpreted as himself or his life) is 'chancy'. Then came an octopus, crab and a cobra which some authorities would understand to be negative mother symbols *(Neumann, 1955, pp. 67, 153, 177)*.

In session 18 Brian created a caterpillar on a twig with a cabbage but, being unable to form the cabbage to his satisfaction, he turned it into an apple. The caterpillar had ample food for its transformation into a butterfly.

The idiom changed to a starship, something that can traverse the heights, and to a snake-dragon-sea-monster. In symbolism, the serpent and dragon are often interchangeable *(Cooper, 1978, p. 146)*, so it is interesting that Brian physically blended them. *Jung (1956, p. 259)* writes about the dragon being a mother-image expressing resistance to incest; the dragon-monster is also something to be overcome, because only the person who conquers the dragon can become a hero or heroine, and all children in deep therapy are, at an archetypal level, likely to undergo the hero(ine) journey. As the sea can stand for flowing emotions, and is also a mother symbol, a sea-monster suggested Brian's problems may have been linked with maternal and emotional issues.

The following week Brian made a less snake-like dragon-monster. The play therapist's record:

The dragon-monster has a string of sausages hanging from its toothy mouth, and a campfire is made, complete with fallen leaves. Brian offered his last snake-monster to me to keep, and I accepted. He asked whether I would take it home; I said I'd keep it in my office for the time being, then take it home.

Finally, Brian modelled a police car (he was doing a police project at school). Next came the devil's slave with an arrow through his head fired by the devil. His final sequence was a seahorse, a boat (he had a safe container to carry him across the waters of life), and a starfish which can be seen as a mandala, a symbol of 'the inextinguishable power of love' *(Cooper, 1978, p. 159)*, and of light shining in the darkness.

Readers may find other 'stories' in the clay models, which in any event warrant more detailed analysis than has been offered here. Whatever the material, readers are challenged to look behind the object to discover the hidden language of symbols.

In Brian's case the play therapist did not offer interpretations to him but observed, made notes and was a receptive companion along the way. In reality it was difficult to evaluate his play therapy as the social worker antagonized the school and mother, and then withdrew. Play therapy confirmed that there was a strong possibility that Brian had been sexually abused, despite formal investigations having been inconclusive. Analysis of the work in the playroom and feedback from the school suggested some positive change in the boy but, because the family moved, there was no follow-up.

SAND AND WATER

Exercise

- Treat yourself to a sandtray (a washing-up bowl or litter tray).
- Experience the texture and movement of the sand.
- What is it like when water is added?
- Make scenes in the sand with bits and bobs.
- Let the play items tell a story so that the scene changes.

Early play

Sand and water are basic materials, preferably sited together in the playroom so that they can be mixed to the child's chosen consistency. Having dry and wet sandtrays is ideal. The majority of children respond to sand and water, using them for age – appropriate play or, more probably in therapy, to rework earlier developmental needs. It is noticeable that children with soiling and wetting problems smear sloppy sand, and play a lot with water, often pouring then controlling the flow. After tentative approaches, many older children love making sand castles and huge boggy messes. Even Gemma, who initially was prim and proper, took off her shoes and wallowed in the squelchy sand.

Sandtrays

Toby was on the verge of being taken into foster care because of his behaviour at home and school (p. 4). The social worker and play therapist thought that his behaviour was largely reactive to insecurity and inconsistent parenting and, in play therapy, Toby showed that he could cope in an environment he could trust. To begin with his sandtrays were alarming. There were devastating floods, frightening landslips and armies fought in hostile terrain. Gradually the elements abated, the armies fought less hard and, although there were spurts of danger, scenarios became more peaceful. It transpired that there was little wrong with the boy, but a lot wrong at home.

Gemma (p. 33) created landscapes mostly of farm animals, but dangerous predators lurked and lonesome creatures were at risk. As time went on, animals were placed in family groupings and could wander safely. At referral, Gemma's foster placement was precarious and she doubtless felt herself isolated, on the fringe of things and 'at risk'. However, as relationships improved, she became part of the family, demonstrating this with the animals. Later Gemma played out Hansel and Gretel in the sand, which seemed to be about ineffectual parents, and children having to find their own way.

Twelve-year-old Martin had a deprived family background and was in a children's home following a second foster home breakdown. The problems at referral were that he stole money and food, was manipulative and got other children into trouble, found it difficult to relate to women, was a handful at school, did not communicate easily, and was unfosterable.

His play therapy included quite a lot of regression and painting, and some sandtrays. The first sandtray revealed a strong fort-castle suggesting a defended person. Inside were unequal opposing forces, but he added more figures and the battle evened out. Towards the end he put in a white horse and rider. (See comments about the fifth sandtray.) The walls were solid and the play therapist made the mistake of asking whether it was a castle to get out of or in to, which triggered Martin to create an entrance. The play therapist should not have intruded. Had she not intervened the walls would probably have remained solid, as they did in the second sandtray which contained three smaller forts inside the main one. These sand pictures suggested that Martin was highly defended, emphasizing that play therapy would be slow. He needed a place, fortified against intruders, where he could find himself. (He did in fact spend quite a bit of time hidden away in the playroom den.)

In his third sandtray, two months later, Martin made a road and oasis in a desert (although desolate, a desert can be a place of contemplation and revelation), and a road suggests that Martin was making passage through his desert. Life-giving water was available. As his sandtray developed:

'It's going to be a farm. Still going to have a pool. Get all the horses. Have a farmer walking round with a gun. A few sheep dotted around. Do you reckon these ducks would float? Soon find out. The farmer's walking out with his gun. There's a lion coming, elephant following him. Here comes a dinosaur out of the water. Then there's a panda sitting on top of the house.' [Yes] I confirm. 'On *top* of the house?' [Anything can happen.] 'It can, but it won't. Snake, Tabitha' and he hisses, holding the snake.

Note the small fort-house and the family grouping of domestic animals. Were the farmer and the gun to keep wilder animals at bay?

A tight square of houses on a semicircular island (sandtray No. 4) suggests a mandala. Instead of a fort there were many dwellings, so perhaps other aspects of himself were becoming available. Inside was a tower, three people and an animal. Outside were trees, strong symbols of the self. It was as though he were still defending himself, but from inner strength rather than fear *(Fromm, 1946)*.

Towards the end of play therapy, sandtray No. 5 started as cowboys and Indians, changing to a wild animal park. It contained a castle with flag, around which were various wild animals, and the final item, a white horse, was placed centrally by the castle. In the hierarchy of animals, the horse is close to humans, the white charger often taking its rider on adventures of conquest. The play therapist speculated that the horse symbolized Martin, noting that it came into the picture at the end as an afterthought, that it was near an inhabited castle, and that maybe dangers lurked but the wild animals seemed peaceable for the time being.

Martin was resistant to discussing the sandtray photos, which could be seen as showing a story of how defences were gradually being lowered, and his world was still a potentially dangerous and insecure place. The symbolism of the white horse was so positive, though, that even if his life did not turn out too well in the immediate future, there was hope in the longer term.

When play therapy had ended, follow-up showed that Martin passed through a tricky time in his next foster placement but that eventually he 'made good'.

The sandtray technique

In child-centred play therapy, children make sandtrays when they wish, and it is encouraging if the materials are situated close together. Lowenfeld's world technique (also known as the make-a-world) offers a non-verbal way of self-expression *(Allan, 1988a, pp. 212–21; Bowyer, 1970; Lowenfeld 1935, 1979; Mitchell and Friedman, 1994; Newson and Newson, 1979, pp. 119–39; Reed, 1975; Ryce-Menuhin, 1988, pp. 234–51; 1992)*, and most children take to the technique spontaneously. '[Sandplay] provides us with a tool which not only facilitates therapy but also gives us a way of studying the healing and growth process' *(Kalff, 1980, p. 22)*. Sandplay often gets down to unconscious levels and is a unique way of helping the child express fears and phantasies that are otherwise elusive and difficult to define *(Irwin, 1983, p. 157)*. The child uses two hands, thus employing both lobes of the brain, and no special skills are required *(Vinturella and James, 1987, p. 230)*.

The play therapist's role is to observe and to support but to avoid interfering or making suggestions. As in other aspects of play therapy, sometimes the play therapist may ask amplifying questions, or invite the child to tell a story about the sand picture. Interpretation is unnecessary and would only rarely be offered. Children should be allowed to let their imaginations rip, and if items are put to unaccustomed use, so be it! A few older children may be worried about the lack of appropriate proportions and scale, for instance a model car may be too big against a small house. Their objections can be accepted, and it could be pointed out that it is like this in dreams, or in some forms of art. Photographs (preferably Polaroid) are a useful record, especially if more than one sandtray is done during the course of play therapy, so that comparison and discussion as to how the sandtray pictures have changed over time can be offered *(Oaklander, 1978, p. 166). Allan (1988a, pp. 215–6)* points out that the common stages in a series of sandtrays are chaos, struggle and resolution.

The sandtray can be a means of assessment and therapy in its own right.

Exercise

Water play!
- Find a bath or big bowl, pond, river or puddle.
- Play in and with water.
- See how various items float and sink.
- Observe how colours and textures change.
- Throw it in the air.
- Stamp in puddles.
- Play with your duck in the bath!

Summary

Based on a few of Andrew's and Polly's paintings, this chapter has described some of the things children express about themselves using creative materials. Many paintings and drawings have a symbolic language, clay offering another medium for catharsis and resolution. The majority of children find sand and water compelling, the Lowenfeld sandtray being a versatile tool in which children create multidimensional scenarios often serving as a commentary on the child's inner and/or outer life. Any interpretation of the child's work should be professionally informed, and used, initially, for the therapist's personal thinking about what is happening. Only rarely, and then cautiously, is an interpretation offered to the child.

Some children stick mostly to roles and relationships, some to play-based activities, and others to art-based enterprises. There are those who prefer a range of approaches, and this can be called hybrid play.

9   Hybrid play: Tim's play therapy

Even when we encounter children who are unhappy or emotionally disturbed, an overall attitude of waiting and trusting is a very good one. Psychotherapy is, after all, not something done to anybody. Therapy is a word pointing to servicing and nursing. Often unaccustomed to receiving adult respect, the child benefits, sometimes immediately, from his association with a therapeutic adult.

(Adams, 1982, p. 14)

• Many children communicate through a range of play materials as well as roles and relationships.

Tim was seven. His mother was a loud-mouthed prostitute and his father had been imprisoned for pimping. Tim stayed out at night whilst his mother 'worked', he smashed bottles, stole and was aggressive, favouring erratic school attendance and inconsistent moral standards. Violence and domestic dramas were commonplace.

Tim was referred by an infant school, and was described as making funny noises; adopting jerky, unco-ordinated limb movements; disruptive in class and aggressive in school, in particular biting teachers and not allowing physical contact. The play therapist hypothesized that Tim had had an erratic home life with little structure or preschool education, and that he was probably frightened of his own violence. It was felt that he may not have had sufficient 'primary maternal preoccupation' (one of Winnicott's concepts, *Davis and Wallbridge, 1983*) and that he might therefore have had to 'contain' himself, adopting an aggressive stance designed to gain security and to hide his inner fear *(Willock, 1983, p. 389)*.

The head teacher acted as intermediary, obtaining the mother's approval for her son's play therapy, and a social worker was assigned to the case. The play therapist met Tim at school, on his territory in the classroom, and he was quickly showing her round, telling her about his activities and inviting her to see his work box where he kept his school books. Tim presented as an imaginative, lively boy with an independent streak, and an ability to 'get on in the world'. The play therapist showed him photographs of the playroom, and confirmed that he could come once a week. She attempted to help him remember when the session would be by linking it with a regular school activity, for example that he would be coming on the day he went swimming.

In his first session, Tim immediately selected Skeletor. Involvement with Action men, tanks and motorbikes followed, then the Incredible Hulk (fetchingly called Hunk). Lively activities ensued, and towards the end the naked Hunk, Skeletor and Action men were repeatedly hurled into water, and Tim washed their clothes. Selection of Skeletor indicated that negative power and strength may be issues, Action men and Hunk being other aspects of strength and power. Tim needed to 'bottom' this, nakedness and immersion suggesting that regeneration may be possible.

The main theme of Tim's play therapy was to do with aggression, some of which frightened him. He identified with Hunk (who turned into his 'brother') and, half way through play therapy, built a den for Hunk and himself. This den developed into a sort of nest from which Tim was reborn, and thus became the means of transforming the power that had ruled him. Tim became more in control of his aggression and less at the mercy of his feelings, eventually behaving in a more integrated fashion.

The second theme of Tim's play therapy concerned dressing-up, donning disguises and trying out different personalities.

In the early sessions there was much violent play, shooting, boxing, daredevil stunts, lurid stories and noise, and the play therapist despairingly wondered whether they were making headway and at times was tempted to consider terminating the work. There were glimmers that progress was possible when Tim introduced, briefly, a lighthouse, and negative and positive archetypal figures (pp. 204–7), so the play therapist persisted amidst what seemed like constant chaos, confusion and attacks.

Although the play therapist did not recognize it at the time, session 8 was a transition. Tim offered her and Hunk sweets, and commented on a helicopter. *He* was feeding two strong figures, and there was a possibility of lift-off! Violent activity ensued:

> Tim thrust a toy knife at my stomach ... and fetched a knife and fork 'to eat you up' ... He stabbed himself, then crawled on the floor pushing a pile of cushions. 'I bet Hunk can jump over. Yes, I know, I'll make a house with 'em (cushions) and jump on 'em. This is going to be a good house.'

The next week, after much activity, Tim twisted himself out of the home corner window, in a way that symbolized rebirth, the play therapist having to catch him carefully as he emerged. He did this several times, the play therapist feeling strongly that she was acting in the role of midwife to the birth of a 'new' infant. Then Tim barricaded the playroom door:

> 'This'll keep them (other people) out ... Who killed my wibbly snake? You did. I just killed him. A big elephant ... Wait till I show you these two baby creatures (prehistoric monsters). Pretend you see them two big creatures' and he made an elephant and dinosaur battle. 'Help, it bit me' as the animals fight and he acts it out. 'Look at that' as the dinosaur grabs the elephant in its mouth. 'My other friend (pterodactyl) – they see them two fight. He wanted to stop the fight but he couldn't.' A big and little elephant fight two monsters. Tim is involved in this. 'Come on, then, me and you', and brontosaurus attacks elephant. 'He's the winner in the fight

– three big chunks out of the elephant's leg. There's that monster again that was fighting with us.' Brontosaurus defeats the elephant, but is overcome by pterodactyl.

The play therapist noted:

Play with prehistoric and large primitive animals is significant. Tim was struggling to come to terms with his own considerable untamed primitive energies, since he lacked adult care and training at the right time.

In session 10, the play therapist responded to what she speculated was a regressive phase by providing unlimited biscuits, implying that babies need feeding when and as much as they require if their instinctual needs are to be met. Tim instigated peep-bo and hide-and-seek with the play therapist. Active, but not violent, play followed during which cushions were assembled:

He jumps from a height on to the pile of cushions. 'This time when I fall I'll pretend I'm dead, shall I?' [You'll pretend to be dead.] 'Let them all fall on to me' as he lies on the cushions and some fall on him. 'This is a nest, a little house. It's warm. Where's the Hunk? Here's his nice little bed. Goodnight. No-one's coming into our little house. Goodnight. You're shy (I suspect he means lonely) – and this is our little house. Push some more cushions on. Try and open the playroom door.' The heap of cushions is almost against it and I'm asked to try to open the door several times, pretending I can only open it a fraction. [It's very difficult.] 'That's because we're here, isn't it, Hunk? You (meaning the play therapist) can't find us. You don't know where we are.' [I don't know where he is. Disappeared.]
   There are some odd noises, then snoring, from under the cushions. [I wonder what's there?] 'Incredible Hunk – his den.' [I daren't go there.] Moaning noises. 'You're looking for him.' I discover Tim and tickle him. He giggles. 'It ain't Hunk's den, it's mine.' [That's all right then.] Tim instructs me to hide him again. 'Pretend you look in and I've gone', and we do this twice more. 'Hunk's tired. If you keep on opening it I'll tell him to beat you up. You say "I'll see if Tim's there" and, when I look, the Hunk leaps out. You don't see me.' [Can't see him anywhere] I respond, in mystified tones, and Tim suddenly emerges from the cushions.
   'Make a different den while I'm asleep. Me and him want to be warm.' [Yes, I'm sure you do.] 'You see if I was here, but I weren't.' [Can't see him – not at home. What's that funny noise?] 'These cushions are nice and warm. You look under the cushions.' I discover Tim, [Oh, hallo]. He tells me 'You say "Where's that Tim?". Hide the gaps (in the cushion-den) with the cushion. You say "I wonder if that Tim of mine is at home". You say "I can't find him". Oh, these cushions are lovely and warm.' Tim makes noises. 'Look for me.' [Tim, are you at home?] 'Look under that big cushion.' I look and say [Yes, he's at home. He looks nice and warm]. Tim informs me 'Hunk's gone. If I don't give him any air he'll die'. [Mustn't have that happen.] 'You didn't see us two for a hundred thousand years.' [I haven't seen Tim and Hunk for 100,000 years. Oh, is that Tim? Hello, Tim?] as a cheeky face peers out, then hides itself. [There's Hunk too. Both

warm together.] Tim asks me to cover the gaps in his nest. 'You don't see us for two years', which I have to repeat. 'A thousand hundred million two years.' There are noises and groans as the cushions move, Tim's face emerging. [There they are.] 'I'm coming out of my house. That's a nice house.'

'Make another house' and I rearrange the cushions, sealing him in, being instructed to hide all the gaps. 'Now you say "Where's that Tim? I haven't seen him for 3,500,000 years".' I get it wrong saying 7,500,000 years, and am instructed, from the muffled depths, to get it right! His hand emerges, scratching the cushion. [What's that? It's a hand]. Tim mutters 'Somebody ... You look under this red cushion'. [There's Tim – haven't seen him for 3,500,000 years. Better shut him in again. Mustn't let him see the light too quickly. Who's that? It's Incredible Hunk] and Hunk disappears. 'Hunk is my brother. Superman.' [I see, of course.] The full face of Tim appears. 'Will you make another den?'

Various other things happen, then he goes into the home corner. 'I'll climb through the window again. You say "What's he going to do?" Tim climbs out a bit apprehensively, asking me to catch him. He kicks over the crib. Angry noises as, in a fairly controlled manner, he knocks a few things over. He takes the roof off the dolls' house and makes roaring noises. 'I'll pick the house up and fling it, pretend. Pretend I've got a sword and cut your finger' and he mimics assaulting me. [You feel like hurting me, do you?]

I tell him there are about five minutes of the session left. 'No' he asserts as he continues to saw my finger. He goes into the home corner muttering 'Hide me. I'm not coming out now'. [No, not for another four minutes.] 'I'm not coming out until home time when my school comes out.' [Oh, I see.] 'Will you pass my drink in? Here you are', as he returns the empty glass. [Thank you.] Tim shuts himself into his den. 'It fell (a cushion fell over), can you put it up? Hunk knocked it down'. Tim declares that he won't leave the playroom. [Shall we make a den and leave Hunk safely?] 'Yes. You'll break it', meaning I will dismantle the den. [Yes, but we'll leave Hunk here until next week.] 'Will you be here later?' [Not today.] 'Make a den and cover him up, so he's nice and warm. He's going to be lovely and hot for next week.' Tim buries the Hunk in the pile of cushions, heaping on blankets for good measure.

When making her written comments on the session, the play therapist noted that hide-and-seek seemed to be about early forms of communication, verbal and non-verbal, and this was carried through at greater depth in the den of cushions, which was more like a nest or womb. Tim was insistent that the cracks had to be filled in, and at times it was difficult to hear his muffled voice. On two occasions when she uncovered him she felt like someone smiling and cooing at a baby, feeling obliged to tickle him, but he didn't like being tickled very much. There was a basic quality to this play. A bit later in the den sequence she sensed him

emerging from it as from a chrysalis – an emergent power ... Quite often during the session he was singing and humming, and communication felt to be flowing at a number of levels.

The following week the play therapist and Tim fed Hunk in the den and, a fortnight later Tim requested 'Make a little house for me, I'm safe'. His play became less violent.

An aggressive child, Tim's play therapy had been active and, at times, disheartening as his rumbustious behaviour was somewhat wearing and he seemed to be working on, and testing, various 'attachment' issues *(Willock, 1983, p. 406)*. However, the Hunk and the den were transforming symbols, and the new house that he made seemed important. These were turning points, and the play therapist became more optimistic as Tim seemed to make progress. Improvements were reported at school and at home, and Tim became less notorious in the neighbourhood.

Exercise

- If you were to have play therapy, what sort of play would you choose
  - as an adult?
  - as a child?

Summary

Tim partly used objects such as Hunk, and partly his relationship with the play therapist to work out issues that were important for him. In the early part of Tim's play therapy, the play therapist felt confused, angry, disoriented, not at all sure what was happening. Eventually play themes emerged and a more positive relationship developed between therapist and child. Learning to read the play themes is sometimes only possible with hindsight, particularly in the beginning stages, but was one of the anchors that helped the play therapist amidst the turmoil.

Another anchor was an understanding of the therapeutic stages traversed by children in play therapy, and this will be examined in the next chapter.

10 The therapeutic process and evaluation

Nondirective therapy has come to be recognized as an important approach to understanding behavior. It makes no attempt to control or change the client's meanings, rather it focusses attention on creating a therapeutic situation which provides experiences that make changes possible and leaves to the individual the freedom to decide the nature and direction of the change.

(Lebo, 1982, p. 71)

- Four therapeutic stages through which children in play therapy typically pass are discussed
- Evaluation of play therapy is gained from knowing
  - whether there have been any changes in the child's presenting problems
  - where the child is in relation to the therapeutic stages.

Exercise

- Do we just 'do' play therapy and trust to luck?
- Do we stop the work when *we've* had enough?
- On what basis would you evaluate the work?
- If you were a child, how would you know when you were ready to stop?

Conditions for change:

- The child needs to feel safe and valued, both in and out of play therapy sessions.
- Commensurate with developmental levels, the child needs to understand what has happened to her or him.
- The child needs to have been able to recapture, express and explore troubling incidents from the past.
- The child needs to have been accepted for what he or she is.
- Play therapy and the play therapist need to have been consistent and reliable.
- The child needs to have had an opportunity to regress, regrow and repair early-life deficiencies.
- The child needs to have age-appropriate opportunities and also to be allowed to behave in a manner commensurate with emotional age, until the two have balanced.
- The child needs to know about the future, especially if there are to be moves, changes, or contacts with former known adults.

FOUR THERAPEUTIC STAGES

Stage 1	The child's behaviour is profuse, diffuse, over the top, or inhibited, targeted appropriately and inappropriately. The therapeutic task is to form the therapeutic alliance.
Stage 2	The child's feelings become focused on definite people and things outside the child. The child's behaviour may appear to get worse.
Stage 3	Positive feelings begin to show, but there is a lot of ambivalence.
Stage 4	Realistic feelings emerge more strongly. The child feels better inside and is more able to deal with life's vicissitudes. The child develops an age-appropriate relationship with the play therapist.

- The stages are not always gone through in this order.
- Stages may be revisited, but usually differently as the child works on further issues.

(From *Moustakas, 1964*)

Children in play therapy characteristically move through four phases *(Dockar-Drysdale, 1968, p. 82 quoted in Aldgate and Simmonds et al., 1988, p. 50; Finke, 1947 reported in Guerney, 1983a, pp. 24–5; Guerney, 1983b, p. 352; Moustakas, 1953, pp. 6–9; 1959, pp. 27–45; 1964, pp. 417–19).* Occasionally the order of the first three phases varies. Although the stages are not always clearcut in practice and are sometimes difficult to discern despite a satisfactory conclusion to play therapy, they are nevertheless sufficiently useful to warrant careful attention. The therapeutic process does not occur automatically and depends, in part, on the working relationship, known as the therapeutic alliance, forged between child and worker. The therapeutic alliance is more likely when the play therapist responds consistently and sensitively to the child's feelings, accepts the child's attitude, and conveys a constant and sincere belief in, and respect for, the child.

Stage 1

This is the stage of profuse, diffuse behaviour targeted appropriately and inappropriately. At referral, behaviour may appear extreme. The child may have lost contact with his or her real self, and unease may be widespread, indiscriminate or unattached to the person and/or situations that provoked the problems. When acting out, children display hostility indiscriminately, including towards themselves, sometimes expressing this in the playroom by attacking the toys and play therapist. Anxious children are diffusely afraid of everything and everybody. They want to be left alone; anything might be harmful.

Stage 2

The greater children's trust in the play therapist, and the more they are sure of being accepted and respected in the playroom, the more will children be able to focus anger or fear on *definite* things or people outside themselves. At first it may be the play therapist who gets the full blast because the child can trust sufficiently to test the worker in this way. Although it can feel uncomfortable and puzzling, the child-centred play therapist accepts calmly and lets it work itself out.

Children may also have the courage to try out their anger or fear at home or at school. At this stage, fears become targeted to the objects that caused the problem instead of substitute figures and situations. Angry children stop hammering the toys and begin to take it out on a sibling or a parent. This can be a critical time because children may appear to get worse from the carers' or school's point of view, and the play therapist must explain that it is a necessary but short-lived stage.

The eruption of fears and anger may be intense, but as children express and release their negative feelings in direct ways, and as these expressions are accepted by the play therapist, the child is not so much at the mercy of frightening feelings which become less insistent. The more children can get their angry feelings out of their system, and the more the play therapist accepts the child, the better the child is able to feel good inside, a worthy person.

Stage 3

Now comes the building of positive feelings. As children gain in their conviction of being worthy, accepted and 'good' inside, they are no longer quite so negative all the time in the expression of their feelings. This is a stage of acute ambivalence. Children may hate and love the same object, which can be puzzling and painful to the child and the object, if it is a person. Children will tentatively test out good feelings of love and trust, asking for things from important people in their lives. As they do not yet trust what will happen if they show true feelings, there are violent swings. Children may care intensely for a baby doll, smothering it with love, then spank it viciously. They may alternatively kick and be nice to the play therapist. They may ask to be given something and then fling it back, or say they do not want it. These ambivalent feelings can be severe in intensity at first but, when expressed again and again in the therapeutic relationship, they calm down.

Children may try to involve the play therapist more actively, or differently. Although the child may be using the play therapist in a number of ways (e.g. as 'mother', playmate, slave, container of the chaos) and may be working on issues to do with trust and mistrust, dependence and independence, there will probably also be the beginnings, if only spasmodic, of a more age-appropriate relationship, and the child may begin to verbalize and discuss concerns to some extent.

Stage 4

Positive, realistic feelings emerge more strongly. Through the first three stages the child has been accepted consistently and wholly by the play therapist, no matter how 'awful'. So, by this time the child has introjected a good-parent image from the adult play therapist and feels a good self-image inside. The child is worthy and secure, with a burgeoning self-esteem, and can now afford to love others from a sort of overflow. As a five-year-old once put it 'I'm going to have a big party and invite everybody, even my brother', a far cry from the child who hated everything and everybody and only wanted to be left alone!

At this stage the child adjusts to reality and sees other people as they are. 'Mummy would have liked to look after me, but she couldn't. I still love her and would like to live with her, but I know I can't.' More importantly, children are better able to accept their own faults and shortcomings without undue anxiety; after all, the play therapist has accepted them, therefore they are acceptable. So this is the stage when specific problems can be dealt with in play therapy without damaging the self-confidence of the child. This, too, is the weaning stage from the play therapy situation.

Children drop away when the play therapist has fulfilled his or her function, carrying away the play therapist's acceptance and respect inside themselves as self-acceptance and self-respect. The children are normally better able to make appropriate decisions, to take some self-responsibility, and to own and respond to their feelings.

EVALUATION

Exercise

- Think of situations where you have been evaluated, and when you have evaluated somebody or something. What were the important issues?
- How would you evaluate play therapy?
  - why evaluate it?
  - what criteria would you use?
  - when would you evaluate?
  - who would know about your evaluation?

'Is play therapy of any use to the child and how do we know when to finish it?' It is important that play therapy does not just wander along, but that it is evaluated and appropriately terminated (Chapter 11).

There are four main evaluative guidelines:

1. The play therapist's understanding of the child's progress through the therapeutic stages, and the nature of the child's relationship with the play therapist.
2. The play therapist's analysis of the process and content of the play sessions, in particular the resolution – or otherwise – of the main themes of the play.
3. The energy the child puts into the sessions, and, if old enough, his or her appraisal about how life is progressing.
4. The perceptions of the child's progress by the referrer and people such as carers and teachers.

To aid evaluation, the play therapist will find it useful at the beginning of play therapy to list the alleged difficulties that precipitated the child's referral, itemizing who said what. Periodically the play therapist should check everyone's perceptions of what is happening, noting any changes.

Toby

The identified problems relating to nine-year-old Toby (p. 4) can be used as an illustration, though it should be borne in mind that it is often the referrer who passes on the carer's perceptions.

At referral

Toby said he was unhappy and bewildered at home; doing badly at school; in scrapes in his social life; could not please his mum.

His mother complained that: Toby defied her, threatened her, said he hated her and told her lies; he associated with bullies and yobbos; he behaved aggressively with men; she wanted him taken into care.

His school reported: Toby misbehaved and had been suspended, though reinstatement was likely. He was underachieving.

First phase of the work, and therapeutic stage 1

In the early sessions Toby was acting out what seemed to be internal power struggles using the playroom soldiers, in particular Darth Vader, but making very little reference to the play therapist. His inner discomfort was symbolically deflected to the toys.

From time to time it is advisable for the play therapist to check with the referrer (and school) about what is happening to the child in his or her environment. The play therapist would normally tell the child that she or he planned to chat to the social worker (or appropriate person), stressing that the content of the play sessions will not be revealed (if that is the case, or unless the child gives permission) but that the play therapist may give general information about how many sessions the child has had, perhaps with a broad outline of the gist of the work, and will be enquiring about what is happening in the child's life. If visiting the school or home, it is important to forewarn the child because it could come as a shock to see the play therapist out of context and in the child's territory.

After seven weeks of play therapy, the *social worker* reported that there continued to be some ups and downs in family relationships, but that things were on the whole a bit better. The *teachers* were positive about the improvements in him, begging that play therapy should not at that stage be terminated (they had been suspicious about it in the first place), reporting that Toby was not causing any worry and that he was obtaining better marks.

Second phase of the work and therapeutic stages 2 and 3

The play therapist noted that Toby was slowly communicating more positively with her, firstly through painting slogans and also through table games. Toby had dealt with much of his cathartic outburst and distress in his battles and sandtray work without direct reference to the play therapist, but now play therapist and boy were beginning to relate to one another as people. There had been some specific communication when the play therapist had said positive things about him, had stressed to his surprised enquiries that she enjoyed his presence and, perhaps significantly, had told him that his second name, Nicholas, meant 'victory of the people' and not Old Nick (the devil), which was his connotation. The play therapist recognized that 'improvements' in children's behaviour and attitudes in the playroom usually extend to their outer life (*Kempe and Kempe, 1978, p. 116*), but that sometimes there is a delay. With other children, 'improvement' may be reported by other people before the play therapist sees it in the play sessions. In Toby's case, therapeutic stages 2 and 3 seemed to merge, his paintings offering a positive indicator that his suspicion and hostility towards the play therapist had changed.

Final phase and therapeutic stage 4

It became apparent from the play that Toby did not carry nearly so much personal and social distress as in earlier sessions, the therapeutic hours became calmer and less insistent, and he seemed, in general, more positive and accepting about life. To help make a decision about termination, the play therapist gained Toby's agreement to contact his mother and the school again, the social worker having withdrawn in the meantime.

This was the evaluation:

Toby said he was: much happier at home; getting on well with mum; surprised that he was doing so well at school; having an agreeable social life.

His mother: reported a big improvement in Toby and in her relationship with him. He got on all right with her recently-acquired male partner.

His school: his marks had improved; he had moved up a group in maths; he was considered to be a useful and valued member of the school community.

Obviously not all referrals are like this, though in the vast majority of children there is often significant improvement. During sessions the play therapist will note changes in the quality and type of play, and the emergence and progress of themes. The evolution of the symbols and of symbolic play can give useful pointers to the child's progress. It takes a bit of practice to understand the language of symbolism and play, but it is worth the effort.

Examine the 'problems' list from time to time and see what progress, if any, is being made. If there has been some improvement and the child is working through the stages reasonably well, you may wish to consider termination. Initially, all-round improvement is unlikely and may be patchy for a time. Sometimes improvements first appear in one area of a child's life (school, home or play therapy). Remember that some children work through in play therapy more speedily than others (often the younger the child, the quicker the outcome), and that factors such as extraversion or introversion, how deeply disturbed the child was in the first place, and whether the child needs a long and maybe testing time before putting trust in an adult, should be taken into account.

If there is no change after a reasonable period of time (say six to ten sessions), the play therapist should discuss this with the consultant and might decide to abandon play therapy or seek additional (psychiatric) assessment to check whether it is worth continuing with play work. Results are not always easily apparent and the therapeutic stages are not always completed in practice, but nothing in the therapeutic relationship is wasted. Any seeds sown may germinate later on, and apparent 'failure' does not necessarily mean that no good has been done.

- Several things help us in our evaluation of the effectiveness (or otherwise) of play therapy.

  - have there been any changes in the child's presenting problems?
  - is the child behaving age-appropriately in play therapy sessions?
  - are the 'themes of therapy' more or less worked through?
  - is the child feeling better about him or herself?
  - evaluating the work gives important information when considering termination.

Summary

At the beginning of the therapeutic process, children are initially troubled, without always knowing why they feel that way. Then feelings become targeted on definite things or people, though these are not necessarily the true cause of the problems. The third stage is often ambivalence when positive feelings emerge, jostling with feelings such as anger and rejection. In the final stage, positive feelings become less erratic and more firmly based, and the child's negative feelings more appropriately focused. In practice, the child's journey through the therapeutic stages is not always so clearcut.

The therapeutic stages, coupled with feedback from the child, and from people such as the carer, school and referrer, form part of the evaluative guidelines that help the decision-making process about when to finish working with the child.

EVALUATION CHECKLIST

1. At referral, list the problems perceived by the referrer and other significant people such as the child's teacher, keyworker and carers, noting who mentioned which difficulty.
2. List the children's account of their problems (if they are old enough to formulate ideas about this).
3. During play therapy, check your own understanding of where the child is at with reference to:
   (a) the therapeutic alliance
   (b) the therapeutic stages
   (c) the content of the play and whether the themes are arriving at some sort of resolution.
4. Periodically seek information from the referrer and other relevant adults about what is happening in the child's life, and their current views on the child's 'problem profile'.
5. What is the child reporting to you about home, school and other important areas?
6. Is the work coming to a conclusion, and should termination be considered?

11 Termination

With his self-capacity available and his self-regard restored, he ventures into new experiences and attains new meaning and value in relation to others.

(Moustakas, 1959, p. 45)

This chapter

- Outlines what should be taken into account when deciding about finishing play therapy with a child
- Contends that children have different needs and ideas about ending
- Suggests how the final stages of play therapy might be handled

---

Exercise

- Feel into and then compare
  - endings that have mattered to you
  - endings you have been glad about.
- What feelings can you recall around endings in your own childhood?
- What will be the issues when a child finishes play therapy
  - for the child?
  - for the child's carers?
  - for the play therapist?
- How will you prepare the child for ending?
- Pretend you are eight years old and have had 12 sessions in the playroom. How will you feel about finishing?

DECIDING ON TERMINATION

Much has been written about the importance of the therapeutic alliance and the consideration that is needed when starting work with a child, and equal care should be given to termination. A technical consideration is whether termination is planned (see Chapter 10 on evaluation), or whether there is sudden termination when, for instance, the child moves away, or someone (usually the child's carer on the rare occasions this happens) decides the child should stop attending play therapy sessions. When termination occurs unexpectedly, the play therapist has to make the best of a bad job and, if given the opportunity, would mark the occasion in some way. If termination is planned a date is set and play therapist and child work together towards the ending.

In most cases, termination is considered when the child is more self confident, exhibits decreased problem behaviour, is more realistic about where the difficulties lie, and shows improvements in social relationships and school work. In play therapy sessions, play has usually become age appropriate, organized and constructive, and there is a feeling of mutual trust in the relationship between play therapist and child *(Reisman, 1973, pp. 185–6)*. There may still be one or two problem areas but 'the therapist negotiates termination with the client when he believes that the advantages of ending the meeting, outweigh what may be gained by their continuance' *(Reisman, 1973, pp. 67–8)*. It is unrealistic to expect that a child will be 'cured' for ever; difficulties may recur at a later developmental stage or if the child's life circumstances deteriorate but, once freed to develop healthily, the growth process is on the child's side. Some children 'mature' when termination is discussed, others are indifferent *(Reisman, 1973, pp. 197–201)*.

Thinking about ending a child's play therapy?

* Is there improvement in most of the child's presenting problems?
* Is the child feeling better?
* Is the child getting on all right at home and at school?
* Does the child have a reasonably realistic understanding of his or her family background?
* Would the child benefit from referral elsewhere?
* Is play therapy proving unhelpful, or is it rejected by child and/or carers?

Following the notion of child-centred therapy, the child is usually involved in the decision to terminate, though with the pressure of a waiting list, pragmatic management pressures may determine that it is the play therapist initially who will begin to consider termination. In giving children some partial autonomy in the termination process, it may be useful to ask them how many more sessions they think they need *(Reisman, 1973, pp. 73–4)*. A definite ending date helps child and therapist to make the best use of the remaining time *(Gillmore, 1991, p. 339)*.

If the effects of previous losses in the child's life have been resolved and the child's progress in play therapy has been accurately judged, termination should not be too traumatic *(Jewett, 1984, p. 139)* and is a normal process. However, if children hide their distress, or reject the play therapist and/or play therapy in an attempt to prevent feelings of being rejected themselves, the play therapist should raise these issues with the child.

Preparation for termination is important, and ending should be discussed at least about half a term (certainly no less than four sessions) before the anticipated closure. Most children will initially experience the approach to termination as rejection. They appreciate knowing they are unique to the play therapist in some way, and value explicit assurance that they and the sessions have been important to the play therapist. Therapist and child may need to think about 'How many more times' in the playroom. Unless a child such as Andrew shows that he needs the sessions to stay the same, it can be helpful to space them out and to moderate the child–play therapist relationship; for example, with Toby and Polly the play therapist let herself be seen in different ways and allowed sessions to spill into the child's outside world.

Anna Freud *(Sandler, Kennedy and Tyson, 1980, pp. 243, 264)* states:

As far as the relationship is based on transference, it should end, but insofar as it is a real relationship, the child should be left to outgrow it gradually … It never seemed quite logical to me that terminating a child analysis should involve the complete separation from the analyst that it usually does for adult patients. With children, there is the loss of the real object as well as the loss of the transference object, and this complicates matters. To make an absolute break from a certain date onward merely sets up another separation, and an unnecessary one. If normal progress is achieved, the child will detach himself anyway, in the course of time, just as children outgrow their nursery school teachers, their school teachers and their friends at certain stages. The analyst can thereafter be visited and remembered on certain occasions, and should be available for this kind of contact.

Preparing the child for finishing play therapy:

- Involve the child in the decision to terminate
  - fix a date.
  - make sure carers, school and so on are aware of what you are doing
  - decide on how to 'countdown' with the child to prepare him or her for the reality of ending
  - remember that children are individuals who will have their own ideas about the best ways of finishing.

The playroom had been important to nine-year-old Brian (p. 89). Discussing the imminent holidays, Brian said he would like to come to the playroom 'until it falls down'. At the next session, his fifteenth, just before Easter, he remarked that he wanted to come 'for ever'. The play therapist reminded him that they would meet in a fortnight, after the holiday, and in alternate weeks the following term, so there would be five more sessions before they finished. It seemed important to handle termination sensitively in view of Brian's earlier comments. A bit later, when talking about ending, the play therapist described finishing as growing up, saying that the playroom is not the sort of place where children come for ever, and Brian appeared to accept this reasoning. In a later session there was a subtle change in the relationship and the play therapist felt challenged by him in a positive way. She was becoming a real person to him, rather than just a therapist figure.

Endings should not further damage the child:

- Particular care should be taken with children who have had bad experiences of previous loss and endings.
- Play therapists sometimes worry that a child who has made an attachment to the therapist may be damaged when play therapy finishes. Attachment is a good thing and, provided play therapy termination is handled sensitively with careful recognition of the child's feelings and phantasies, the child's ability to attach is transferable.
- Play therapists need to ensure that they do not become over-involved and hang on to the child.

Countdown

Most children know about school terms and school holidays, and these can be a useful framework when deciding when to terminate once it is agreed that this is the correct strategy.

When discussing termination, the play therapist can ask the child what he or she feels, and may suggest that the child is doing well (if that is the case), is growing up, that children do not come to the playroom for ever, and that the difficulties (these can be identified) that precipitated the referral seem to have diminished (if this is true). Holidays or half-term provide a useful interruption to the normal flow of sessions, after which an agreed number of sessions can be offered on a weekly or fortnightly basis until, perhaps, the next school holiday when they will finish with, if appropriate, the offer of a follow-up session a few months later. (Check, though, that the child comprehends what is meant by 'fortnightly'. This proved a difficult concept for ten-year-old Pam who eventually understood with a jubilant 'I've cracked it!'). It is helpful to tell children (or work out together) how many sessions they have had, how many there are still to come, and how many there will have been altogether. They are often impressed! Younger children may welcome some tangible form of countdown and the play therapist can usually find an idiom that suits the particular child. Ideas include drawing a train with a number of carriages equalling the remaining number of sessions. In the run-up sessions the child draws something in each carriage so that the train is complete on the final day, and the picture can be taken away. There are many variations, e.g. a child holding balloons that can have faces drawn on them and are coloured in, horses jumping over hurdles eventually arriving at the winning post, photos of different parts of the playroom. Let play therapists and children indulge their imagination!

Disrupted sessions

Occasionally, children abruptly stop coming to sessions when termination is broached. The child may be angry that play therapy will be stopping, and it feels safer for him or her to take control and say that he or she will not attend any more. Or perhaps an important issue, such as abuse, has not surfaced sufficiently for it to be dealt with; at some level the child realizes it needs attention but is too scared, so, in a rather upside-down way, chooses not to continue with the final sessions. If the child has had difficulty in coping with previous losses of, and separations from, significant adults and is insecure in outer life, he or she may take the decision to terminate forthwith. Disrupted sessions rarely happen if termination is approached sensitively, and at the right time. Of course sessions can be disrupted at any time by the child refusing to come, or by carers, teachers or someone important to the child preventing attendance. This needs handling differently.

THE BRIDGING PHASE

> - Make the therapeutic process more explicit. The therapist tries to help the child be-come more consciously aware of some of the issues and processes in the play therapy.
> - Some children like to gather concrete reminders of their sessions, such as photos, drawings, a story of their time in the playroom.
> - Other children want to go out of the playroom, e.g. to a park, cafe, or place of interest.
> - A few children use the last session or two to re-run the major, or beginning, stages of their playroom work.
> - Some children do not wish to make any changes in their sessions.

The bridging phase, towards the end of play therapy, is when the therapist can become a 'real' person to the child, mediating between the child's inner world and playroom activities, and the expectations of the outer world. During this time, especially with older children, the play therapist may want to make some of the therapeutic process more explicit to the child. How the bridging phase is attempted varies according to the unique nature of each child and each child/play therapist relationship (Smalley, 1971, p. 102).

Making the therapeutic process more explicit

Play therapists may consider it appropriate to share with the child some of the issues on which they have been working. Paintings, sandtrays or clay models can by surveyed together, exploring what the subject matter might have repre-sented, and how things have changed. Some children like to remember what they have done with specific play materials. Others are interested in remind-ing themselves: 'When I first came here I did ..., I felt ..., I thought ...'. 'Do you remember when ... ?'. Yet others may be problem based: 'It was like this before I came here: I was in trouble at school, mum hated me, I was nicking things, I got into rows with by brothers ... Now I'm OK at home, and it's brilliant at school. Yes, we did play a lot about me being angry with my mum and that she'd put me away'. There are some children, however many ways the play therapist tries, who have no wish to reflect on their time in the playroom.

Tangible reminders

Some play therapists abhor the idea of giving children presents, but others would see reasonable gifts as positive and therapeutic (Adcock et al., 1988, p. 132; Jewett 1984, p. 141). Birthday and Christmas cards, together with small presents (not the edible kind as the idea is to give the child something tangible to serve as a reminder of the play therapist and the play sessions) can be mementos that the child appreciates and collects. Another useful aid is to take a photograph in the playroom so that both can have a copy 'to remember you by'. The photograph, often snapped during the final session, and a small 'playroom present' chosen to complement the themes of the child's play therapy, are usually taken away with pleasure.

Eight-year-old Ann was in the tenth of 14 sessions:

'I wonder what present you'll give me when I leave?' [We'll have to think about that.] Ann: 'Mummy and Daddy came here, didn't they? Did they come to the playroom?' I said I hadn't seen them, but I didn't think they came to the playroom, and that this was Ann's room. A sigh of satisfaction. One session had been lost due to a school play so, on what was planned to be our final session, Ann wanted to confirm that this would be the last time. 'Have you got my present? I've got one for you.' Ann unwrapped her present (a doll) and was delighted, saying I'd chosen just the right thing. For the first time she sat on my knee and I rocked her. We talked about the sadness of ending, how endings can be beginnings, about what we had done together, and the reasons she had come to the playroom. She was extremely sad about finishing, and I said I was sad too. At the end of the session Ann packed the new doll's things into the box and, fetching a blanket, covered herself with it and sat on my knee and rocked. I offered to see her once more the following term, the aim being for her to tell me how she had been getting on. I stressed that this would be a one-off event, and it seemed as though I had got it 'just right' for her.

The play therapist's comments on the above session read:

The sessions had obviously meant much more to her than I realized, and I was surprised at the intensity of feeling, both verbal and bodily. It was unfortunate that I had not been able to do the usual countdown because of the school messing up appointments as I felt we hadn't been able to prepare ourselves properly.

The follow-up session was successful.

Environmental change

For some children it is appropriate to introduce a change of environment during the bridging phase. Towards the end of his work Toby (p. 4) had accomplished much, in particular vanquishing strong, angry inner and outer forces. His school was amazed at his improved performance and behaviour, and progress at home was reported. At this stage Toby began to use the sessions differently, choosing games he and the play therapist could play together. Instead of being an observer, the play therapist was drawn into his play. She felt that his 'trial of strength' was on a different level and that she was being involved in real-life way.

Around Christmas there was a natural gap in the weekly sessions, and Toby and his play therapist agreed to meet fortnightly until Easter, when they would probably finish. In the penultimate session, the play therapist reminded him that a fortnight's time would be their last regular meeting, but that there would be a couple of follow-up occasions after that. Toby said he would be sad to finish, the play therapist stated that she would be sad too.

The play therapist's notes of the last session:

He painted a bold human figure that said 'I am Toby and I will be gone soon'. We talked again about parting and finishing, and how the experiences he had had with me cannot be taken away. I offered to do a painting saying 'I am sad Toby is going soon', but he didn't take this up. I enquired what had been important about coming? 'I don't know. It's just been good'. He beat me at draughts! On the table I'd left his photographs and two parcels, a present for him and one for his family. I told him he was the only person to whom I'd given two presents.

On his first follow-up session Toby and his play therapist had an outing to a steam railway, and when the play therapist collected him for their second trip to a theme park he gave her a present (wrapped in wedding paper!) containing an ornament of a smart young man. The label read 'To a very *special* friend'. The play therapist told him she would treasure it greatly. She understood it to be a present of 'himself', a symbol of the young man he had been freed to become.

Six-year-old Polly (pp. 33–4) was an example of how environmental change was threaded into her sessions. A child whose play therapy was vivid, exciting, difficult and pathetic, Polly had pluck and stamina and within nine months of weekly sessions she was learning at school and a potential adoptive family had been found. However, there was a delay of several months before the latter was confirmed, and the play therapist's role was to help Polly through her depression and anxiety, and to prepare her, alongside the foster mother and social worker, for the transfer to her permanent home.

Having had a few interruptions to their weekly sessions, in the fifty-fifth session the play therapist discussed seeing Polly fortnightly. 'Oh no, don't leave me' she responded in desperate tones with a look of dismay. The play therapist explained that she would not leave her as long as Polly wanted her. Later Polly agreed to fortnightly sessions, the play therapist offering to send her a postcard the weeks she would not be coming for play therapy, and this pleased her.

By session 60 the potential adoptive placement was looking positive, and Polly was going through agonies about whether she would be 'good' enough for them to want to keep her. Towards the end of the session Polly hid, and the notes read:

For a while she has me foxed as she's hidden herself inside a drawer. She protests about coming out and I start getting firm. I say 'You want to stay in the playroom?' Polly nods. I continue 'Well, you've got the playroom inside you; you've got the biscuits, you've got me, you've got your memories of what we've done'. Gradually she yields and puts on her coat. She wants to be picked up, snuggling into me.

Shortly before the sixty-third session, Polly had confirmation that Mr and Mrs Taylor would be her new parents, though it would be some time before she could live with them permanently. At the beginning of that session Polly requested that, if they finished early, could she and the play therapist visit the houses she lived in before going into care. The play therapist cautiously said she would have to ask the social worker. Much of that session was about visiting:

> Polly: 'I'll come for tea in your home. I'll get the dinner. What would you like?' and we decide the menu. 'If you want me, you knock. Pretend you're a visitor and I invite you for tea. Pretend tea's nearly ready. Get the tea.' I take some bits of Lego (cakes) on two plates. 'Not that tea! I meant the sand, you idiot. You say, "I'm not an idiot".' I fetch the sand. '*This* side' exasperatedly, as I sit at the 'wrong' side of the table.

Winnicott (1977, p. 195) emphasizes how important 'visiting' can be in the bridging phase.

The play therapist had a discussion with the foster mother and social worker, and they agreed that, as Polly was requesting it, they would embark on an active life history *(Ryan and Walker, 1993)*. It was decided who would do what, the play therapist's task being to accompany Polly to previous houses, schools and nurseries. Photographs, mementoes and anecdotes would be collected and placed in a book that Polly would compile. All this was to be done in a child-centred way at her pace.

There was the delicate matter of confidentiality. The play therapist reminded Polly that, as she knew, what happened in the playroom was private, unless Polly wanted to tell people, but the play therapist would inform her social worker and foster mother about the visits they might make. Polly accepted this. After further conversation she asked if she could have next-time's (eight months hence) birthday present 'because I won't be coming to see you then. You'll have Tracey [another girl in the home] or someone like that instead'. It seemed as though Polly was beginning to accept the reality of ending play therapy.

Session 64 was largely spent visiting her former house, an important shop and her infant school, returning to the playroom for refreshments. In session 66 Polly asked if they could go to the park 'or summat'. The play therapist mooted an expedition to town to buy things for the book Polly would be making and she jumped at this, being keen to return to the playroom for the usual refreshments. In these sessions there was a balance between playroom and outside world, between going out as companions and the regressive elements she still sometimes displayed by wanting to be carried and drinking from feeding bottles.

The next (and last main) session was three days before her move, and the play therapist recorded:

> Polly told me about how she'd be going to the Taylors on Friday. I reflected that she was excited, but perhaps a bit sad too? She denied sadness. 'Ann will still be my social worker and you'll still be my playworker.' I reminded her that I wouldn't be having her back in the playroom until the holidays, and then probably only twice; but I'd give her a card with my work and home address and telephone numbers so that she could contact me. She looked at the welcome-to-your-new-home card and the six photos we'd taken to mark events like birthdays. She asked that together we make the life-story book, so we punched the paper, placing it in the binder. 'It's like an office,' she exclaimed.

We picnicked outside, and returned to the playroom: 'This is your house and this is mine'. After other activities, she swept the home corner so that 'It will be clean for when I next come'. As Polly prepared to leave she exclaimed 'I'm a new lady'. I asked her if she wanted to take the card, photos, and life-story book, but she piled them up, indicating that they should remain. However, she gleefully claimed a blanket which many months ago I had told her she could take when she moved to a new family. This had been an attempt to give something personal to her with, at a deeper level, a recognition of the symbolism of the regressive work she had done with me, regrowing herself from the baby to the more or less adjusted child of today.

The play therapist sent her another card to arrive at her new home on the first morning. At 9.10 a.m. that day, Saturday, the play therapist's phone rang; and again the next day: 'You told me to ring!'.

Individuality

The way termination is handled is unique to each child–play therapist relationship, and it is not always necessary to do something different in the final sessions. In view of the improvement of seven-year-old Andrew at school, the play therapist told him that she would finish seeing him regularly in the playroom at the end of the summer term but that, with the co-operation of the junior school, she hoped to see him twice the following term. Although the play therapist felt that she and the playroom were important to Andrew, he appeared unperturbed in the run-up to the final session. He used the last two sessions to recapitulate much of the work he had done, the play therapist experiencing a condensed version of the previous sessions. He was pleased with his present of some toy cars (much of his play centred on vehicles – pp. 79–80).

The ending of the play work with six-year-old Abigail had been discussed for some time and the student's notes of the penultimate session read as follows:

> Abigail wants to sit by the fire to have the food and drink. I remind her that it will be our last time next week and I say I will miss her. She sits close to me while we eat. I suggest we could have a party next week, if she liked. Abigail responded 'We could have the story'. [What story is that?] 'The one you are writing about me coming here – about all the things I have done while I am here.' The student said she thought that was a good idea. Abigail continued 'Then we could tidy all these things away and clean everywhere.' The student responded [If you like I won't bother to put the toys out, we'll just have the story]. (Note how the student missed the point, but Abigail knew what she wanted). 'No, put them out and then we can put them away together.'

In Abigail's final session the toys were in their usual places. As well as food and drink, there was a gift of a book, and Polaroid photos of Abigail and the student were taken. The student recorded that Abigail was cheerful and chatted about the photographs. The student mentioned once again that she would miss her, and Abigail responded 'I won't see you ever again, will I?' (The student was leaving the area and this had largely been worked through earlier.) [No, I will miss you but you have a present from the playroom to take home with you, and we both have a photograph to help us remember.]

In her reflections on the session the student commented:

> Abigail seemed psychologically prepared for the ending of the sessions. I suggest that the photographs and the gifts were useful in providing her with something material to take away and remember the sessions by.

Many children like to do something different for their last session, most preferring a party in the playroom, but a few opt for an outing. (If an outing is offered, the play therapist needs to check with appropriate adults that this will be in order.)

Six-year-old David lived in a children's home, having been poorly treated by his mother who subsequently abandoned him. He had had 23 therapy sessions over seven months and his student play therapist was important to him, as David was to her. They handled the countdown by taking a photograph at each of the last four sessions, mounting them on a specially prepared board and David knew that at the last session he could take them away. As well as the playroom present, the student had prepared a party table replete with tasty food. David could eat as much as he wanted, in whatever order, and this he hugely enjoyed! The sadness about ending was talked about together, and his play therapist offered David two follow-up contacts: taking him to the cinema and attending his birthday party.

Eleven-year-old Jean (pp. 65–6) organized her leaving party with great excitement. She contributed towards the food, brought along a music tape, invited the secretaries (proffering refreshments to the team manager who acted as receptionist in their stead!), and got everyone involved in party games.

Recapitulation

For some children, before a holiday or on termination, ending is marked by a fairly condensed recapitulation of the play therapy sessions, and the play therapist may experience a feeling of 'We've been here before'. However, this time it is different as play therapy has run its course and the child is merely replaying, albeit unconsciously, some of the key elements of the work.

Writing up the penultimate session with Jean, the play therapist noted:

> There was an air reminiscent of the first few sessions when she didn't quite know what to do, an air of recapitulation and, at some level, of sadness. Hide-and-seek and making greetings cards were déja-vu, harking back to earlier sessions. Supporting this was her reference to

another child she knew who had been in play therapy and had moved successfully to a foster home. Would it be like that for her? Jean had gathered me up in the carpet sweeper and I felt that this was her way of controlling the ending. She can sweep me away; I don't then have to chuck her out. On the face of it, she's accepting termination well, but I must make space for expression of sadness, hers and mine.

FINAL SESSION

Exercise

- What memories do you have about the last session of something special that you had been doing?
- Can you remember, or imagine, what the 'last time' would have felt like when you were a child?
- What are the play therapist's feelings likely to be?
- How would you like to say 'Goodbye' to the child?
- Pretend you are a child. What feelings would you have in the last play therapy session?

If the child does not specifically raise the fact that this is the last session, some play therapists may take the initiative (*Reisman, 1973, p. 197*) and ask 'What do you want to leave behind you here? What would you like to take with you?'. The play therapist expresses his/her mixed feelings about the ending, pleasure at the child's progress, but sadness at missing the child (if that is the case). 'I've learned a lot from you. Take care of yourself' (*Jewett, 1984, pp. 140–1*). Sometimes the final session, if located in the playroom, may be a party, or at least significantly different from the beginning sessions. However, *Haworth (1990, p. 24)* advises:

> The final session often recapitulates the presenting problems, with the child using the toys most frequently used in the past as well as giving some indication of the progress made. Often the final session can be quite a discouraging one for the therapist, in that the child may appear to be regressing, especially if the final session mirrors too closely the initial session in tone and content ... It may take strong resolve on the therapist's side to resist the urge to retract and decide to resume the sessions, partly because the therapist, also, may be reluctant to terminate the relationship.

If offered, arrangements are made for follow-up sessions, and the child informed how the play therapist can be contacted. Some children like to take home things they have made in the playroom such as paintings or clay models. One girl had written and drawn her own book of key events to take away with her.

It is important to observe sensitively what termination means for play therapist and child, and to give permission for sadness, anger, loss; or perhaps relief?

- Acknowledge this is the last session and share feelings, perhaps reviewing what has happened in the play therapy sessions.
- Ensure the child understands about any future contact with the play therapist.
- If being referred elsewhere, celebrate what has been achieved in play therapy.
- Let the child know that he or she has been special and important to you in some way.

Summary

Evaluation of the work is usually a precursor to termination. Decisions have to be made about the best way of finishing the work. During the bridging phase the play therapist becomes a 'real life' person rather than the all-accepting (well, almost!) therapeutic figure. For some children, sessions continue as usual in the final stages. For others, some of the work may be located out of the playroom. Children may appreciate some tangible mementoes of their time in the playroom. In the last session or two, some young people play out a review of the work as a whole, or in kaleidoscopic flashbacks and there can be a feeling of going back to the beginning. The majority of children ask for a party in this last session. Farewell cards and gifts may be given. A few children may be offered a follow-up session.

So far in this Part we have looked at various stages of the therapeutic process, and gained glimpses of how the work may be accomplished. The next chapter raises some contingent issues of incidents that arise at some time or another in the playroom, and are of direct relevance to the work.

TERMINATION CHECKLIST

1. Has termination been precipitated by the child, the family, or someone else? How should you respond?
2. Normally, termination should be planned.
   (a) Do the child's play and progress in the session suggest that the work is coming to a normal conclusion?
   (b) Does feedback from the referrer (school, family) indicate that the child is less harassed and troubled?
   (c) Do you think that, although perfection may not have been achieved, the child has progressed as far as can reasonably be expected at this stage?
   (d) If children are not making any progress, or are getting worse, do they need referral elsewhere? In which case, how will you handle play therapy termination?
3. How do you propose to involve the child in the termination decision and process?
4. Whom should you inform about the termination?
5. Is any form of tangible countdown useful and, if so what form will it take?

6. Would locating some of the final sessions out of the playroom be helpful?
7. Are the giving of gifts, cards and photographs appropriate?
8. During the ending phase, do you need to modify your relationship with the child?
9. Who requires reports of the work?
10. Is any follow-up necessary?
11. How do *you* feel about the proposed termination?

12 Some specific issues

A crucial requirement is the ability to enter into a significant relationship with a child and to bring to the therapy meetings a blend of personal and professional talents and skills, a natural integration of knowledge, understanding, and experience.

(Moustakas, 1959, p. 360)

This chapter identifies some of the issues that arise in play therapy and suggests ways of responding to them

- language and questions
- gifts
- the playroom and other children
- restatement about the purpose of sessions
- repeated material and 'stuck' play
- holidays
- missed sessions
- aggressive play, violence and 'bad' toys
- broken and stolen toys
- what do we do if children start acting out sexually
- what happens if children reveal abuse

Exercise

- 'I wonder if … ever happens?' How many eventualities can you think of?
- 'How would I respond if this … happened?'
- What is your worst scenario?
- At what stage, and from whom, would you seek help?

LANGUAGE AND QUESTIONS

Exercise

- What do you know about the development of children's language, memory and thought processes?
- Are you aware that some troubled children suffer from speech problems?
- How do you communicate so that children understand you?
- Can you communicate effectively with children for whom English is not their first language?
- How would you adapt your communication skills when working with children with hearing or sight problems?
- Would you allow the child to swear, or to use offensive language in sessions?
- Observe how children of different ages, races and ability, communicate with
  – their peers

- bigger children, smaller children
- authority figures
- animals
- people they do not like.

In play therapy there are three levels of verbal communication. There is the regressive baby stage with sign language, babbling or baby talk, where communication is often hidden. Then there is the level of phantasy, and the message the child is giving may be conveyed through idiom and symbols. The play therapist needs to support the child, encouraging communication in the idiom of phantasy, art and imagination (Gondor, 1964, p. 376). Thirdly there is direct, logical age-appropriate communication. By the end of play therapy, older children should be able to talk out their difficulties rationally and consciously, bringing them into verbal awareness.

When talking to children, play therapists would normally try to use the child's vocabulary and expressions (Klein, 1955, p. 233). Many children referred for play therapy have language deficit with, maybe, restricted conceptual ability (Berry, 1972, p. 16; Rich, 1968, p. 41), and the play therapist may be responding to a child's emotional, and not chronological, age. Some children talk relatively easily about facts but find it difficult, perhaps impossible, to share feelings, whereas others are lost in their inner world and facts are hardly worth the bother. In adult psychotherapy questions tend to be deflected back to the client, but if children ask factual questions there is an argument for giving realistic, though not necessarily detailed, answers because the child's cognitive awareness is less well developed than an adult's. However, before offering responses, it can be useful to try to elicit the child's own answer:

Child: 'What's that for?'
Therapist: 'You wonder what it's for. What would you like it to do?'

But the child may really want to know what 'it' is for, and a simple answer may be in order. Play therapists need to be able to handle the following – and worse! Peter:

Two old ladies sitting on the grass – you'll laugh at this. One stuffed her finger up the other one's arse. Old Mother Riley, she got drunk She fell in the fire and she burnt her cunt. My aunty learnt me all these jokes.

Smelly little Stuart (aged six) used some fragrant language:

'I heard my heart talking. It says 'Don't listen to your mind.' The therapist asks why not? 'Because you'll start fighting ... Bloody squodgy paint. Can we say naughty words here?' [Yes, you can say what you like in this room.] 'We daren't talk bloody like that to our teachers ... If we start arguing we turn the world upside down ... I'll marry you. Do you want to be married? That means kissing. I've got to live with you.' He gives the play therapist a big kiss. 'I'm married to you and I've kissed you.'

Swearing and racially and sexually offensive language are acceptable in child-centred therapy, with the proviso that the child is told that whilst it is all right to say these things in the therapy room, they should not be said elsewhere, and the offensiveness of certain words might be explained.

Interestingly, and perhaps in defiance of development norms, some children, as they grow older and more verbally skilful and defensive, become less verbally expressive in the play therapy setting *(Lebo and Lebo, 1957, p. 753).*

GIFTS

Exercise

- Would you allow the child to give you a present? If so, in what circumstances?
- Would you give the child a present? If so, when?
- What might a present signify?

Gifts for special occasions may be acceptable, provided they are not overdone *(Adams, 1982, p. 115)*, and can be an important mark of respect for the child, giving some tangible sign of the relationship *(France, 1988, pp. 134–6)*. Less often do play therapists receive gifts. If offered a present, the playworker might reflect the child's feelings about giving the present, find out why, and decide whether to accept or reject it. If play therapists are attuned to the child and to the work they are doing, they will be able to judge how to handle the giving and receiving of gifts.

THE PLAYROOM AND OTHER CHILDREN

- 'Am I the only child (I hope I am the only child) who uses the playroom?'
- Do you see any other children? If so, who are they? Why? What do other children do?
- What do you know about
  – sibling rivalry?
  – jealousy?
  – needy children who feel they are not getting sufficient care and attention?

At some stage in their play therapy the majority of children enquire whether other children use the playroom. Some are curious, others jealous, and the play therapist needs to be sensitive to the child's enquiry, which may be a reflection of sibling rivalry.

Wendy asked about the other children who come here. 'When do they come? Different days like me?' I replied that children come here on different days and at different times, and go to different schools, and that Wendy comes on Wednesday – every Wednesday except for holidays – for one hour. 'Yes', and she smiled happily. She made a sandcastle but messed it up because the next child would knock it down. 'Do you take my paintings down when the other children come?' I said I did. 'That's fair, isn't it? I'll paint a house like I did before. My pictures are nice, better ones than the others, aren't they?' [You're saying that your pictures are better than the other children's], I reflected.

Gemma:

'Do other people come here too?' [You wonder whether other children come here as well?] 'Yes, I want to know whether other children come?' [Some other children do come here, but this is your time.] She points out scribble on the wall and I say that someone else has done that, but Friday afternoon is for her. 'Do other children come this afternoon?' [No, no-one else this afternoon. Do you mind sharing? Sometimes it's nice to have things to ourselves.] 'Mm.'

Exercise

- How have you felt when you have had to share someone precious to you?
- Can you remember someone who was important to you when you were little?
- What did you feel about him or her, particularly with regard to other children?

RESTATEMENT ABOUT THE PURPOSE OF SESSIONS

> - Child and play therapist can sometimes get wrapped up in the play therapy process. They may
>   - enjoy being together and 'forget' the problems outside
>   - be finding the therapy sessions difficult or boring
>   - have lost focus and are not sure why they are there.
> - It helps if play therapist and child occasionally talk about why the child is coming to the playroom.

From time to time it can be useful to recap what the sessions are for. Play therapists can elicit the child's views, or offer their own version, or both. Children may be engrossed and involved in the work, or may not be fully engaged; the child may not really understand what the sessions are about, and it is helpful to give the child an opportunity to indicate this. As play therapy proceeds, children's perceptions of the therapeutic process may alter.

The previous session had been cancelled by the children's home because Martin had absconded, and when he arrived the next week the play therapist noted:

He came into the room looking happy and composed. I said I was glad to see him, and obviously knew something must have happened last week. He replied that he'd been in trouble – people had been picking on him and another lad. He didn't know why he had run off, nor what was bothering him, except for being picked on. I reminded him that the play session is a place where he can bring his annoyance, angers, upsets; that perhaps he can express in his session what is upsetting him, or he can use me to talk about, or work at, whatever is bugging him, if he wants. I said I wasn't there to tell him off about what had happened, but perhaps he could avoid these incidents if he could express what was bothering him. The playroom is a place where he can bring, and leave, his troubles.

As an older child, this approach was tapping his conscious awareness, but it was also implicitly suggesting that even if he did not overtly know what the trouble was, there was a chance that it could be resolved in the play setting.

REPEATED MATERIAL AND 'STUCK' PLAY

> • The child is practising something.
> • The child needs to keep going over a shocking event.
> • The child returns to a former situation, but differently.
> • The child repeats something that the therapist has missed.

There are four types of repetition.

1. Based on the mastery principle, some play or affect will be repeated until the child has fully experienced and integrated it or, on the other hand, like a well-worn coat that has been outgrown, can discard it.
2. Grossly abused children affected by post-traumatic stress disorder may replay many times the events that shocked them so much.
3. Play therapy can be like a spiral: the child experiences something, then the same incident is repeated, but differently, and again, and again as various dimensions are assimilated into the child's repertoire. When this happens, the play therapist acknowledges and accepts the almost-repetition, encouraging re-emergence of the material and extra dimensions as it seeks integration.
4. However experienced, play therapists will 'miss' important material that a child presents. Children can be obliging beings and usually re-present the material, albeit unconsciously, until the dumb play therapist suitably acknowledges it. Sometimes a particular piece of play may seem trivial, but if repeated several times the play therapist is urged to examine it carefully to see what it is saying (Berry, 1971, p. 326).

Despite the above, play sometimes seems to get 'stuck', and the child appears blocked and unable to continue, or to alter, the play. The play therapist has to decide whether to wait and see what develops, or whether to try to facilitate the child (cf. Gil, 1991, pp. 73–5). In most circumstances we would 'wait and see', but occasionally facilitation seems appropriate.

– We may try to help the child verbally, by asking about what has happened, and what the child's feelings are. Sometimes a verbal commentary sufficiently disrupts the child's play to allow a change to take place.
– We could suggest some directed play, for instance around a particular issue.

- If a play episode has been repeated but the ending has got 'stuck', the therapist might suggest several endings and invite the child to choose.
- Transferring the play episode to other media, e.g. puppets, storytelling, dramatic role play, sometimes enables the play to become unstuck.
- Inviting the child to take on someone's or something's role may shift the blockage.
- The therapist could physically move some of the play materials, or cast someone or something into a different role. 'What would happen if …?'
- Video the play, then watch with the child, discussing feelings, perceptions and intentions.
- Ask 'If you could do whatever you wanted to change things, what would it be?'.
- The therapist could introduce a story in which the characters have similar problems to the child.
- Offering materials related to the five senses can sometimes give a different perspective.

HOLIDAYS

Exercise

- You are doing something that is really important to you, and the person you are doing it with says he or she is going on a family holiday so cannot see you for a few weeks.
  - How would you, as an adult, feel?
  - Imagine how a child might feel. Might he or she think 'It's my fault. I'm no good. She [or he] doesn't care. If I'd done … this wouldn't have happened.' What else?
- How would you feel, as a play therapist, when the child tells you that he or she cannot come for a few sessions?
- Do you know what it is like for an adult in therapy when the therapist takes a break?

For some children, holidays need as much sensitive preparation as termination (Chapter 11), especially if the *play therapist's* holiday is breaking the continuity. It is not always so painful if the child's holiday causes the break as there is often excitement about visiting the sea, or gran, or whatever. However, play therapists need holidays too, which should be planned to cause the children as little dislocation as possible. It is good practice to warn children in advance that there will not be any sessions for however many weeks, but that sessions *will* resume after the break. Some sort of countdown is helpful so that children know that they can come to the playroom, say, three more times, then the play therapist will be away for two weeks, and that they will come back again after then as usual. Play therapists may offer to send a card during the weeks when they are unable to see the child *(France, 1988, pp. 133–4)*.

There are occasions, particularly if a child is in deep regression, when the play therapist would try to avoid breaking the continuity and, unless away from the area but otherwise on holiday, the worker may choose to keep that particular child's sessions running. Similarly, play therapists should avoid going away in the first few weeks of a child's sessions.

Some children, when faced with the 'loss' of their therapeutic time, react by needing to take control and they choose not, for instance, to attend the last session before a break (cf. *Horne, 1989*). Other children do not seem to mind the disruption and carry on as normal. Yet others present a kaleidoscopic synopsis of the work they have done in the playroom. In all cases it is not uncommon for an apparent deterioration in the first play therapy session after the holiday break, but normally there is a satisfactory pickup after that. If not, such children are probably working on issues of loss and separation that are part of the therapeutic process.

- It is important for child and therapist that there are some holiday breaks in long-term play therapy, and that these breaks are prepared for and approached with sensitivity.
- The play therapist will try to take holidays to cause the least disruption to the child, and to avoid a long absence if the child is going through a regression.
- The therapist might send a card to the child during the holidays as a way of keeping a link.
- On the first one or two sessions after a holiday break, allow the child to express and act out feelings about the gap. The child may revert to earlier playroom behaviour.
- Play therapists would not normally start with a new child shortly before a holiday.

MISSED SESSIONS

Exercise

- You, the play therapist, are suddenly taken ill
  - what will you do about tomorrow's play therapy sessions?
  - will you expect any repercussions when you next see the child?
- You have to go into hospital next week. How do you prepare the child?
- You are seven and are told that you won't be able to go to the fair tomorrow, which you had been looking forward to, because the person who was taking you has to do something else. How might you feel?

Sessions may be missed for a number of reasons. Holidays and the occasional conflicting appointment are usually known about in advance so that child and play therapist are prepared, and are aware when the next session will occur. It is trickier if missed sessions happen unexpectedly. The play therapist who is suddenly ill would inform people concerned with the child's session, and could send a card or note of explanation to the child. Occasionally the child suddenly misses a session, and at key points in the therapy this could upset the therapeutic work. A card from the play therapist saying that the child is expected the following week may help.

After a session when Wendy did not arrive, the play therapist said [Hallo, Wendy, I missed you last week. Were you ill?] 'Yes. Did someone else come?' [No, because that time was for you and me.]

The play therapist will take it up with the person concerned if a session has been prevented or 'forgotten'.

Sometimes the child decides not to come to the playroom. This may be a bid to independence, or there may be a counter-attraction, in which case the refusal is usually short-lived. However, when the child's refusal is more determined, some play therapists may take the line that it is the child's right to decide, accepting the decision at face value. Or the referrer could be asked to see the child and assess what is happening. Additionally the play therapist might write to the child, saying that the sessions are being held open and that it is hoped the child will attend at least once more. Some children may be testing out the concern and interest of the play therapist, so do not always accept apparent withdrawal at face value.

- It is only as a last resort that play therapy sessions should be cancelled.
- In emergencies, let the child know why the session is cancelled, and when the next session will be.
- If necessary, follow this up with a letter or card, mentioning feelings as well as facts.
- Allow the child to express anger and to feel you have let him or her down.

AGGRESSIVE PLAY, VIOLENCE AND 'BAD' TOYS

Exercise

- What do you do when you feel, and are, angry?
- What do children do when they feel, and are, angry?
- How would you feel if, in a play session, a child was angry about
  – his or her family?
  – school?
  – you?
- How would you deal with
  – violent feelings and thoughts within yourself during a play session?
  – the child's violent behaviour?
- What ways are there to help a child identify, and express, anger?

There is a difference between symbolic dangerous or violent play, when things are being acted out and everyone concerned knows that no real harm will be done, and the occasional potentially damaging play entered into 'for real' by an angry or disturbed child. It is in no one's interests for children to damage themselves, the play therapist or the playroom, and situations should be averted before they get out of hand. Most children respond to a quiet verbal caution, with reasons given as to the potential danger, and the play can perhaps be deflected, for example so that the child hits the doll instead of the play therapist. On rare occasions, a piece of equipment that is being dangerously used (for example, a sword) may be placed out of bounds and, even more rarely, the child may have to be restrained or removed.

Fairly early in her therapy Polly was in an angry mood, and a 'bad teddy' seemed an appropriate target for some of her anger.

I'm asked to be a ghost, and she says she's a 'bad girl'. She tells me to be a bad ghost and she'll be my bad-ghost baby. Polly sits on my knee, insisting that we cover ourselves with blankets. She suggests that we make a house behind the curtain, so we drape the curtain in front of us, cover ourselves in blankets, and utter 'bad ghost' noises. We have to make nasty faces too. We look for bad babies (dolls) and she clutches two of them, plus a woolly ball. The teddy becomes the *really* bad thing, and he tries to steal the good babies (as the dolls have now become). He makes fearful noises. Eventually the bad teddy is stabbed … Then we have to look for a bad-ghost baby. We sit in the sun and Polly breaks the baby's neck. There is more violent play and, towards the end of the session when she goes to the toilet, I suggest that before she leaves the building we'll go back to the playroom and magic everything better. We pick up the beheaded doll and the teddy, making them better, then cast a happy spell over the whole room.

There may be patches of violence or sadism in some children's play and play therapists might query the wisdom of allowing it. However, provided it is kept within bounds, if the child needs to play it out then it is important, and may prevent violent urges from being acted out in other areas of the child's life. When accepted, violent themes usually diminish. Violence often results from learned behaviour or from intolerable stress and failed communication. Play therapists should be aware of their own violent feelings so that children do not need to act them out on the therapist's behalf (*Dockar-Drysdale, 1990, pp. 126, 129, 133; 1993, pp. 123–36*).

- Aggression is a normal part of human behaviour.
- Physical violence against people is not allowed in the playroom, but the child should be encouraged to identify, own and express angry feelings.
- You may have to model alternatives to physical violence.

BROKEN AND STOLEN TOYS

Exercise

- As a child, you desperately want to take a small toy from the playroom.
  - what are your feelings about this?
  - why do you want to have something?
  - where will you secrete it?
- If, as a child you broke a toy in the playroom
  - how would you feel?
  - what would you expect should happen?
- As a play therapist, what would you do if a child steals something from the playroom?
- What would you do if a child brings a stolen toy into the playroom?
- Do you replace stolen or broken toys?

Toys rendered dangerous should be removed or replaced, but views vary about broken toys. Sometimes an object should not be thrown away if a child breaks it, as the play therapist might be understood as saying, symbolically, that the playroom is not a place for broken, 'bad' things. Children might therefore, at some level, feel that they cannot bring the 'bad', broken aspects of themselves into that setting. Also it can be important, for some children, to find ways of playing with, and in a sense restoring, the broken toy. It is perhaps easier to accept this philosophy if children have their individual toy boxes, but it is more problematic when toys are used by other children. In practical terms, a compromise may be employed whereby careful judgement has to be made. Some broken toys are removed and replaced; some made available to the child who broke them but with a replacement for other children; or, rarely, the broken toy might remain for all children for the time being.

It is often difficult to know how to handle the issue of stolen toys. If the play therapist is sure that a certain child has stolen something, the child or carer can be contacted and the item retrieved.

> Polly (pp. 33–4) had been dressing up and loved wearing a bracelet. At the end of the session I noticed that she was still wearing it and, after I had commented on it, she said 'Oh, the bracelet, so you remembered it.' I was with her all the time, but at one stage she turned towards a curtain, so was partly hidden. When tidying up I couldn't find the bracelet and telephoned the foster mother who said Polly had it, so we agreed that she take it from her and that it would be returned to me.

Sometimes there is just a nagging suspicion that something might have been, or is being, stolen. The play therapist might say 'I wonder where such and such is? I wonder if it's slipped into your pocket?'

A few sessions previously:

> Polly had wrapped up some plasticine into a parcel. Towards the end of the session my ears tell me that she's putting the parcel in her coat pocket. 'You stay over there. You'd better be asleep when I come back', she uttered. After going to the toilet, it's time to leave and she's got her coat on. I know she's put the plasticine parcel in her pocket and want to give her the opportunity to get out of the situation gracefully. We have a plasticine search. 'I don't know where it is', she says. We look in the sand, the dolls' house, the crib. I suggest [Perhaps Polly knows – can she find it?] 'You stay there, Mrs' and I hear rustlings. My ears tell me she's removed half the plasticine, and this is evident when she gives it to me. I'd already suggested that she wants to take something from the playroom away with her but that this is not allowed, and I remind her that she can take her memories and the things she has eaten inside her, and that she already has some playroom presents. I ask for the other half back, but she refuses to return it. I tell her we're not leaving the playroom until I have it, and that if time is wasted it will be docked off next session. Then I get angry as she becomes more awkward and tell her I don't like things being stolen and I want it back. She shamefacedly gives it to me, obviously being shaken by my

anger. I knew, from previous experiences, that whereas some children might be cowed, Polly often responded, in the long term, to genuine anger.

Twelve-year-old Martin (p. 92) had been playing with the Incredible Hulk, Darth Vader and a small black figure in the sand. When I came to clear up I could not find the small black phantasy man, and suspected Martin might have taken it. I wondered what to do, particularly as this had occurred before a holiday. Eventually I decided that I needed to acknowledge what *might* have happened, so I wrote to him. Martin was somewhat sheepish at the beginning of the next session, and thanked me for his birthday card and present. Halfway through the session I realized I hadn't mentioned my letter about the missing black man, and wasn't sure whether it had been appropriate not to raise the matter. I decided to let it drop, and my consultant commented that it must have surprised him that nothing had happened, bearing in mind inquests he had experienced in other settings.

Some children are extremely adept at secreting toys in their clothing. A few deprived children desperately need something tangible to take home. After careful assessment, the play therapist might provide a small item specifically for the child to take away *(Swanson, 1970, p. 74).*

- Sometimes children steal playroom equipment. The play therapist will tackle the child, concentrating on the child's feelings about the misappropriation and of being found out.
- Despite a rule of not damaging people and things in the playroom, toys may get broken accidentally, or on purpose. Help the child to calm down, discussing circumstances surrounding the event and reminding the child of the playroom rules.
- When encouraging the expression of anger, it is sometimes appropriate to select a certain toy that the child can pull to bits, break, hit mercilessly, etc.

WHAT DO WE DO IF CHILDREN START ACTING OUT SEXUALLY?

Exercise

- What do you know about childhood sexuality?
- How would you feel, and what would you do, if a child
  - touches your genitals or breasts?
  - strips off, inviting you to look at, or fondle, his or her genitals?
  - wants to 'love' you and/or to be physically intimate and/or to have intercourse?
- What titillates, or intrigues you, about the sexuality of children?

At some stage in their therapy a very few children try to engage in direct sexual touching or explicit sexual behaviour with the play therapist, sometimes removing their clothes and trying to take off those of the play therapist. There is a fine dividing line between letting the child express what needs to be expressed, but with safety and propriety. *Sexual involvement with the play therapist is prohibited*, but in such a way that the child is not made to feel ashamed, 'naughty', or puzzled – after all, this is how she or he might have got used to pleasing adults. The play therapist might say something like 'I can see you want to … but I can't let you … because …'. The therapist may suggest 'We need to learn to keep our bodies safe'; 'In the playroom we don't touch each other's private parts' (or whatever words the child uses); 'Our body is our own and it's OK to say no' *(Bannister, 1989, p. 81)*; 'You can tell me/show me with the dolls/draw me a picture'.

Importantly, play therapists need to be safeguarded against allegations from the child, and should inform their consultant and line manger if the child is trying to enter into explicit, body-to-body play. The use of video- or an audio-tape, with the date and times of starting and stopping the session clearly recorded, or an observer, may be appropriate. If *a play therapist feels he or she is responding to the child's physical or sexual demands, it is imperative that this should be discussed urgently with the consultant and the play therapist's counsellor.*

There are some sexually abused children who are eroticized, who seduce adults and try to enter into sexual relationships with them. If thwarted, such children can be frustrated, angry and puzzled when their learned behaviour of a way to please a grown-up is rejected.

Eroticized children become stimulated as they form close relationships. For therapy to be effective, the therapist must foster a close relationship with the children. Eroticized children react to therapy as if the therapist were soliciting their sexual favours … they are also testing to see if the therapist will act in the same fashion as the last incestuous partner. When the therapist is consistent, kind and firm, the children gradually desist, but not until every strategy has failed. If the therapist is of the other sex from the original molesting partner, the children display fewer sexual and more aggressive manifestations early in therapy. Eventually the relationship deepens. Sexual themes emerge regardless of the gender match between client and therapist *(Yates, 1990, p. 327, 328, 331)*.

Eroticized children often herald their sexual overtures by playing hide-and-seek, by burying their play therapist in cushions, by turning the play therapist into a horse and riding him or her, or by urging the play therapist to 'go to sleep'. When engrossed in such 'play', children do not seem to be aware that 'sleeping;' or 'blind' play therapists can still feel and hear!

Children sexually abused as infants may, when older, act out sexually without verbalizing *(Donovan and McIntyre, 1990, p. 69)*. This can be frustrating when the play therapist becomes aware that something untoward has happened, but clarification may not be forthcoming as the therapist cannot allow the body-to-body play that would probably enable the child to tell the story.

- You should have an understanding of normal childhood sexual development, and of the effects and manifestations of child sexual abuse.
- You should also have some knowledge about children who sexually abuse.
- From the referral information, you should be aware of any known sexual abuse.
- You must have clear strategies for dealing with children who approach you sexually.
- If you find yourself being titillated, or wanting to be sexually involved with a child, you must discuss this urgently with your consultant/supervisor or personal therapist.

WHAT HAPPENS IF CHILDREN REVEAL ABUSE?

Occasionally children's play may indicate that they have suffered abuse. In the case of a child known to have been abused, the adults have to determine whether the child is playing out previous events about which the authorities are already cognizant, or whether this is 'new' material. A different problem is posed if children not known to have been abused produce play that gives rise to suspicions that they have been abused (*Haugaard and Reppucci, 1988, pp. 133–47*). In either case, play therapists have to weigh up their duties and responsibilities to the child with their professional accountability and responsibility, and tell the child that this matter will be reported. (Hopefully the play therapist had warned the child at the beginning of the work that there might be something that had to be told to another grown-up.) Very occasionally it might be appropriate for the play therapist to inform the social worker of her concerns, but not the child, in the hope that the child will spontaneously produce more information in due course.

If the child does not have a social worker, the play therapist's concerns should be passed to the professional involved with the family, or to the social services department in whose area the child resides, NSPCC or police, or to the appropriate person in the play therapist's place of work. If the play therapist discovers a suspicious physical injury, the play therapist should immediately inform the social worker (or keyworker, or school), ensuring that the possibility of abuse is investigated straight away and that the child receives appropriate medical intervention.

Exercise

- How do you know if a child is disclosing new information, or is acting out 'old' disclosures?
- What are the procedures for reporting suspected abuse?
- What should you tell the child if you suspect abuse?
- Is urgent action needed?

Summary

This chapter has looked at various issues that crop up in the course of play therapy, some more than others. The use of language (see also Chapter 15) is crucial as this is one of the means of communication, and it is important that we are able to relate to children at all developmental levels. The giving and receiving of gifts requires careful thought; what is right for one child may not be right for another. Many children are concerned, or interested, about other children using the playroom; this may partly be curiosity, but may also express sibling rivalry. It is important for therapist and child to bear in mind the reasons that brought the child into play therapy; sometimes children are not always as clear about this as we assume, and it behoves us to check this out now and again. Some play therapists are perturbed if the child repeats the play, and we consider why this might happen. Preparing for holidays, and dealing with planned and unplanned missed sessions, are also important elements of the therapeutic process. Violence and aggressive play need to be handled bearing playroom limits in mind (pp. 175–9), and we consider the child's anger in a bit more detail. At some time most play therapists have to decide what to do about toys that are broken or stolen from the playroom, this varying from child to child. Play therapists are advised to have a strategy for working with children who act out sexually, and should know the procedures that have to be undertaken if a child reveals abuse.

Play therapy can be applied to small groups, and this aspect of therapeutic intervention is discussed in the following chapter.

13 Child-centred play therapy groups

Children are our first teachers. They already know how to grow, how to develop … All they need is the space to do it.

(Oaklander, 1978, p. 324)

In this chapter we think about

- An introduction to play therapy groups
- Deciding whether a child should have individual or group play therapy
- The composition of a play therapy group
- A format for studying the group process
- Things to consider when starting a group

Exercise

- What is a play therapy group?
- What do you already know about groupwork theory?
- Would what you already know help, or hinder, a play therapy group?
- Why might you want to run a play therapy group?
- Make a list of the things you would need to do
  - before the group begins
  - during the group
  - after the group.
- If you were eight years old, what would you expect would happen if you were told you might be going to a play therapy group?
  - what would be your worst fears?
  - what might be good about it?

Although there is not much written in the literature, play therapy can be undertaken in small groups (*Gazda, 1978; Ginott, 1968; O'Connor, 1991, pp. 323–45*). The same basic theoretical principles apply as for one-to-one work, but the level of play in small groups is understandably more interactional than in individual therapy. Instead of directing attention to just one child, group leaders have to be aware of and work with the dynamics of the whole group and subgroups (perhaps several at any one time), and with the 'space' between the children, as well as the individual child. Group leaders need to be alert to the fact that there is greater potential for behaviour to get out of hand because the child's usual controls can be swept aside in the tide of joint activity, thus creating greater scope for hyperactivity and destructiveness (*Slavson, 1979, p. 242*).

This chapter should be viewed as an introduction to therapeutic groups, and interested workers are urged to seek further information through the group-work literature (e.g. *Benson 1987; Doyle, 1990, pp. 66–79; Dwivedi, 1993a; Glassman and Kates, 1990; Haugaard and Reppucci, 1988, pp. 261–92; Houston, 1984; Lennox, 1982*) and other professional sources. In group play therapy, the children are in the playroom with plenty of material for expression. Group leaders (two are recommended) are 'good' parental figures, listening and helping if the children want this, or interpreting if necessary – but rarely. Children often interpret for each other. A group worker who is uncertain what is happening can usually check by asking another child. In a group, many problems are worked out between the children, but they derive a sense of security and freedom if they play freely in the presence of understanding adults. Interestingly, the treatment focus in play therapy groups often remains the individual child *(Slavson, 1979, p. 245)*. Unlike groupwork with adolescents or adults, group goals and group cohesion are likely to be of secondary importance. Some children will not play with the others at first, but may sit silently in a corner. In a child-centred therapy group they are left free to do as they please, and after a while they join in.

AN EXAMPLE

Two group leaders worked for ten sessions with four six and seven year olds with social and educational difficulties. The children were a mixed bunch! Stuart was smelly, a bit odd-looking, and somewhat withdrawn. He had been a battered baby and was touchingly amazed when anything good happened. John was a boisterous, aggressive extravert, who took the world by the horns. Narinda was a quiet but sociable child, and Amarjit was obsessional about cleanliness and order, constantly washing her hands and tidying up.

Sessions were full and, as far as the group workers were concerned, demanding. Each child expressed his or her individual needs, strengths and weaknesses. The quiet girls became more outgoing and assertive and there were times when angry John was soft and gentle. Towards the end Amarjit revelled in messy sand and water play. The referrers commented positively on the changes they perceived in the children, and the group seemed to have been a worthwhile experience.

The group leaders felt that Stuart needed further therapy and, after the group finished, he was overjoyed to find that he would meet with one of the group workers for individual work. (He had not been told about this *before* the end of the group as it was felt it might destroy the dynamic of the termination process.)

In the first of his individual sessions:

'Poor Tabitha' (one of the group workers). [Why?]' 'Because there's only one person.' The next week he unexpectedly met Pauline, the former group co-worker, and denied having seen her, but the following week, wistfully, 'Pauline – I'm dreadfully sad.' [Would you like to tell me about it?].

INDIVIDUAL OR GROUP PLAY THERAPY?

Children who may benefit initially from individual play therapy

- Very chaotic, acting out children.
- Children with a lot of emotional problems.
- Children with early parental deprivation who cannot share.
- Severely abused children.
- Children who abuse.
- Children with an isolated problem.

Usually the more disturbed children, those with deep-seated emotional diffi-culties and those who had an unsatisfactory early-parenting experience, are taken individually, at least initially, as they may be too upsetting, or too upset, in the group context, and anyway they may need to work out a parent-relation-ship with the play therapist first, after which they can be transferred to a group. Less disturbed children and those with social and behavioural difficulties often do well in a group right from the start. If the group is balanced and carefully chosen, children learn from each other and adapt to peers (siblings) as well as to parent-figures. Group members are receiving feedback from, and giving feed-back to, their contemporaries, and the child will be encouraged to adjust to group norms, however 'permissive' the atmosphere. Children will be learning from, responding to, and testing out new behaviours on their peers, allocating roles to themselves and other children which uncannily reflect each child's problems.

GROUP COMPOSITION

Exercise

- How many grown-ups and children should there be in a play therapy group?
- Does it matter what the children's ages are?
- Would you look for children who have similar problems?
- What rules would you have in group sessions?
- As a seven year old, please decide
  – what rules you would have in your group sessions
  – what you think should happen in the sessions.

In the younger age range where children are more dependent on adults and less reliant on their peers, groups normally comprise between four to seven children and two group workers. Attitudes vary as to the age range that a particular group should encompass but there is evidence to suggest, because of need and developmental stage, that there should not be much more than a two-year gap between the older and younger members of the group. It is important that the children should be on roughly the same developmental level, though in sibling groups there may be a bigger age span.

Although there may be children who are unsuitable, groups usually comprise children with a variety of problems as it is helpful for the child to be exposed to a range of behaviours. Groups with all withdrawn children, or all hyperactive children will have their own momentum, but a better therapeutic balance is more likely to be achieved if there is a mix, including one or two reasonably stable children who are often a helpful influence and usually remain 'untainted' by children with more obvious problems. The inclusion of an 'odd one out' (such as only one boy, or only one child from a particular racial grouping or school) should be avoided. Some group workers recommend mixed-sex groups for preschool children and single-sex groups for school children, though opinions vary.

There is a difference between on-going, open groups which children attend for a period and which newcomers join, and closed groups for a fixed number of sessions where membership remains constant. There are also technical differences between stranger groups (children who only know each other within the group) and intact groups (where children have contact with each other outside the group). The implications of these various possibilities need to be worked out beforehand. *Dwivedi et al. (1993)* have a helpful chapter on the structural and organization aspects of group work.

Suggested group composition

* Two adult co-leaders.
* Four to seven children, usually within a two-year age span.
* Each child should have something in common with at least one other youngster.
* It helps if there is a range of problem behaviours; beware taking a child with a unique difficulty.
* Is it an open or closed group?
* Do the children know each other outside the group?

THE GROUP LEADERS

Exercise

* What qualities would you look for in a co-worker?
* Make a plan of what the group workers need to do
  - before the group starts
  - during the group
  - after the group.

Running a group is different from individual work, calling for additional skills *(Reid, 1988)*. It is recommended that when working with a group of young children there should be two group leaders, preferably male and female, who know each other, share the same theoretical perspectives and can work harmoniously. In discussing adult groups, *Smith (1980)* points to the importance of the group leaders offering a blend of confrontation (letting group members experience the impact of their behaviour) and support in enabling group members to maximize the group opportunity. A pair of workers give a greater chance of the play therapists being able to provide proper attention to the concerns of the whole group, the subgroups and the individuals, but is only beneficial if the two workers are in accord with each other. If they, or even one of them, have a hidden agenda and are trying to show the other up, or score points, or have a different perspective about what the group is about and how to run it, then disaster is imminent *(Brown, 1979, pp. 52–5; Heap, 1985, pp. 166–71; Whitaker, 1985, pp. 11–12, 93–6)*. 'The unconscious preoccupation of the groupworkers becomes the conscious preoccupation of the group' is an adage which sums up the pitfalls of unsuitable leadership pairings. If a group goes haywire the group leaders should look to themselves and not just blame the children!

Groupwork takes time and is not an expedient to deal with a number of children. The groupworkers should meet before each session, sharing their current concerns and preoccupations so that these are kept out of the group therapy room. They are also advised to spend time together after the session, not just surveying the aftermath and wondering how they are going to clear up, but exchanging how they are feeling and their views of the session.

There has to be agreement about how to record the session (pp. 182, 217–8), and consultation, with the co-workers being seen together, should be available initially on a weekly basis. All this involves a substantial time commitment.

It is helpful if, before embarking on the group, each group worker acknowledges his or her weak spot(s) so that the other worker knows when it might be appropriate to offer assistance. For instance, with one set of co-workers, one play therapist admitted that she was edgy and found it difficult to tolerate children who deliberately infringed the geographical boundaries and made a dash out of the playroom. This was not a problem for her co-worker. However, her partner was uncomfortable when children climbed on the furniture and, as it were, swung from the rafters, but the other worker could take this in her stride. Inevitably the children sensed and tested out the co-workers' respective weaknesses but, because the workers knew each other's limitation, they were able to help each other out. The children's exploitation of and perhaps strong interest in splitting the co-workers (many of the children come from homes where manipulation of the parent figures is the order of the day) can be countered and prevented, provided the group leaders work closely together. Frank discussion about what has happened in the group, how each worker views the performance of the other and the co-working relationship, and what the workers plan for future sessions, are vital.

- Two compatible group workers are more or less essential in a play therapy group.
- It is important that co-workers have mutual aims and share the same theoretical frameworks.
- Co-workers must respect each other, be able to share their own feelings, and talk about how they experience each other.
- Co-workers should have consultation/supervision as a twosome.

PLANNING A GROUP

The success of a group depends on preparation, on the group leaders' ability to organize and plan effectively *(Gumaer, 1984, p. 219)*, on their capacity to support a group of children, on the mutual respect they have for each other, and on agreed joint aims.

(a) There should be consensus about the purpose and theoretical orientation of the group, and each child will have his or her 'targets of change'.

(b) In time-limited group work the number of sessions is established in advance so that children and others (such as parents and school) know what the commitment will be. If the number of sessions is not agreed beforehand individuals could, arguably, have different ideas as to how long they want to continue meeting. In an open group, sensitivity is required about the best time to introduce new children.

(c) The group should be organized at a regular time and on the same day, or days, each week. An hour is usually the minimum time span, some group leaders finding 90 minutes preferable.

(d) The group workers need to ensure that they have adequate premises and suitable equipment. A soundproofed room is ideal, not too cluttered to make tidying away easier. Toilets should be nearby and, if necessary, adequate waiting facilities for escorts or carers.

(e) Consultation prior to and during the currency of the group is an urgent priority.

(f) Agreeing on how to evaluate the group should be an integral part of the planning process, as it will influence data collection and recording *(Preston-Shoot, 1988)*.

(g) The co-workers need to determine how they intend to record group sessions (pp. 182, 217–8).

(h) How to recruit children and obtain parental approval has to be decided *(Manor, 1988)*. Most group leaders wish to interview prospective children prior to the group, and to make contact with the referrers and parents. The leaders therefore need to work out who will conduct the pre-group interviews (will it be one or both play therapists?), and what information should be conveyed, or sought. (See Chapter 4 on the referral process.)

(i) It is advisable to think about limits and boundaries (Chapter 16).

(j) Is it ever appropriate to remove a group member? What effect would such an action have on the group?

(k) Within the overall theoretical framework, is it necessary to have goals for each session?

(l) Should children in the group be having, or be able to have, individual play therapy? Is the expectation the same for all children?

(m) What are the rules of confidentiality, and how will these be explained to children, referrers and carers?

(n) Once the group has started, is it all right for a child not to participate, or to leave? How would such an eventuality be handled?

(o) What will you do with the information you have gained about the children during the group, and what will happen about children who seem to need continuing help?

(p) Is it expected that the carers will also receive some sort of intervention, for example from a social worker?

(q) Will there be any opportunities for carers and/or referrers to meet in a group with the group leaders? Or with someone else? If so, when, and why?

Group planning: things to work out in advance

- Who will run the group?
- Recruitment of children, plus arrangements for getting them to the group.
- Will it be an open or closed group?
- What is the theoretical base of the group?
- How many sessions will there be?
- Times, dates, place of sessions.
- Planning the format of the sessions.
- Play materials required.
- Refreshments.
- Group rules.
- Confidentiality.
- Follow-up arrangements.
- Recording the group.
- Evaluating the group.
- Feedback about individual children to referrers/carers/school.
- Can children in the group also have individual therapy?
- Contingency arrangements for children who still need help when the group has finished, or for children who should be referred out during the currency of the group.
- The group workers' own consultation/supervision.

GROUP PROCESS

Exercise

- Can you just go in and 'do' a play therapy group?
- Is common sense sufficient?
- What theories of group process would give you a framework for understanding what is happening in the life of the group?

Workers who have previously been involved in group work will have their own theoretical framework for studying the group process. Play therapists uncertain about group work are advised to consult some of the existing texts, to find a consultant, and seek professional training. Having some similarity to the therapeutic stages in individual play therapy (pp. 101–3), *Gumaer (1984, pp. 221–36)* takes the reader through a child-centred time-limited group, suggesting four phases:

(a) *Establishment* which is the preliminary phase during which the children become familiar with the setting and each other, and decide whether the group experience is for them.

(b) *Exploration.* Having progressed beyond initial apprehension and excitement, group members begin to test more seriously what the group is about and how much of themselves they can put into the sessions, so this sometimes seems to be a turbulent period.

(c) *Work* is the main phase where the children bring to the group the various issues that, consciously or unconsciously, need to be worked out.

(d) *Termination.* In this phase the children have integrated some of the exploration and testing that featured in the previous stages and the group is brought to a planned end. One or two children may throw up new problems in an attempt to prolong the group's life, and the co-workers need to consider whether these difficulties should be acknowledged and no action taken, or whether alternative provision such as individual therapy or transfer to another group should be offered. Other children may withdraw prematurely, either by not turning up or by non-participation, particularly if previous endings in their lives have been painful. Full recognition should be given to the 'mourning' process.

However, groups do not just have a linear life, and stages can be repeated, but differently, during the group's lifecycle.

- Stages of a play therapy group *(Gumaer, 1984, pp. 221–36)*
  - establishment
  - exploration
  - work
  - termination.
- There may be individual rather than group goals.
- Watch that behaviour does not get out of hand!

ANOTHER EXAMPLE

Six-year-old Patricia was referred for violence towards her small brother. Patricia was a 'nasty, vicious child', and her mother openly favoured the boy, cuddling him lovingly and spending all her time on him. As she was tired after a day's work, she had no time or energy left over for cuddling Patricia or putting her to bed. So Patricia, seething with fury, took it out on her small brother to such an extent that it was unsafe to leave her alone with him. Patricia had individual play therapy for several weeks, during which, given the undivided attention of the play therapist, she worked off the worst of her rage, stamping around and tearing a teddy bear to pieces. There had been some question as to whether she was dyslexic since she wrote a few of her letters back to front. During the latter part of play therapy, however, she freely admitted that she knew how to write them, 'But I do them backwards to spite Mummy'. It was only after some degree of love, trust and confidence had been established that it was considered safe to let her join a play therapy group. First she was placed in a small group in which she was the youngest. Only after some time in this group, where she gradually became socialized, was she tried in a group in which children younger than her were present. The group effected the desired result. Patricia was 'safe' with the younger children, and no more trouble at home.

Summary

This chapter highlights some of the differences between child-centred play therapy undertaken individually and in groups. Criteria are established about the type of child who would not initially be suitable for a group, and we consider the recommended group composition of two group co-workers and four to seven children, the latter being within a two-year developmental span. The professional relationship between the co-workers is discussed, and the reader is taken through initial group planning. Gumaer's model of group process is outlined: establishment, exploration, work and termination (1984, pp. 221–36). Finally, a separate groupwork checklist is available.

In Part Three the therapeutic role is examined.

GROUPWORK CHECKLIST

1. Do the children need individual therapy, or are there some who might benefit from a group?
2 Who would be your co-worker?
3. Do you have time for the necessary preparation and consultation, as well as for regular group sessions?
4. Is there a suitable consultant?
5. What are the theoretical frameworks for the group?
   (a) What are the group's aims and objectives?
   (b) What type of group leadership do you envisage?
   (c) What sort of involvement do you expect from the children?
   (d) What framework will you use to help you understand the group processes?
6. How will you evaluate the group?
7. What recording format will you use?
8. How big will be the group?
9. Who will be in the group, and do the children have varied problems?
10. What is the age range?
11. Where will the group meet, and do you have appropriate equipment?
12. Will you provide refreshments?
13. When will you hold the group (time and day), for how long and for how many sessions? What will happen during holidays?
14. What are the rules for confidentiality?
15. Who will be expected to escort the children?
16. What preparations do you need to make?

17. What limits will you impose?
18. What will happen to group members who seem unsuitable?
19. Is it in order for some of the children to have individual therapy?
20. What provision, if any, will you make for children who still seem to need help after the group finishes?
21. What contact will you have with referrers and parents?
22. What feedback will you give to referrers, parents, schools?

PART THREE

The therapeutic role

14 The aspiring play therapist

We must take with us two things if we would enter into the inner world of childhood: love, and an understanding which includes both intuitive perception and deep technical knowledge of those forces which rule our conscious and our unconscious life.

(Wickes, 1977, p. vii)*

In this pivotal chapter, we consider

* The personal qualities of the 'ideal' play therapist
* The importance of the play therapist's own personal therapy or counselling
* Training and preparation to become a play therapist
* Ways in which children might 'test' the play therapist
* What happens if the child ignores the play therapist
* Change of play therapist

Exercise

So you want to become a play therapist!

* Describe the ideal play therapist - qualities, education, family background, life experience.
* What sort of training and preparation are required?
* Outline the difficulties and challenges that might be offered by the children with whom play therapists work.
* What do you think and feel about children? About troubled children?
* In play therapy, children need ...

'You're awful. I hate you and want to go home' shrieked Peter, throwing things and trying to kick and bite the play therapist between screams. Gemma somewhat snootily berated the play therapist for having a messy playroom. Polly informed the play therapist she was a witch. At times Andrew appeared to ignore her, playing quietly and seemingly self-contained.

There seem to be four sorts of adults: those who think that working with children is easy and 'any one can do it'; those who find children fearsome creatures to be avoided at all costs; those who 'know' that children need control and correction; and those who relate naturally to and enjoy being with children. Some adults transfer easily to the play therapist role; others, perhaps more used to socializing, disciplining and teaching children, find the transition more difficult; others experience the approach as uncongenial. It is sometimes difficult for play therapists who have children of their own when they learn what may be a different way of interacting with, valuing and validating children in play therapy.

Play therapy must never be undertaken lightly, and sufficient training and supervision are vital, plus the right innate personal qualities to enable intending play therapists to support, and be accepted by, troubled children. External reality is important, but it is the child's inner response to that reality, or to what the child perceives or has perceived as reality, that is the area of work.

'Being' skills of the play therapist

• Ability to get on, and communicate, with children.
• Genuineness, authenticity, congruence.
• Positive regard, non-possessive warmth.
• Accurate empathy.
• Reliability.
• Respect for, and non-exploitation of, children.
• Awareness of, and ability to respond to, one's own inner child.

Knowledge required by play therapists

• Children's developmental ages and stages.
• Effects of faulty early parenting, attachment problems, trauma, loss, abuse, multiple placements.
• Theory and practice of child-centred play therapy.
• Allied knowledge, e.g. systems theory, family therapy, cognitive and behavioural therapies, expressive arts therapies, child psychology.
• Awareness of issues to do with race, gender, disability, power.
• Ethical and legal issues.

In child-centred play therapy, the play therapist has genuine interest in, concern and respect for the *whole* child, but would normally only work with the child within the play therapy context *(Goldstein et al., 1986, pp. 81–3)*. 'It is not always easy to see how to offer a child … a relationship where his emotional needs can be considered and understood in cases where the worker's role includes urgent decision-making on his behalf' *(Copley and Forryan, 1987, p. 4)*. Underpinning play therapy are the faith, acceptance and respect highlighted by *Moustakas (1953, pp. 1–5)*. Faith that children have the ability to grow and become fully themselves; acceptance of children as they are, without criticism or disapproval; and respect for children's rights as individuals.

• Faith, acceptance and respect *(Moustakas, 1953, pp. 1–5)*, with suitable technical knowledge, underpin the play therapist's approach to play therapy and the therapeutic process.
• Keyworking and management responsibility for the child should be undertaken by someone other than the play therapist.

PERSONAL QUALITIES

Exercise

- List the personal qualities that
  - should be helpful to the play therapist
  - may hinder the play therapist.
- If you were a troubled child aged six, what would your best play therapist be like?
- Draw your ideal play therapist!

From the outset, what the play therapist says and does is important, and the feelings behind the play therapist's statements and actions, the bridge between two people intrinsically bound up in the play therapy process, are important. Working within a child-centred framework, intending play therapists relate through feelings, accepting the child's acting out and strong emotion without retaliation. *Astor (1991, p. 415)* points to the importance of intuition – 'the matrix out of which thinking and feeling develop as rational functions' *(Jung, 1921)* – as a central part of the therapist's repertoire. Intuitions, hunches, need to be tested against what the child presents in play, sandtray, artwork and dreams. The play therapist respects the child's pace, without pushing for a speedy 'cure', having confidence that the child's psyche will know when the time is right for some sort of resolution to the conflicts *(Winnicott 1971b, p. 2)*. One of the personal challenges for intending play therapists is to recapture the world of make-believe in which they lived as a child *(Fraiberg, 1968)*, and to harness an intuitive understanding of the child's inner world with a willingness to learn the youngster's method of communication.

Play therapists are required to work on their experiences in and feelings about their adult and early life so that, with sufficient personal maturity and self-knowledge, they can begin to come to terms with their own childhood and family, their child-selves and life circumstances *(Lewis, 1985, p. 179)*. Personal stability to work alongside suffering, unhappy, disturbed children and to acknowledge that the worker will sometimes feel confused, belittled, angry, ineffectual *(Bandler, 1987, p. 81)*, mirroring the child's experiences, does not always come easily. It is particularly poignant and delicate if, through their work, play therapists come to the realization that they have been (sexually) abused. The assistance of a skilled counsellor or psychotherapist is vital in helping the worker explore and come to terms with what happened to him or her, and the aspiring play therapist will seriously want to consider whether, at that point in time, play therapy with an abused child is an appropriate occupation for him or her.

The oft-quoted qualities of genuineness, acceptance of and positive regard towards the child, non-possessive warmth, empathy *(Katz, 1963)*, a non-judgemental attitude, and belief in the process are core essentials in the therapeutic relationship *(Rogers, 1957; Truax and Carkhuff, 1967, p. 25)*. To these can be added such characteristics as sensitivity, responsiveness, flexibility, patience, humour, confidence, intelligence, reliability, integrity, resolution to keep confidences, with relaxed acceptance of oneself and the child.

Play therapists should beware of over-sympathy or over-identification with the child, and of using play therapy to meet their conscious or unconscious needs (such as vicarious or compensatory satisfaction, prestige, being wanted) rather than the child's needs *(Ginott, 1961, pp. 129–34)*. The work is taxing because the play therapist is responsive to the child's pain, anger and deprivation *(Hoxter, 1983)*, at times experiencing strong feelings of revulsion, pleasure, annoyance, anger, fear, pity and concern *(Simmonds, 1988, p. 16)* as children play out, and evoke feelings about, some of the traumas through which they have lived *(Lanyado, 1989, p. 97)*. It is important to accept children in all their moods, and not to collude in masking their (painful) feelings *(Copley and Forryan, 1987, p. 32)*. Peter, for instance, would sometimes shout at, tell off, countermand, hit and generally belittle his play therapist, and the play therapist felt that she was probably experiencing to some extent what the child had endured with his mother.

People undertaking play therapy require careful objectivity and the ability to be both in and alongside the process between play therapist and child, so that hypotheses can be formulated and checked and responses adjusted accordingly.

Offering a code of ethics, *Reisman (1973, p. 91)* suggests that play therapists should:

- Be modest and dignified without guaranteeing results.
- Respect the tenets of confidentiality.
- Not exploit children.
- Seek suitable consent to see child clients.
- Be aware of their own limitations; endeavour to increase their knowledge and skills.
- Behave within the law.

Personal qualities of the play therapist include the ability to

- Relate to, through and with feelings.
- Understand and come to terms with what has happened in their own childhood, adolescence, and adulthood, including child-rearing and parenting issues.
- Work within a child-centred framework.
- Communicate with children.
- Play.
- Work alongside troubled children without being damaged by the child's pain.
- Act as an advocate for the children they have in play therapy.

It perhaps goes without saying that enthusiastic, committed play therapists have a better success rate than bored, pessimistic workers *(Rutter, 1975, p. 305)*, and some research studies claim that it is the worker, rather than the technique or theoretical persuasion, that has most effect *(Smail, 1978)*. Children are percipient, often seeing through to the essence of adults, and the workers themselves are perhaps the greatest tool, underpinned by sensitive theoretical knowledge.

From the above description it may sound as though only paragons are acceptable for play therapy! It is important, serious work requiring important, serious preparation; trained adults who maturely have come to terms with the vicissitudes of their lives have a lot to offer.

PERSONAL PSYCHOTHERAPY OR PERSONAL COUNSELLING

Personal psychotherapy or counselling is a requirement for most professionals working psychotherapeutically with children. *Jennings* urges 'if we choose to work with damaged children then we must be prepared to acknowledge our own internal damaged child, and seek personal therapy for ourselves. If we avoid this, then we are in danger of exploiting the child – of searching for our own resolutions through our work with children' *(1993, p. 147)*. Everyone has relics from their own childhood and family life that, if not released, resolved or reframed, might impair the aspiring play therapist's ability to be child-centred. Personal therapy affords the opportunity to undergo therapeutic regression and to re-experience babyhood and childhood so that, instead of reading about the child's inner world (e.g. Fraiberg, 1968), the play therapist can have first hand knowledge of the processes at work within the child. Therapeutic effectiveness is often proportional to the therapist's personal 'togetherness', and to the success with which rejected or discarded parts of the being have been welcomed back into the adult's personality with love, tolerance and understanding.

Personal therapy also provides an opportunity to work on current issues and life experiences, which should help guard against play therapists using children and play sessions to meet their own needs. Therapy gives busy, harassed adults the luxury and opportunity of paying attention to themselves; after all, most of their professional life is spent giving out to others, so why should the play therapist not receive something personal?

- Play therapists and intending play therapists should have personal psychotherapy or counselling.
- They should get into direct touch with their own childhood.
- They should come to terms with what life has thrown at them, in particular experiences of abuse and/or loss.
- Psychotherapy or counselling helps to keep the balance if the play therapist now sees things differently about child rearing, and worries about what he or she might have done in the past to his or her own children.
- It can help with feelings and transferences thrown up in play therapy sessions.

TRAINING AND PREPARATION

Exercise

- Should a play therapist have qualifications? If so, what?
- What would you expect a play therapist to know if you were
  - the child's parent?
  - a professional who referred the child?
  - the child?

At the time of writing, training in play therapy is slowly becoming available in the UK. It is vital that intending play therapists prepare themselves as fully as possible because children will, cannily and accurately, discover and exploit weak spots. When dealing with adults, professionals may be able to effect a reasonable facade, but with children such a cover-up is quickly seen through, then exploited and demolished. Play therapists require informed knowledge, and need to accept and work on *themselves*, if they are fully to accept the children.

Traditionally, social workers have been involved with clients in their social surround, and psychotherapists with the intrapsychic conflicts and inner worlds of their clients *(Konopka, 1968; Simmonds, 1988, p. 16)* pointing to the blurred boundaries and resultant confusion that may exist when professionals dabble in each other's fields. In any sphere therapeutic effectiveness can be jeopardized by faulty knowledge and poor skills *(Reisman, 1973, p. 90)*.

Training and preparation fall into three main areas *(Ross, 1991, p. 619)*

• What one 'is': personal qualities, especially unconditional regard, warmth and integrity, and the ability to be child-centred.
• Theoretical knowledge guides and explains, shows the way and aids evaluation.
• Technical knowledge: e.g. types of play work, principles of child-centred play therapy, what one does.

The following is a recommended training format for professionals wishing to undertake play therapy:

1. *Their own professional qualification.*
2. *Training in person-centred counselling.*
3. *Personal counselling, psychotherapy or psychoanalysis* of a type that includes an opportunity to work on issues surrounding the worker's childhood.
4. *A thorough course in, and understanding of, normal and abnormal child development* including observation of and involvement with children of all ages (not forgetting children with learning difficulties, physical disability and psychiatric disorder) in a variety of settings. This would give norms for different developmental stages, the various milieux in which children live, and how the behaviour of distressed children might vary from that of 'normal' children *(Rich, 1968, pp. 110–14)*.
5. *Knowledge of*
   (a) different types of family structure
   (b) disrupted and abusing families
   (c) male and female adult perpetrators
   (d) children who abuse other children and animals.
6. *Knowledge of the principles and practice of communicating with children.*
7. *Understanding about and possession of the personal qualities and attitudes necessary in play therapy.*
8. *An historical overview of play therapy, and an awareness of play therapy within the context of other provisions for children.*

9. *Principles of child-centred play therapy; the types of children that are suitable and how to obtain referrals: the therapeutic process: evaluation: termination.*
10. *Different idioms in play therapy* (such as art work, sandtray, therapeutic regression, dance movement, music, drama, play, storytelling, puppetry).
11. *Agency implications:*
    (a) staffing
    (b) facilities (e.g. suitable room, equipment)
    (c) liaison with referrers, other professionals, families
    (d) recording
    (e) consultation
    (f) accountability
    (g) supervision and training.
12. *Case supervision seminars.*
13. *Written assignments.*
14. *Relevant reading* including texts on play therapy and child development should be studied; the reading list could usefully incorporate children's books and comics.
15. *The services of an adequate consultant.*
16. *Opportunities for personal play and for exploring different play materials.* Being a play therapy client is an important aid to training.
17. *Understanding the legal framework.*

Guerney (1983a, pp. 27–8) points to the value of:

– the worker's openness to the approach; the quality of training and supervision
– the worker's personal qualities, including the acceptance of and non-authoritarian approach to children
– the worker's self-exploration and self-awareness.

Ultimately a therapist's best instrument is the trained and responsive self *(Lewis, 1985, p. 179)*.

Training should include

- Values and ethics.
- A thorough knowledge of normal and abnormal child development.
- Childhood trauma (e.g. abuse, loss, disability, disease, neglect, poverty, powerlessness, unpredictability).
- Child observation studies.
- Children and the legal system.
- Children in society, and within the multiracial community.
- Children and family life.
- Children living in someone else's home.
- Theory of child-centred play therapy.
- Practice issues in child-centred play therapy.
- Supervised practical work.
- Personal experience of play, art, drama, music, sandtray, etc.
- Personal psychotherapy or counselling.

THE PLAY THERAPIST AT WORK

So there is this paragon of virtue! The child-centred play therapist is an accepting, understanding, warm, helpful, adult who is concerned about children and has come to terms with his or her own child-self; reasonable, non-punitive, consistent; giving the child freedom but invoking limits if necessary. The play therapist should remain a neutral figure (not neutered and expressionless, for personality is important), as a backcloth against which the child can project images, fears and phantasies, and should avoid giving unnecessary personal information. The preparations have been accomplished and the play therapist is in the playroom. What happens?

The play therapist attempts to provide a warm, understanding relationship (*Dorfman, 1951, p. 241*), underpinned by Axline's eight basic principles which are a major theoretical mainstay for child-centred play therapists (*Axline, 1969, pp. 73–4*):

---

1. The therapist must develop a warm, friendly relationship with the child, in which good rapport is established as soon as possible.
2. The therapist accepts children exactly as they are.
3. The therapist establishes a feeling of permissiveness in the relationship so that children feel free to express their feelings completely.
4. The therapist is alert to recognize the feelings the children are expressing and reflects those feelings back to them in such a manner that they gain insight into their behaviour.
5. The therapist maintains a deep respect for children's abilities to solve their own problems if given an opportunity to do so. The responsibility to make choices and to institute change is the child's.
6. The therapist does not attempt to direct the child's actions or conversation in any manner. The child leads the way; the therapist follows.
7. The therapist does not attempt to hurry the therapy along. It is a gradual process and is recognized as such by the therapist.
8. The therapist establishes only those limitations that are necessary to anchor the therapy to the world of reality and to make children aware of their responsibility in the relationship.

These neatly summarize the main tenets of child-centred play therapy. The play therapist tries to 'feel into' the child, accepting the play and reflecting something about the child's actions and feelings, attempting to attune to the child and to work with non-verbal as well as verbal cues. However, the play therapist is not a piece of blotting paper, passively absorbing what the child offers, nor merely a scene setter, for whatever the play therapist does (or does not do) is a response of some sort. The play therapy relationship (therapeutic alliance) is a kind of duet, or dance, between two participants in which they (often skilfully) interweave.

In child-centred play therapy the play therapist is working with what the child presents in the here-and-now, being aware that the present is shaped by past experiences. The play therapist's presence is supportive, and respect for the child and the therapeutic process means that the play therapist does not intrude. There is a delicate balance between play therapist activity, which may be seen as dominance, and play therapist passivity that may be interpreted as disinterest. Polly and Peter interacted with the play therapist from the start. If involved by a child, take care that it is the child who makes suggestions and gives directions. Gemma and Andrew initially related more to the toys. Whatever the style of the session, the play therapist does not obtrude, unless for the sake of safety. As some of the case examples show, the play therapist's role changes to fit the child's needs. It is the continuing, steady, trustable relationship that is as important as the actual nature of the play. After the first few sessions, which are mainly the accepting, assessing phase, there may be occasions when the play therapist wishes to offer alternative responses and behaviours, and may choose to introduce some specific play *(Schaefer, 1985, pp. 98–102, 105)*.

Sometimes it is only with hindsight that the play therapist recognizes a mistake has been made. In the previous session Polly had asked the play therapist to be a ghost, and the play therapist had somewhat clumsily declined, feeling that if Polly wanted a ghost, she (Polly) should take that role. In the following session the child raised the ghost again and, having subsequently realized that Polly, at that stage, needed to play out the ghost theme but was probably too scared to do it directly, the play therapist said: 'I've been thinking about the ghosts. Last time I said you had to be the ghost. Well, I'll be the ghost if you like and when you want to you can join in.' Sure enough, within a short while Polly was able to become the terrifying ghost.

Before beginning a session, it will pay dividends if the play therapist spends time in self-preparation for that particular child at that specific time, by reading the notes of the previous session and recapping points raised in consultation. Some children continue their play from the previous session (so it behoves the play therapist to remember what happened), but for others each session is a new experience and the play therapist should be open to what the child brings *(Dorfman, 1951, p. 241)*. Similarly it will help if there are a few quiet minutes after the session to concentrate on feelings and thoughts about what has happened. During the session the play therapist's concentration is centred on the child and the room, and distractions from outside such as thinking about the next appointment, or the shopping that needs doing on the way home should be banished.

Margaret Lowenfeld (1935, p. 44) summarized important aspects of the play therapist's role:

(a) Physically the adult should be on the child's level, or below. It is bad practice for the play therapist to talk down to a child, metaphorically or literally.
(b) In the playroom, the adult does as the child asks, unless dangerous or unethical.
(c) Standards of behaviour in the playroom are the child's, not the play therapist's (but remember the limits – Chapter 16).
(d) The play therapist allows the equipment to be used unconventionally, unless there is likelihood of danger or damage.

(e) Avoid blaming or reproving children; awkward situations should be evaded rather than directly opposed.

Madge Bray (1991, pp. 10–19) gives a vivid account of the changes and accommodations that adults commonly undertake when adopting a child-centred approach. In sessions, it is not unusual for play therapists to feel bewildered, disorientated, angry and helpless, and they may have phantasies about wanting to rescue some children from their situations *(Chethik, 1989, pp. 23–5)*.

The play therapist at work has considered

- The relevance of Axline's eight principles.
- Mistakes play therapists sometimes make.
- Preparing for play sessions.
- The adult's 'shift in role' in play therapy.

TESTING THE PLAY THERAPIST

Exercise

- Have a game with yourself! Pretend to be a seven year old. How many ways can you find to outwit, outsmart, grown-ups?
- How do you feel if you're successful? Or unsuccessful?
- What changes could grown-ups make so that you don't have to outsmart them?

Reisman (1973, pp. 17–81) points out that play therapists are not infallible, listing six 'tests' to which child clients may subject them:

(a) The attention test. The child may quiz the worker, checking whether the latter has been attending to what has been said and/or done.
(b) The memory test. The child checks the worker's memory of previous sessions.
(c) The anger–tolerance test. The child taunts the play therapist. Will the play therapist take reprisals?
(d) The love test. Does the play therapist suitably recognize birthdays, special occasions?
(e) The rejection test. Children may require verbal confirmation that the worker is not rejecting them; or, if rejection is suspected, the child may forestall and reject the play therapist. Rejection may be triggered if termination has been inappropriately approached, or if the child feels insecure.
(f) The confidence test. The child may disclose a secret or precious piece of information, and wait to see if it emerges elsewhere.

It is important that play therapists pass these 'tests'. With older children, the testing-out mechanisms can be acknowledged, brought into awareness and discussed.

Reisman (1973, pp. 179–81) suggests six 'tests' to which children might challenge their play therapists

- The attention test.
- The memory test.
- The anger–tolerance test.
- The love test.
- The rejection test.
- The confidence test.

NON-INVOLVEMENT OF THE PLAY THERAPIST

Exercise

- Why do you sometimes choose to ignore people?
- Try ignoring someone close to you, and see how she or he reacts.
- Why might a child ignore you in the playroom?
- How would you respond?
- If you are a child in a play session, what reasons would you have for wanting to ignore your play therapist?

A few therapists (*Ginott 1964a, pp. 127–8*) recommend that the play therapist should be passive and not become involved in the child's play, but many child-centred play therapists feel it is right to respond to the child's idiom. Sometimes a child may appear withdrawn, or plays silently and alone. This may be experienced as rejection and thus might be difficult for the play therapist (*Boston, 1983a, p. 62*), who should maintain focused awareness on what is happening, empathizing and accepting (*Ginott, 1982a, p. 206*) without intruding (*Dorfman, 1951, p. 246*). Play therapists may feel they have not been 'doing their job' if the child has not engaged in 'meaningful activity'. Difficult as it is for some workers to accept this, it is all right if the child does not apparently 'do' anything.

Whatever they choose to do in that hour, even sulk, day-dream or leave early is meaningful at an unconscious level to them, whether or not I (the therapist) understand it. For once this is their space, their chance to explore and discover themselves … . (*Gillespie, 1986, p. 23*)

Some introverted children, or children who are hounded in their daily lives, revel in the freedom to be themselves in the playroom. Andrew and, in the early stages, Toby, were aware of the play therapist but did not directly include her in their play.

However, if there is an air of discomfort in the room (either the child gives the appearance of feeling embarrassed or under scrutiny, or the play therapist feels unduly uncomfortable), it may be appropriate for the play therapist firstly to verbalize what she or he is experiencing and how the child might be feeling. If this does not help, the worker might choose to indulge in parallel play of some sort. This means that the play therapist could take up some alternative quiet activity that does not 'show up' the child by being so much better, or so much more skilful, but often creates a companionable feeling which makes the therapist more approachable (provided the play therapist does not become too engrossed in the play!). Sometimes silence is comfortable, with the play therapist just accepting what is happening. Sometimes, though, silence feels rejecting. During a silent spell a play therapist reasoned:

> How much do I take the initiative? Was I feeling like his mother, i.e. that the child does not give me anything. But his *being is* important.

Some children withdraw after active play. They reveal themselves then retreat until the next flash of activity.

- If ignored, sit quietly and observe. Sort out how you are feeling.
- If the child is new to the work
  - empathize about how he or she may be feeling
  - remind the child that he or she can choose what to do
  - say it's OK if the child does not want to do anything
  - make a more directive suggestion if the child appears 'stuck' and uncomfortable.
- If the child is excluding the therapist, test whether the intrusion of words will be tolerated. If so, orally reflect on what you have seen the child do, and the feeling content. 'How are you feeling?' 'I'm feeling a bit … and wonder if …'
- Are you being 'tested'? (pp. 156–7)

CHANGE OF PLAY THERAPIST

Exercise

- How have you felt when somebody, some professional, has transferred you to someone else?
- How might a change of play therapist affect children who have already had many adults come and go in their lives?
- If you were a six-year-old, what would you think, and how would you feel, when your play therapist tells you she will be leaving and you will have a new play therapist?

Good practice is for the child to have the same play therapist throughout, but there are rare occasions when the child has to be transferred. Changing to a different play therapist sometimes creates a setback in the child's play therapy *(Bixler, 1982, p. 247)*, and the introduction of the new play therapist should be sensitively handled.

Nine-year-old Brian (p. 89) was in his twelfth session and his play therapist, Pat, had to move unexpectedly, having consulted a colleague to whom Brian would be transferred. Brian's father was about to return to the family from prison and the first play therapist used this, plus some visual aids, to explain to Brian what would happen:

> I sit beside him and talk about his dad coming home. He's looking forward to it and I talk about families being complete. I then ask if he's

heard that I might be leaving. He says 'No'. I tell Brian that my husband is working in another town and that we have got to move there. 'Why?' I explain that his work is there and that we want to be together as a family, just as his family will soon be complete. As I talk, I use the animals and village toys. I make his family up from horses, and then I put my family together of sheep, with my husband on the far side of the town. I will be going on a little wooden train. Brian likes this, but decides to change his family to lions. He gets a big lion for his mother, altering it to one in a sitting position. I talk about the good and bad things of leaving, saying that although he and his mum will be pleased to have his dad home, there may be some friends of his dad's in prison who'll be sad that he's going, and although my husband is pleased I'm joining him, Brian will be sad that I'm leaving. He agrees.

I talk to Brian about having a new playworker so that he can have his sessions each week, and he says he would like to carry on, so I tell him about the new worker and bring her into our animal play as another sheep, like me. There's some discussion about when the new arrangement might start, and he agrees to meet the new person.

When the new worker took over she put an additional 'bad' figure in the playroom so that, if he wanted, Brian could act out his anger and aggression at his first play therapist leaving.

The transfer was handled differently in the case of a younger child. Her play therapist told her that she would be having a new playworker, as he was leaving and the new worker would join them for a handover session (Reisman, 1973, p. 179). Six-year-old Susy was curious to meet this 'new person' who, in the transfer session, entered the playroom soon after the child and original worker arrived. Susy dealt with the new female worker by sending her to bed, but asked her to take off her shoes in which Susy slopped around; at some level there was identification in progress. A bit later, the new worker was invited to share food, and the three of them went to bed. Susy was Santa Claus giving the first play therapist a bag of furniture for his present, and her new worker a bag of people. It seemed, on the face of it, that Susy was keen to explore relationships with her new play therapist. Photographs were taken of Susy and her former and new play therapists; she was told that the playroom would remain the same and that the new therapist would be there next week.

In Tom's case there was a two-way screen in the playroom and he knew that the observer, whom he had met each week, would become his play therapist when his original therapist left the area. O'Connor (1991, pp. 315–8) suggests three possibilities for a joint handover session:

– the new therapist is mostly passive
– the two therapists interact equally
– the former therapist takes a passive role. The new therapist and child might plan a 'goodbye' party for the departing therapist.

The child should be adequately prepared for transfer, given ample opportunity for displaying feelings about the change, and it helps if children know that key figures in their lives have met the new play therapist *(Reisman, 1973, p. 179)*. When accepting a transferred child, it is useful to know about the structures surrounding the previous sessions, and about the major themes of the work. The 'new' therapist could have a profitable meeting with the former therapist, and the child may wish to join in and explain what has happened. Within the first or second sessions after the changeover, the 'new' therapist will probably give the child the opportunity to express how s/he feels about the loss of the former therapist, and what it is like to be with the current therapist.

Children's responses to their new play therapist will vary according to their previous experiences of personal loss. Some may mourn the former play therapist, unfavourably comparing their new worker and withholding from or even appearing to reject the new person as a defence against further rejection *(Reisman, 1973, pp. 174–6)*. Others may fling themselves over-enthusiastically into the new relationship. It is imperative that former and new play therapists should acknowledge their feelings, fears, phantasies, resentments, pleasure and sadness about the child moving to someone else.

- A change of play therapist only happens in exceptional circumstances.
- Encourage the child to express feelings about losing the 'old' play therapist, and concerns about the 'new' therapist.
- Work out with the child the best way of conducting the handover.
- Try to ensure that the child does not feel it is his or her fault that the 'old' play therapist is leaving.
- What does the 'new' play therapist need to know?
- How will you and the child adapt to the transfer?

Summary

It is easy to sound prescriptive, with lots of 'shoulds' and 'oughts' for the intending play therapist. A relaxed yet informed approach is ideal, plus a good helping of intuition and sensitivity. Play therapists spend much of their professional time with deeply troubled children, and need the resilience to remain consistent, supportive and enabling without being intrusive. Certain personal qualities are required, plus professional training, self-work and personal psychotherapy. A potential play therapy training programme is outlined, and Axline's eight principles (1969, pp. 73–4), which underpin much of the therapist's inter-action, are quoted (p. 154). Children may subject the play therapist to various 'tests' including, occasionally, the uncomfortable one of ignoring the play therapist. Changing play therapists during a child's play therapy is not normally recommended but, if it does occur, sensitivity is required in introducing and handling the transfer.

The actual words and responses the play therapist uses are an integral part of the therapeutic process, and counselling skills are discussed in the following chapter.

CHECKLIST: SO YOU WANT TO DO PLAY THERAPY?

1. Have you worked on, and come to terms with, your own early childhood and current life experiences?
2. Can you relate warmly and intuitively, but non-possessively, to a range of children, in all their moods?
3. Are you trained in one of the 'helping' professions?
4. Are you prepared to spend time equipping yourself to undertake play therapy?
5. Can you remain alongside hurting, troubled, sometimes badly abused, children?
6. Do you have, or will you arrange to have, personal counselling, psychotherapy, or analysis?
7. Will your agency allow you appropriate facilities and conditions to undertake the work?
8. Can you locate a suitable consultant?

15 | Counselling skills

We need to seek contact with the suffering part of each child, because locked up in the suffering is each child's potential for living and for feeling love as well as for feeling fear, anxiety or hostility.

(Winnicott, 1984, p. 20)

Within the child-centred framework, we study

- A counselling model
- The use of questions
- The role of silence
- The place of interpretation
- Some examples of verbal interactions with children
- Transference and counter-transference

Exercise

- Are counselling skills 'everyday common sense'? How might they differ?
- If you were seeing a child in play therapy this afternoon
  - what sorts of things would you want to communicate to the child?
  - why?
  - how could you attempt this?

Counselling is a therapeutic way of communicating, verbally and non-verbally, on inter- and intra-personal levels, with another person. Grown-ups are accustomed to teaching, training, helping, socializing, reproving children; adults' language, behaviour and attitudes usually express that they know best and are to be obeyed. The child-centred therapeutic relationship is different. Child and play therapist come together as a partnership, as co-workers. Validating the child is the central focus.

Counselling skills – first principles (adapted from *Jacobs, 1993*)

- *Listen and watch* – give undivided attention to the child
  - for the child's feelings, and inner and outer reactions
  - for your feelings, and inner and outer reactions.
- *Remember* what is going on. Make contemporaneous notes, if this helps and the child does not object.
- *Relax and stay calm*
  - avoid speaking too soon, too often and too much
  - avoid loaded remarks
  - be confident that you have a sufficient theoretical understanding of the play therapy process.

FOUR LEVELS OF THERAPEUTIC INTERACTION

Four levels of therapeutic intervention (adapted from *Brady and Friedrich, 1982*)

I   Physical interventions
    Simple verbal interactions
    Listening
    Attending.
II Reflecting
    Paraphrasing.
III Third-person interpretation, from the child's point of view (primary empathy).
IV Cautious direct interpretation (intuitive advanced accurate empathy).

Brady and Friedrich (1982) usefully identify four levels of therapeutic interaction. It is recommended that beginning play therapists concentrate on level I skills first, gradually including the other stages. *Level I* covers the *play therapist's physical presence, non-verbal gestures, and simple responsive or reflective statements* such as 'You're tidying up', 'Mm, yes, I see/hear what you're doing/saying'. The main task is to *'attend'*, to focus on the child's verbal and non-verbal communications through listening, watching, eye contact, gestures and posture.

> Eight-year-old Gemma (p. 33) entered the playroom clutching an immaculate doll in a carrycot which she put carefully down, her eyes surveying the scene. 'What a mess!' she declared of the home corner, and set about tidying it in minute detail.
>
> The play therapist watched, feeling somewhat inadequate, for Gemma did not involve her in the orderly domesticity. At last Gemma asked for a dustpan and brush which the play therapist gave her, venturing [You felt the home corner was messy and you wanted to tidy it up].

Level I skills. Listening and attending

- Requires intense concentration from the therapist.
- Allow the child time and space to share what he or she wants.
- Note the personal and specific significance of what the child says and does. This is not necessarily commented on immediately.
- Be alert to non-verbal cues.
- Work on feelings, as well as what the child does and says.
- Look for incongruities, e.g. between words and body language.
- Concentrate on the here-and-now.
- Listen to your own feelings.
- Check whether you understand how the child feels.
- Stay with the child. Do not introduce new variables or your own agenda unless embarking on focused work.

Level II skills (Brammer, 1979, p. 156; Mearns and Thorne, 1988; Schaefer, 1985, p. 103) go further in helping the child to own and locate statements, actions and feelings. In addition to level I skills, the play therapist *reflects* (by repeating what the child has said, perhaps altering the inflection, or putting the child's actions or demeanour into words), *paraphrases* (using different words to those spoken by the child), *summarizes* words or deeds, and *amplifies,* encouraging the child to expand something that has been said or done.

> Gemma is in bed and hears a noise. 'Is it my horse? No, he's all right. I can still hear the noise – better check the baby. He's fast asleep. Is it the rabbits? Oh, yes. One's hurt its leg. I'll get into my car and take it to the vet.' Gemma and the rabbit set off on the tractor. 'At last we're here' as she enters the den that serves as the vet's house, and she hands the rabbit to the vet. Collecting the playroom broom from a friend's house, Gemma bikes home, saying she's 'awfully tired, I've had no sleep' but, unfortunately, her bike runs out of petrol. [When you were in bed you heard a noise, and you checked round, finding the rabbit had hurt its leg, so you took it to the vet. On the way home you ran out of petrol, and felt very tired. I wonder when you've felt like that before?]

Confrontation may occasionally be used, not in the oppositional sense, but to bring out underlying contradictions in the child's speech and/or behaviour *(Beail, 1989).*

> Having previously eschewed the punchball along with other 'messy' things such as paints, sand and water, in this session Gemma, giggling, ran to the punchball, asking the play therapist to watch her boxing. She was fighting Harry. There were lots of bouts, Gemma being knocked out several times but recovering to continue fighting, and Harry was battered. [Often you like to be neat and tidy in the playroom, but there's also an angry bit that needs to come here as well, and batter Harry.]

Overt questions, informing, directing, controlling, or problem-solving observations are rarely used.

Level II skills
- These go further in helping the child to own and locate statements, actions and feelings.
- In addition to level I skills, in level II skills the play therapist
  - reflects
  - paraphrases
  - summarizes
  - amplifies (comments that try to expand on what a child is doing or feeling)
  - uses confrontation only rarely (confrontation draws attention to mismatches between the child's words, play, feelings and non-verbal cues).

Level III responses or *third- person interpretation* are equivalent to primary empathy, where the play therapist tries to reflect the child's thoughts, feelings and affect in the session from *the child's point of view,* but not directly focused on the child. It is often 'The baby ...', 'Some little girls ...', 'The mummy ...', 'Sometimes children feel ...'.

There were noises outside my 'house' in the playroom and I discovered a baby Gemma had left in a pushchair, so I took her home. I had to ring the police to say that the mother had disappeared. The baby was crying, screaming, tipping up things, hitting older children, and I was instructed to put her back in the pushchair as punishment. When I went to bed the baby and pushchair disappeared, and I rang the police. The baby returned to my house: 'I go into your house and was naughty, doing something I shouldn't, and I smash things'. [Maybe the baby feels angry and upset because she's lost her mummy.] The baby ran away at night, climbed to the top of some high flats and fell off, being taken to hospital, where I visited her. [The baby must feel very sad, lonely and hurt.]

Level III skills. Primary empathy
- Through third-person interpretation, the play therapist attempts to respond to the deeper, underlying content of the child's play.
- It is important to follow the child's lead.
- The therapist reflects his or her understanding, free from blame or criticism.
- The therapist avoids advising, asking lots of questions, reassuring or comforting.
- It is not a good idea to generalize about the child's experiences.

Level IV is the area of *direct interpretation,* is usually cautious and is based on what the play therapist sees, deduces or feels.

Gemma reorganized the home corner, tutting a bit at the mess. She improved the area, adding a table cloth, wanting the corner to look nice but, before anything else, she made sure that the baby's needs were met. Gemma set the table, saying that visitors were coming, and started cooking while her baby was in the garden. Gemma rang me up, inviting me to go round, and I was treated with courtesy, ushered to the table, and served with some food that she was trying for the first time, the shopkeeper having recommended it. Gemma talked about how much she had to do at home and what hard work it was. Two or three times I offered to babysit, and to help her. She resisted these offers, but then let me help a little, and eventually agreed that I could babysit so that she could go out and enjoy herself. [It feels as though you've an awful lot to do. You don't always have to take responsibility and do everything; there are some people who can help, if you'll let them.]

Level IV is more akin to intuitive advanced accurate empathy where the play therapist takes the child's world into account but conceptualizes differently, tentatively attempting to address what might lie beneath the child's behaviour. 'Advanced empathizing builds on information made available over a number of sessions in which the therapist has concentrated on making primary empathic statements' *(Davis, 1990; Davison and Neale, 1982, p. 574; Egan, 1982;* cf. the empathy scale in *Mearns and Thorne, 1988, p. 42).*

As play therapy progresses it may be appropriate for the play therapist to express feelings of, for example, boredom, annoyance or pleasure whilst not rejecting the child. Ten-year-old Craig was engaging the play therapist in mechanical, repetitive play of a very boring nature and, having weighed up the situation, the play therapist felt that he perhaps needed the stimulus of her genuine reactions. [We've been playing this game for a long time and I'm getting a bit tired of it. I wonder if you are getting tired too?] This is where personal therapy is important as it helps to distinguish between what is congruence and legitimate feeling and should be used in the interests of genuineness and advanced accurate empathy within the session, and what is really the personal, private business of the play therapist.

Consider this scenario: Toby accidentally scatters sand on the floor. He looks anxiously down, then vehemently throws the mother doll away, saying 'I don't want her'. The therapist could respond:

Level I – 'It's OK to put sand on the floor in here.'
Level II – 'You're throwing the mother doll away as you don't want her.'
Level III – 'Sometimes children feel angry with their mother.' Or 'Sometimes children are scared when they do something their mother might not like.'
Level IV – 'I wonder if you feel angry with your mother sometimes, or maybe me?'

Congruence, authenticity and recognition of personal feelings

* If the play therapist is emotionally engaged with the child, and has worked on his or her own inner child in personal counselling or psychotherapy so is as clear as can be of projections, it is probable that the play therapist may feel what the child feels.
* It can be helpful at times to acknowledge, test out and share such feelings with the child, respecting the unique nature of the child's experiences.

POSITIVE AND NEGATIVE REINFORCEMENT; COGNITIVE RESTRUCTURING

---

* I affect you by what I say, the words I use, and the tone of my voice.

Counselling skills inevitably contain elements of positive and negative reinforcement, for example at the simplest level the play therapist will comment on certain things and ignore others (*Herbert, 1975*), which may influence how the child reacts. As *Patterson* says (*1986, p. 559*) 'All therapies that focus on the relationship – for example, client-centred therapy – include cognitive elements'. The play therapist's choice of words can have important effects. For instance, when paraphrasing the play therapist might reframe, restructure, 'positively connote', what has happened. Within the child-centred approach, the play therapist can verbally correct children's distorted perceptions and evaluation of reality, thus reducing illogical thinking which, in turn, affects children's feelings and actions *(Di Giuseppe, 1981; Patterson, 1986, pp. 1–62).*

QUESTIONS

> - Questions should be asked sparingly by the play therapist.
> - Open-ended questions are often best in play therapy.
> - Avoid too many direct questions, unless you are amplifying and trying to enlarge on what a child has said and/or done in the playroom.
> - Children generally find 'What?' questions easier to answer than 'Why?' and 'How?'

We often ask questions to satisfy our own needs or curiosity, or because we want to gather information for an assessment or proforma. In play therapy, we try to be child-centred and not to ask favourite adult questions such as 'Have you had a good day at school?', 'What did you do for your birthday last week?'. In play therapy sessions, we keep questions to the minimum, using open-ended questions to clarify the child's behaviour and speech, and to test interpretations. If the child does not respond we check, mentally, whether we have used appropriate language, whether we have asked an inappropriate question at an inappropriate time, or whether the child is blocking.

When children ask questions to therapists, therapists have to decide whether to give a direct answer, whether to solicit the child's answer to the question, or whether to reflect the question back to the child without answering, e.g. 'You are curious about whether I have a husband'.

SILENCE

Exercise

- What does silence indicate in a play therapy session? Consider this from the perspective of the play therapist, and of the child.
- Should the play therapist attempt to break a silence?
- Pretending to be a child, when would it be appropriate for the play therapist to break a silence, and when would it not?

Never underestimate the value of silence. It can be a sign of withdrawal and rejection *(Boston, 1983a, p. 62),* but it can be an opportunity for creative inner work. A comfortable silence during a conversation or activity can encourage children to explore deeper into what they are feeling or trying to express *(Gumaer, 1984, p. 41),* and play therapists should avoid rushing in with words or actions. Just to lie quietly with the play therapist *there,* in silence, can be healing. So much goes on in silence. One girl aged 11 used to travel 50 miles once a week to lie in silence for 40 minutes.

INTERPRETATION

- Some child-centred play therapists do not make interpretations.
- If offered, interpretations should never be hurried, and always tentative.
- Third-person interpretations are safer; e.g. 'Some children feel …'.
- Never attempt to push an interpretation if a child rejects it.
- There is no place for clever interpretations that make the therapist feel good.
- The best thing is when a child discovers something for him or herself.

Reflection of feelings is more commonly used, and clever interpretations are not the order of the day, the *reception* of the play often being sufficient. In child-centred play therapy it is not essential to interpret to children what their play means or indicates, though it is helpful for play therapists to have experience and understanding of a 'deeper' level of psychotherapeutic work and symbolism. However, there are times when verbalizing what the play therapist thinks or feels might be happening can be appropriate. Children do not always have the vocabulary or concepts to explain their experiences, and it may be helpful for them to know that an adult understands enough to try to put what is happening into words. Interpretations should not be made at the last minute and should be ego-building, not designed to strip or unmask the child *(Wolff, 1986, p. 239)*. Some play therapists worry that, if offered, a wrong interpretation will upset the child and interfere with the therapeutic process. This is unlikely *(Winnicott, 1971b, pp. 9–10)*, unless the play therapist insensitively tried to hammer it home. If an interpretation makes sense to the child, so be it; if not, the interpretation will probably be shrugged off or the child will re-present the material in a way that the play therapist can perhaps better understand.

In his third session nine-year-old Toby had been engrossed with making Darth Vader vanquish Action men and tanks. The play therapist sat on the floor with him and suggested: 'There has been a lot of power, Darth Vader has a lot of power, and we sometimes feel as though we've got some angry power ourselves'. Little had been said during the session, and the play therapist was attempting to put into words what might have been an important theme of the play.

Gemma seemed to have the burdens of the world on her shoulders and had given herself a mammoth task of putting all the furniture into the dolls' house.

> [Do you remember the first time you came when you asked for some extra furniture?] 'Yes.' [Do you sometimes make life difficult for yourself?] Nod of recognition. [Perhaps you could put some in this bag, then you wouldn't have so much to do?]

Andrew had been playing intently:

> 'Is that made with gold?' pointing to the inside of a lorry cab. [Pretend gold. They're very powerful, these lorries. They can drive through all sorts of places.] He makes whizzing noises and picks up the yellow car. [That's a very strong car. It's had some splendid adventures. I've been watching you race it.]

He demonstrates how it runs around the dolls' house and the floor.

In her notes the play therapist wrote:

> In my comments I was trying to reflect back to him what I thought to be the themes of the play, his patience and persistence – he doesn't give up easily. I acknowledged the power of the car, how it crashed through the dolls' house and swept aside furniture and people. He may feel like crashing through his house sometimes and may want the power to move/destroy/change his family?

TRANSFERENCE AND COUNTER-TRANSFERENCE

Let us introduce ourselves to two technical, but nevertheless important, concepts that spring from the psychoanalytic tradition. Transference, usually unconscious, is when we 'transfer' thoughts, behaviours and feelings arising from one situation or person from the past, to another situation or person in the present. Toby might have had a childminder with fair hair and spectacles who shouted when he went to the biscuit box. When Toby first saw me (I have a similar physical description) he may automatically have expected, and may have invited, me to shout and behave like the child minder when he approached the biscuit box in the playroom. If confronted by something unexpected in a child's play therapy, we should speculate about a possible transference. O'Connor (1991, pp. 273–6) highlights common transferences made when children

- Mirror their experiences of parenting, sometimes casting the therapist into unexpected roles.
- See their play therapist as all-powerful and knowing everything.
- Expect the play therapist to rescue or persecute them.

These, and other transference phantasies, should be acknowledged to the child as phantasies, and untrue.

Counter-transference comprises the emotions, thoughts and behaviour, arising from past baggage, that the play therapist brings to the therapeutic encounter. It is essential to identify our personal residual issues. For example, our parents may have taught us it is improper to allow children to argue with a parental figure *but* it may be beneficial to let a child argue with the 'mother' in play therapy, even though part of us may feel this is an inappropriate thing to do. So we need to overcome our own parental and other injunctions that may interfere with our work, and to take responsibility for tackling them in our personal therapy.

Toby's vocabulary and tone of voice may remind me of another child and, if not careful, I may respond to him as if he were that other youngster. It is important that I recognize what I am doing, and respond to Toby in his own right; and that I work out the reasons why I have made the link. Is there something about the other child that is as yet unresolved in my psyche? Supervision is a vital aid in identifying and monitoring counter-transference (Webb, 1989).

Transference

Thoughts, feelings, emotions, images that you, (the child) unconsciously attribute to, or feel about, someone or something because of your previous experience(s) with similar people or situations.

Counter-transference

Thoughts, feelings, emotions and images that
– I, the therapist, unconsciously attribute to other people or situations because of my previous encounters with similar people or situations.
– I experience when I am with other people; some of their feelings might be located within me.

HOW NOT TO DO IT?

Resist the temptation to teach! A student with a six-year-old boy:

'Money spiders bite when they crawl in your hair and make honey.' [I told him that bees make honey, but he insisted spiders did.]

Child: 'There's a £100 note – look!' [It's 100p.]

Child: 'There's no way you can hold to get down these steps because they're a bit slippy.' He slips, frightening himself. [I told you! You'll have to come down backwards. You'll remember next time.]

A BETTER EXAMPLE?

This was a first session with a student and a four-year-old boy who was behaving at the two-year-old level in some respects:

[You are not sure what to do?] The boy looks at, then plays with, some cars. [Is that the car you wanted? ... You want to go up the ladder, but you are not sure whether you ought to? You want me to come with you? We can go up there together. Do you want me to help you? You made it on your own ... Are you trying to get the wheel off? Are you wondering what that is? Now you're behind me, aren't you? I will have to turn round if I am to see you. You like that car. The wheels don't come off the car, even if you pull them very, very hard.]

The child plays in the sand and the spade broke.

[That spade is not strong enough for you, is it? You can hit the sand quite hard. You can get a lot of sand in there.] The boy indicates that he wants to take some toys out of the playroom. [You want to take something out. Even if you want to take something out we can't allow it, otherwise there will be no toys left.]

The student's comments can be understood as affirming and interpreting the child's actions, thereby giving the boy a sense of being himself, which is vital for any child, but particularly for one described as being, among other things, 'all over the place'.

Difficulties in play therapy counselling

- Don't attempt to move the child too quickly by suggesting a solution.
- Avoid initiating the 'good parent' role. Follow the child, rather than teach or stimulate.
- Work with your own feelings and intuitions, screening them for counter-transference.
- Try to reflect feelings non-judgementally rather than giving the child your own interpretations and opinions.
- Pitch your interventions appropriately.
- Is your body posture child-friendly?
- Remember that the child's experiences are his or her experiences of life. The child may not know of an alternative.
- Avoid asking direct questions. Questions of clarification are all right, but not too frequently.
- Resist giving advice and 'clever' interpretations that make you feel good.
- Staying alongside the child can be difficult. Do not rush in to reassure and comfort.

Summary

Counselling skills for the child-centred approach have been described, based on four levels of therapeutic interaction *(Brady and Friedrich, 1982)*. Brief mention has been made of the contributions to counselling skills from behavioural and cognitive theories. The role of questions and of silence in play therapy has been explored, and the relevance of the appropriateness, or otherwise, of interpretation has been broached. Transference and counter-transference have been discussed, and the chapter concludes with some examples of therapists' verbal interchanges with children.

However skilful the play therapist, the work is likely to be jeopardized if playroom management, case recording and case consultation – topics of the following chapter – are faulty.

16 Allied practical considerations

Children become wonderfully alive when they are listened to, understood, and accepted.

(Moustakas, 1953, p. 206)

The practice of play therapy is supported by important infrastructures

- Playroom management
  - playroom premises
  - refreshments
  - limits
  - tidying up
  - time keeping
  - waiting room and escort
- Professional considerations
  - recording the work
  - consultation/supervision

PLAYROOM MANAGEMENT: PLAYROOMS

Exercise

- Forgetting budgetary constraints, draw the plan for an idea playroom complex.
- Imagine you are seven years old: describe and draw your best playroom.
- What are the similarities and differences between the seven-year-old's ideas and your views as an adult?
- How will you manage if you do not have access to a special playroom?

The child enters a hallway with pictures representing the multicultural society, and coat hooks at child height. The waiting area is child-oriented, warm and welcoming, and the toilet is clearly marked. Opening the playroom door, the child sees a light and airy room with views of a garden. The home corner has its own private space because the child can shut the play house door and draw the curtains across the window. In the 'wet' area of the playroom stand a sink, sandtray and easel. In another corner are the dolls' house, puppets, musical instruments, punchball and 'aggressive' toys, and the fourth area is 'quiet' with beanbags, cot, dolls, cuddly animals, baby and toddler toys and a few jigsaw puzzles. Against one wall are a child-sized table and chairs. Another wall is pinboarded for children's paintings and drawings (other pictures are usually excluded), and at the opposite end is a one-way screen doubling as a mirror. The playroom is the child's domain *(Ginott, 1982b: Landreth, 1982, pp. 152–4; Reisman, 1973, pp. 115–6)*; the playroom, toys and a calm, non-judgemental ambience creating a therapeutic atmosphere *(Hoxter, 1981, p. 210; Moustakas, 1959, pp. 7–9).*

A pleasant room, free from intrusion, with good light, heating and ventilation, without outside distractions and preferably sound-proofed (or not adjacent to offices, classrooms or domestic accommodation) offers a suitable working environment. Windows will have safety glass with high-up areas protected. It is better if the decor, though not drab, is not too stimulating. Curtains or blinds are useful so that the child can draw them, if so inclined. It helps if walls and floors are easy to clean and the floor is non-slip and water repellent. A movable carpet square or rugs add comfort, together with beanbags or cushions. A mirror is an asset. Suitable storage containers are necessary, some portable or on wheels if used in more than one room. Running water is important, a watertray or baby bath is second best. A lavatory and wash basin *en suite* are desirable. Video equipment and a one-way screen help with training, observation and recording. To preserve a neutral space, the room should be free of the worker's possessions.

Some agencies have rooms for different kinds of play, for instance a sand room, water room, a quiet room, a noisy rough room, a woodwork room, and the child selects where to go. Other agencies have one large or two adjacent rooms in which equipment is accessible so that the child can select various materials. Other agencies may have dual-purpose rooms with toys in transportable boxes.

Playrooms are not always available and some play therapists work in their office with a restricted choice of toys *(Oaklander, 1978, pp. 191–2)*; others have a box or drawer for each child *(Klein, 1955, p. 226)*, or a portable play kit *(Axline, 1969, p. 55; Bray, 1986, p. 19)*. Peripatetic play therapists find their own play areas *Cattanach, 1994, pp. 51–2, 70)*. (Appendix 2 suggests play equipment for different types of playrooms.)

Select toys carefully, and do not just accumulate them *(Lebo, 1979)*. Purely mechanical toys should be avoided. Two of certain items (e.g. feeding bottle, dummies, soft balls, weapons, dolls, soldiers, vehicles) are recommended so that the play therapist can play alongside if so directed by the child. *Sinason (1988)* found that some children need communal toys and that children may portray physical or sexual abuse more readily using dolls of different ages and sexes, and a range of toy animals.

At the beginning, play therapists might like to establish a simple, standardized play setting so that familiarity can be gained with the way different children respond to the same play materials *(Beiser, 1979)*. Initially, dolls' house, sand and 'world' toys, aggressive equipment, scary things and items for the home corner may be found useful, as well as materials for painting and drawing.

Playroom characteristics

- Safe, warm and private.
- Child-centred; looks welcoming.
- Contains play materials that allow self-expression, with adequate storage space.
- Boasts an area where the child can make a mess.
- Can be easily cleaned.

If working elsewhere

- Assemble a portable play kit.
- Find ways of changing the ambience of the play space so that it can be experienced as different and 'therapeutic', rather than relating to its previous function.

PLAYROOM MANAGEMENT: REFRESHMENTS

Exercise

- Feel yourself into being seven years old. Would you like something to eat and drink in the playroom? What would make this different from going to a friend's to play?

Provided there are no dietary problems, some play therapists offer drinks and biscuits for children to consume when the child chooses (*Haworth and Keller, 1964*). Alongside safety, warmth and acceptance, food is a basic requirement which the play therapist is acknowledging (*Adams, 1982, p. 115*) and, if hungry or thirsty, the child's needs can be met within the session. At a deeper level, the child's approach to food, and how that approach changes during play therapy, may aid evaluation (*Haworth, 1990, p. 172*).

Some children ignore the food. This may imply that food is not, and has not been, a difficulty in the child's life though, conversely, it could indicate a severe problem. (Or it could be that the child does not like what has been provided, or is too busy to bother!)

Some children use the food in moderation, helping themselves during the session. Others binge, or store some for 'later' or to take home. It is interesting to note whether the child shares food with, or offers it to, the play therapist. Remember though that some children may feel inhibited about offering food to a grown-up, and may need to be reminded that they can help themselves. To give children the freedom to choose when, if, and how much food and drink they consume is perhaps an unusual experience.

Toby's approach to refreshments varied, sometimes taking biscuits to eat by himself, sometimes sharing them. Polly liked to eat hers alongside the play therapist and in front of the fire, which had to be full on even in the height of summer. Occasionally she took some biscuits home.

In the early sessions, Andrew tended to ignore the biscuits and drink until towards the end of the hour, when he would retreat to his 'base' for a biscuit in between violent boxing. Later in play therapy he put biscuits on a plate. 'So when you want one, they're on the plate' he informed the play therapist. 'I'll have one now. Here you are. I'll pour your pop out.' In his final session: 'I'll pour your pop for you. I've got a bit bigger than yours' and he equalled the amounts. 'Let's measure. Yours is bigger. Take one (biscuit).' He gave us equal quantities.

Andrew had changed from eating almost secretly when he needed comfort to sharing the food with his play therapist. Gemma often wove the refreshments into her play by feeding her 'children' and 'visitor' (the play therapist). Twelve-year-old Martin transmitted important personal information around requests for food and drink; other children like to be able to offer the play therapist something.

If there are to be refreshments, you will have to decide

- What will be available.
- Whether there is an unrestricted supply.
- Whether refreshments are freely available, or at a specified time.
- Whether children can help themselves.
- Whether the child is expected to share the refreshments with you.

PLAYROOM MANAGEMENT: LIMITS

Exercise

- 'It's all right, this child-centred stuff, but does it really mean that children can do what they like?'
- Are there any playroom rules you might consider? If so, what?
- If you were a child, how would you feel and behave if you were unclear about the rules?
- As a child, you have perhaps found that grown-ups don't always stick to what they say. How would this affect your attitude to the play therapist?

Although adopting a child-centred approach, the play therapist will be working with troubled children. To give security, a sense of containment and of 'holding', and to keep child and play therapist safe, the wise worker will bear a few limits in mind *(Ginott, 1961, pp. 101–23)* as 'limits define the boundaries of the relationship and tie it to reality' *(Moustakas, 1959, p. 11)*. The few play therapists who do not believe in restrictions *(Rosenthal, 1956, pp. 215–32; Schiffer, 1952, pp. 255–61)* can skip this section. The play therapist aims at creating a warm, accepting, non-judgemental atmosphere where more or less anything is acceptable, but the 'more or less' is important. Children can feel scared if left totally free, particularly those with poor differentiation between themselves and other people, and children who can become violent and 'act out'. Many play therapists, too, might become anxious, wondering whether a certain situation should be allowed to continue. Such anxiety and uncertainty take energy that deflects from the therapy, so an awareness of boundaries, at least on the play therapist's part, can be freeing and enabling.

Establishing limits

Limits largely revolve around personal safety, protection of the playroom and toys, maintaining the integrity of the play sessions and on curbing anti-social behaviour such as defaecating or urinating in the playroom.

The following are amongst the most commonly imposed limits:

1. Children should not wantonly damage themselves, physically attack the play therapist, or create a dangerous situation.
2. Children should not drink or eat unsuitable materials.
3. Children should not damage the playroom or the toys. (Some play therapists may provide toys or crockery specifically for breaking.)
4. Playroom toys should not be taken away.
5. Children should remain within the playroom, with access to the lavatory (or waiting room if there are special reasons for this), but should not be permitted to wander around the building.
6. Play sessions do not usually overrun, and children will normally only be seen at the appointed times *(Bixler, 1964, pp. 134–47; Ginott, 1964b, pp. 148–58; Moustakas, 1953, pp. 15–16).*
7. Play sessions will not be interrupted by phone calls or outside interference.

Additional points that the play therapist might care to think about include:

– What happens if children want to paint the playroom, or the play therapist, or themselves?
– Is there any restriction as to what can be done with sand and water?
– Can children take home things they have made? (It is probably better if they leave paintings and items such as clay models in the playroom, partly because they may be wet, but largely because a sequence of paintings or models can often be useful in the assessment of a child's progress.)
– Can children undress? If so, to what extent? Can they undress the play therapist? If so, to what extent?
– What degree of physical intimacy such as fondling or cuddling is permissible?
– What happens if children introduce explicit sexual play?
– Is there any restriction on noise?
– Should children be prohibited from fiddling with the audiovisual aids?
– What happens if they bring their own toys, books, friends or refreshments to the playroom?
– Are swearing, racial expletives, or sexually explicit language allowed?
– What about throwing things out of windows, or shouting profanities at people in the street?
– Is there anything else that might be contra-indicated?

Play therapists are human and have their own levels of tolerance, and what might be a problem for one play therapist is not necessarily a difficulty for another. Obviously, play therapists imposing too many restrictions need to check out the reasons for this with their consultant or personal therapist, but play workers should give themselves the opportunity to prohibit things which they find intolerable in what is, after all, their work place.

Sometimes the unexpected happens and the play therapist has to think quickly about whether to prohibit or allow specific behaviour. There are occasions when, with hindsight, the play therapist might decide that a situation has been misjudged, and it might be appropriate to say that, having thought about what happened last time, she (or he) has had a change of mind. For example, Polly declared that she wanted to visit the cellars beneath the playroom, and this was prohibited on the grounds that such an exploration would violate the boundary about remaining in the playroom. On reflection the play therapist felt that Polly was expressing a need to overcome her fears of going down into the darkness, the unconscious, so it was explained to her that the play therapist had thought again about her request the previous week, and had decided that, if she still wanted to go into the cellars, this would be allowed. Obviously care is needed when 'rules' are changed because manipulative children would have a whale of a time, and the play therapist would find her- or himself stranded without any clear framework. However, flexibility is often the essence of play therapy and there are times when rules can be altered, and when *ad hoc* rules need to be instituted. One play therapist suddenly made up a rule that orange squash was not allowed in the sand!

Explaining limits
Having decided the limits, the play therapist needs to work out how the child is to be informed of them, how limits are to be enforced, and what happens if they are infringed.

Play therapists vary about what they tell the child. Most children know about 'rules' so useful phraseology may be something along the lines: 'The playroom is a place where you can do almost what you like, and say and feel what you want, but there are one or two rules ...'. Most play therapists outline the main rules concerning the parameters of the session at the beginning of the first session, such as the parts of the building to which the child has access, the timing of the sessions, and anything else that the play therapist considers vital to the actual conduct of the work.

A student play therapist explained:

> I gave Christine the few rules I felt were required. I explained she could do almost what she liked and play with whatever she wants, and eat her biscuits and have a drink when she decides, and that we'd have an hour.

Other limits can be invoked when necessary. This seems an acceptable procedure if it was made clear at the outset that the child can do *almost* anything in the playroom.

> Child: 'I'm going to bash the windows.'
> Therapist: 'Only pretend – that's one of the things we don't do, break the windows.'
> Child: 'Can I bang the garage?' but it's a bit fragile and I say I don't want it broken, suggesting he bang the window-seat as hard as he likes instead.

It is wise to tell children that although in this playroom, in this special place, they can do almost what they want, the rules at home and at school, and elsewhere, will continue as usual. Youngsters can normally differentiate between acceptable behaviours for different places.

Enforcing limits

Children should feel accepted, understood and not shamed, even if their behaviour is rejected. It is important, too, that the play therapist should be consistent and, if expressed by the worker, anger should be controlled so that children know where they stand but also feel safe.

If children set out to do something that is going to break a playroom limit, the child-centred play therapist has to decide what to do:

(a) The child's wish or intention can be verbalized in the hope that this will help the child come to terms with his or her feelings and actions. This is sometimes sufficient. The child might habitually manipulate his or her parental figures and might be testing the play therapist, and perhaps be relieved that the worker remains firm.

(b) However, if the child continues, the play therapist should make the limit explicit and continue to verbalize the child's feelings or intentions, and perhaps his or her resentment at being thwarted. The play therapist can offer an alternative strategy that would be more acceptable. In extreme cases, some play therapists might place the toy or part of the playroom in question out of bounds (*Moustakas, 1953, p. 16*).

(c) If the child ignores this and proceeds to do the forbidden thing, the play therapist has to determine the ultimate sanction *and be prepared to enforce it.*

(d) The therapist should help the child express feelings about what has happened.

Determining the ultimate sanction is difficult. Does the play therapist end the session, or remove the controversial toy, or take the child elsewhere? The ultimate sanction for most play therapists is to curtail the session by removing the child from, or getting him or her to leave, the playroom. Evicting the child from the playroom can be problematic if the child has to wait for the escort; a helpful receptionist can be invaluable and, once evicted, the child often behaves impeccably, having (usually) appreciated that the play therapist has behaved fairly and respectfully. However, for some play therapists ousting is not an acceptable procedure (*Moustakas, 1959, p. 16*) and they find ways of keeping the child in the playroom but also of prohibiting the undesired behaviour.

Some play therapists seem to get into confrontational situations more often than others. The choice of language and tone of voice can sometimes avoid a head-on clash, though it has to be said that however verbally skilful the play therapist, some children are hell-bent on a collision course. How they bring it about, and how the play therapist handles it, are part of the therapeutic process. The play therapist, ideally, can say something like 'You feel like … but we don't do … here', or 'The paint needs to be used on the paper', or 'Toys are for playing with, not breaking', or 'I understand that you don't want to finish today, but I'm afraid we have to stop at three o'clock'. 'You're not to …', or 'You shouldn't …' are to be avoided as such sentences create conflict if the child decides to test out the play therapist. Enforcing limits is not always easy, but the play therapist stands a greater chance of success if the potential issues have been thought through beforehand.

> • *Establish limits* – usually to protect child and play therapist from danger, damage and impropriety, and to maintain the boundaries of the session.
> • Decide when and how limits are explained to the child.
> • Determine your ultimate sanction.
> • Warn, remind, action.

PLAYROOM MANAGEMENT: TIDYING UP

Exercise

• As a child
  – would you expect to tidy up the playroom?
  – what would be the best/worst things about tidying up? and not tidying up?
• As a play therapist, should tidying up be done by
  – the child?
  – yourself?
  – someone else?

Views on tidying up vary. Some play therapists do not tidy the playroom between sessions, the theory being that whatever the child does, and however the child experiences the session and the room, are part of the play therapy. The majority of workers feel that the playroom should be in a reasonably tidy state so that it is more or less constant at the beginning of each session. This gives some stability and the child's own resources are immediately tapped, rather than reacting to the state of the room. A minority of play therapists ensure that the room is exactly as the child left it on the previous occasion. It is usually not feasible to leave a particular piece of play set up from one session to another and, although they may ask for this, children are mostly reasonable and understanding when it is explained that this is not possible. If it is necessary to reconstruct a particular scenario, a Polaroid photograph or sketch preserves a record. Paintings, drawings and models should be retained and displayed for their intrinsic value and so that the room is 'personalized' for that particular child.

The options for tidying up seem to be (a) someone else does it; (b) the child tidies up; (c) play therapist and child clear away together; (d) the play therapist tidies up and sees if the child will help; (e) the play therapist does it after the session *(Reisman, 1973, p. 116)*.

If children are expected to tidy up there are some snags. Asking the child to clear away may inhibit the play; the rebellious child may test the play therapist by refusing or, indeed, adding to the mess; clearing up may prolong the session; or the session may never get properly under way because the child may insist on tidying up from the beginning.

Ideally, the play therapist should not have to clear up either. The play therapist may even unwittingly inhibit a child from the wilder excesses of sand and water play and the general mayhem that sometimes occurs in the playroom. Also, the play therapist needs time between sessions to reflect on what has happened and to prepare for the next thing. Playroom maintenance is hard work and should be undertaken by ancillary staff, otherwise it takes a disproportionate amount of the play therapist's time.

Play therapy frequently occurs in less than ideal conditions and often it is the play therapist who runs the session and maintains the playroom. The play therapist is recommended not to clear away routinely *during* the session *unless* there is an element of risk, in which case the worker could non-judgementally say 'I'll mop this up so that we don't slip', or 'The paint got spilt'. Adequate storage bins are useful so that toys can be speedily stowed away. A portable fan heater can be directed to wet patches for quick drying. Periodically the playroom and equipment should be thoroughly cleaned.

Views and practices vary about tidying up

- Tidy up once a day; don't bother between sessions.
- Tidy up before each child comes.
- Tidying up may be done by
  - the child
  - the child and play therapist
  - the play therapist, inviting the child to help
  - the play therapist, or someone else, after the session.
- Some people think that
  - Children need to see that mess and turmoil can be restored to order.
  - Having to tidy up may prohibit a child from indulging in messy play.

PLAYROOM MANAGEMENT: TIME KEEPING

In so far as is humanly possible, play therapists should be punctual for sessions, thus showing respect for, and commitment to, the child and helping to maintain a sense of safety and reliability. If the play therapist has to cancel or delay, warn the child in advance, in emergency by telephoning home or school, and give full or even written apologies.

The play therapist is responsible for ensuring that the session finishes on time. Near the end it is advisable to give the child a 'five-minute warning' and say something like 'We'll have to stop in five minutes and you'll go back to school for dinner'. This allows the child to finish off any vital bits of play, or energetically to dream up prolonging tactics. Even if the child keeps an eye on the time, it is still the play therapist's job to bring the session to a close. Occasionally the nature of a session may mean that it could be appropriate to let it over-run.

Children arriving late can be a problem, particularly if the play therapist must adhere to a time-table. The general rule is that the session finishes on time.

- Play sessions should start and finish on time.
- The therapist usually reminds the child a few minutes before the end of the session.
- A clock is useful in the playroom.

PLAYROOM MANAGEMENT: WAITING ROOM AND ESCORTING THE CHILD

A welcoming receptionist and cheerful waiting room, warm and well lit with a few toys, games, magazines and comics suitable for all ages is ideal. Playrooms should neither be adjacent to nor directly opposite the waiting area, so that children are less likely to feel that the escort can hear what is happening, nor will intrude into the session.

Depending on the age and circumstances of the child, a carer (or escort) may remain in the waiting room (though some play therapists prefer that carers should not stay on the premises in case the child feels inhibited by their presence). It is helpful if the child can see where the grown-ups will be and, in cases of extreme dependency, younger children often settle better in the playroom if they know that they can quickly check that the adult is still there. Given adequate waiting facilities and a sensitive perception of the child's needs, the play therapist is usually able to come to the best arrangement for all concerned.

In the early stages of play therapy a young child might be reluctant to separate from the carer. It is often sufficient to allow the child access to the carer in the waiting room, the adult having been primed to encourage the child, kindly but firmly, to return to the playroom. If that does not work the adult could be invited into the playroom, with the option either of staying for a short time and then leaving *(Reisman, 1973, p. 130)*, or remaining but deflecting the child to the play therapist. A small number of dependent children feel happier if the carer joins them in the playroom for the last few minutes of the session.

It is inadvisable for the play therapist to escort the child as this means, in effect, the worker has two roles: travel escort where the child's safety and that of other road-users is paramount, and child-centred play therapist. It does not need too much imagination to realize that there is some incompatibility in these roles! It is better to ask for a volunteer driver or a taxi if no one else seems to be available. If the play therapist *has* to escort, one way round this undesirable situation is to inform the child that there are rules for the road (car, bus) where certain standards of safety and behaviour will be required, and which will differ from some of the rules for the playroom. This usually works, though on a rare occasion a play therapist has been seen dancing down the road in an Ascot hat preceded by a highly delighted child!

> Andrew picks up an abandoned tyre from someone's front garden, which I prohibit, saying that he can do what he likes in the playroom, but that we have different rules for outside.

- Adequate waiting facilities are necessary for the person who brings the child.
- The waiting room should not be
  - Too near the playroom in case this inhibits the child.
  - Too far away because some children benefit from the security of knowing that their parent/escort is reasonably close.
- It is inadvisable for the play therapist to escort the child to sessions because this blurs roles and boundaries.

PROFESSIONAL CONSIDERATIONS FOR THE PLAY THERAPIST: RECORDING

Exercise

- Why record?
- What aids would help you record?
- Who would see your notes?
- Pretend you are a child. What would you like to record about your play therapy sessions?

Recording should meet agency requirements and be useful for the worker. It is recommended that notes should be made of each play session, with summaries about every three months (or once a term) and on termination. The initial summary, completed after the first four or six sessions, can often be predictive about the type of work that will follow.

To help the evaluation process (Chapter 10) it is wise, at the beginning of a case, to list the presenting problems as seen by carers, referrer, teacher and child. Also itemize the play materials that are available, noting in subsequent sessions any major removals or additions.

As much detail as is feasible about the first session (Chapter 5) can be useful in helping play therapist and consultant determine more clearly than is possible from referral details the sort of child with whom they are working. Record the first thing the child does, as this may hold the key to the work.

Some workers scribble quick notes during the session and most children find this acceptable. *Cattanach (1994, p. 19)* contemporaneously writes the story of the child's play, then reads it back. Such material can be worked on in several ways. Other play therapists find that note-taking gets in the way of concentrating on the child, and they obtain adequate recall by sitting quietly in the playroom after the session and looking at the equipment that has been used, which, in turn, triggers verbal and non-verbal interactions. Other play therapists have recourse to audiovisual equipment from which they can make their notes. Workers using video equipment will need to get appropriate consent forms signed. Quick sketches and Polaroid photos of sandtray, dolls' house or floor play are sometimes helpful. Play therapists should be aware that case records, video- and audiotapes, can be seized by the court, should the child be involved in, or subsequently party to, legal proceedings. With the arrival of open recording, therapists also need to familiarize themselves with what can, or might, be made available to the child, to the child's family, and to the child when he or she becomes an adult. Suggested recording formats can be found in Appendix 1.

Recording

- Should meet agency requirements.
- Should be suitable for recall by the courts.
- Sessional notes are recommended.
- Termly summaries are good professional practice.
- Would your supervisor/consultant see the records?
- Who else could see your records?

PROFESSIONAL CONSIDERATIONS FOR THE PLAY THERAPIST: CONSULTATION

Exercise

- What would you expect from
  - the consultation/supervision process?
  - the consultant/supervisor?
- Is your line manager the best person to supervise your play therapy?
- Draw a diagram of the rights and responsibilities of line manager, consultant/supervisor, play therapist, child, child's family, referrer.

'Where there is lack of containment and continuity for workers [in supervision], it is hard to provide these for children' *(Sainsbury, 1994, p. 166)*. Play therapy can be a tricky business and it behoves the agency to ensure that workers and children have the best possible deal. If line managers do not have the requisite skills and knowledge to give professional help with play therapy (and few do), it is imperative that a suitable consultant is found to whom the professional aspect of the work can be contracted *(Hawkins and Shohet, 1989; Houston, 1990)*.

A consultant may be defined as an expert with relevant knowledge and skills, from the same or a related profession. Fees may have to be paid, and consultant and play therapist usually enter into a specific, possibly time-limited, contract. It helps if the consultant has knowledge of normal and abnormal child development, children's emotional and behavioural disorders, the theoretical base of play therapy, and practical techniques for handling various situations. Ideally, the consultant should have undergone personal therapy, counselling or analysis.

A congenial consultant is worth his or her weight in gold as he or she assists the play therapist to deal with the personal, technical and professional challenges of play therapy. 'Psychotherapy ... cannot be *taught* but it can indeed be *learned*. The [consultant] *allows* the therapist to learn and grow, to glean ideas, to correlate them and adapt them to the therapy process' *(Swanson, 1970, p. 10)*. In some settings the consultant may be required to report to the line manager, but normally would not have any other formal responsibility *unless* the child revealed hints or allegations of abuse which the play therapist had failed to act upon, or where there was suspicion of the play therapist's improper behaviour or incompetence.

The aim of consultation sessions is to focus on the interaction between play therapist and child, and on the process and content of the play sessions. The play therapist may provide evidence of sessions by videotape, offering live observation to the consultant, or written records, and is expected to initiate much of the content of the consultation meetings. Play therapists should be prepared to tease out what they think is happening in their work and point out problems or specific areas for discussion, though obviously the consultant may have some sort of agenda too. In consultation meetings the atmosphere should be such that, together, consultant and play therapist can honestly and directly examine and mutually evaluate the play therapist's work.

Group consultation is often effective, provided that the workers are willing to share their practice and their problems, as well as their successes. Group consultation offers opportunities for mutual sharing, learning, information-giving and support.

Play therapy can be taxing, evoking primitive (perhaps buried) responses in the play therapist, and the consultant may help tease these out. However, it is not the consultant's task to undertake the worker's therapy, and such issues should be discussed with the play therapist's personal therapist or counsellor.

Consultation

* The supervisor/consultant is not necessarily the line manager.
* The consultant should have expertise in children and/or in play therapy.
* Consultation can
  – open up blind spots
  – teach
  – act as a sounding board
  – help the play therapist reflect on the process between child and therapist
  – help clarify what is happening
  – enable action to be taken if the play therapist's work is not satisfactory.
* Group consultation, or peer group supervision, may be appropriate.
* The consultant should not be lured into acting as a personal therapist.

Summary

In this chapter we have considered the important ancillary services that surround and support play therapy sessions. Playroom management includes maintaining user-friendly playrooms, or creating a suitable play space if people work elsewhere or are peripatetic. Decisions have to be made about whether to provide refreshments. Limits and boundaries need to be established to keep the play space safe, the key ones being to protect the child and oneself from danger, damage and impropriety. Who tidies up can be a vexed question! The therapeutic importance of time keeping, of maintaining a suitable waiting room and having an appropriate person to bring the child to and from sessions are discussed. Professional considerations for the play therapist cover recording, and consultation/supervision.

In the following Part we will go beneath the surface to find out a bit more about the theoretical reasons why we do things in certain ways.

PRACTICAL CONSIDERATIONS CHECKLIST

1. Is there a suitable playroom?
2. Can I acquire adequate play materials?
3. Can I guarantee to be on time for, and keep, regular sessions with the child?
4. Shall I provide refreshments? If so, how will they be obtained?
5. Who will tidy up?

6. Is the waiting room adequate for the escort?
7. Have I the time, facilities and commitment to record the sessions?
8. Does my agency provide a suitable consultant or supervisor, or do I have to find one myself? If the latter, will the agency pay consultancy fees?
9. Limits
   (a) Decide whether the seven generally accepted limits are appropriate for you (pp.175–9), and determine what additional limits you want to impose.
   (b) When will you inform the child about the limits?
   (c) What will you do if the child infringes the limits? *Warn, remind, action* are useful key words.
   (d) What is your ultimate sanction?

PART FOUR

Contextual issues

17

Historical and theoretical background to play therapy

As I see it, the best work can be done when the professional nature of the role is fully accepted – because it has built into it a discipline based on knowledge and objectivity.

(Winnicot, 1984, p. 23)

This chapter offers a more detailed look at some of the theoretical issues surrounding play therapy

- Firstly, it argues against oppositional theories, suggesting that there is a growing move towards integration
- A historical review of the development of play therapy is attempted
- The predominant theoretical base – the Rogerian person-centred approach – is outlined
- Contextual issues of attachment and loss are discussed

Theories

- Have a value base.
- Explain situations.
- Are predictive.
- Offer a rationale for intervention.
- Can be tested, evaluated and measured.

THE RAPPROCHEMENT OF PSYCHOLOGICAL THEORIES

There seems to be a growing sense in social work and psychotherapeutic practice of moving towards holistic paradigms *(Egan, 1982, pp. 8–9; Fischer, 1978; Guerney, 1984, p. 317; Haworth, 1990, p. 7; Maier, 1978, p. 191; O'Connor, 1991; Patterson, 1980, pp. 559, 571; Ryce-Menuhin, 1988; Shaw, 1987)*. While drawing largely from the person-centred approach derived by Carl Rogers, child-centred play therapy is enriched by knowledge of other disciplines *(Hardiker and Barker, 1981 p. 27; Schaefer, 1988, pp. 1–4)* such as the psychodynamic, behavioural, cognitive, gestalt and transpersonal schools of psychology.

Exercise

- Which theories are relevant for play therapists?
- If you were to write a play therapy textbook, what would you include, and why?
- Become a child:
  - What are the three most important things for you in play therapy?
  - What three things don't matter that grown-ups might consider important?
- What relevance would the child's views have for the theoretical rationale of play therapy?

THE DEVELOPMENT OF PLAY THERAPY

The history of child therapy and analysis is summarized in *Dorfman (1951)*, *Guerney (1984)*, *Haworth (1990, pp. 1–90)*, *Lebo (1982)*, *Schaefer et al. (1991, pp. 1–4)*, *Wilson et al. (1992, pp. 5–10)* and *Wolff (1986)*.

Anna Freud (1895–1982) *(Freud, 1959, 1980; Peters, 1985)* and Melanie Klein (1882–1960) *(Klein, 1932; Segal, 1979)* drew on psychoanalytic principles pioneered by Sigmund Freud (1856–1939) *(Brown, 1964; Fancher, 1973; Thompson and Rudolph, 1988, pp. 147–66)*, who worked mostly with adults, and they realized that, whereas adults used language for free association and telling their troubles, play could fulfil a similar function for children. Freudian psychoanalysis was reductive, usually tracing current malfunction back to early life trauma. Psychoanalytically based therapists predominantly work through the child's transference, through counter-transference, and interpretation.

Moving forward, Alfred Adler (1870–1937) in his 'individual psychology' stressed the relevance of the child's family and social context, and emphasized the importance of the child in his or her own right *(Bottome, 1946; Thompson and Rudolph, 1988, pp. 193–218; Yura and Galassi, 1982)*, some of his ideas having parallels with person-centred and cognitive psychologies *(Mosak, 1979, p. 50)*. Rank (1884–1939) highlighted the relevance of the therapeutic relationship *(Rank, 1936)*, considering it was not necessary to go actively into the past unless the child indicated this was appropriate, so the thrust in his therapeutic sessions was on the child's emotions and feelings in the present, observing that '… once the child has undergone some personal change, however slight, his environmental situation is no longer the same' *(Dorfman, 1951, p. 239)*.

Carl Jung (1875–1961) *(Fordham, 1966; van der Post, 1976)* too viewed people holistically. He accepted the formative influence of parents in their child's development *(Fordham, 1969, p. 133; Jung, 1954, pp. 49–62)*, and recognized that children's energies and growth impulses are forward-looking and developmental, so that it is not always necessary to go backwards to uncover the cause of conflict. It is not thought that he undertook much direct work with children, but some of his writings are seminal *(Jung, 1954, 1961)*. An awareness and appreciation of symbolism, an area to which *Jung (1964)* and the Jungian child and adult analyst, Frances *Wickes (1963, 1977)* made great contributions, is a rich offering. Children's play has symbolic content and, although symbols are not customarily interpreted to the child in play therapy, a knowledge of symbolism can bring added meaning to and understanding of the play.

The school of behavioural casework, based on learning theory, had a strong following *(Herbert, 1981; Hudson and Macdonald, 1986; Thompson and Rudolph, 1988, pp. 124–46)* and play therapists should be aware of the relevance of its major tenets. In summary, it proposes that children's behaviours are often learned responses moulded by their environment; behaviour can be modified by punishment or reward, with modelling and negative and positive reinforcement having powerful effects. General systems theory *(Barker, 1981; Skynner, 1976; von Bertalanffy, 1948; Walrond-Skinner, 1976)* informs that people are not isolates, and that children are affected by the groups within which they live (family, school, community), and vice-versa.

Piaget (1896–1980) investigated norms and expectations in children's cognitive growth *(Ault, 1983; Piaget, 1962)*, and using mosaics and sandtray worlds, Margaret Lowenfeld (1890–1973) enabled children to communicate when words were inappropriate or unavailable *(Bowyer, 1970; Kalff, 1980; Lowenfeld, 1979; Reed, 1975)*. Although mostly applied to adults, the cognitive schools *(Beck et al., 1985; Di Giuseppe, 1981; Ellis and Grieger, 1977; Kelly, 1955; Patterson, 1986 pp. 1–62)* point to the importance of self-talk and suggest how language (and actions) can be reframed and restructured to positive effect.

Further contributions have come from Erik Erikson (1902–1979) whose thesis proposed that, with reasonable opportunities, children progress through inherent levels of development. He formulated eight psychosocial stages *(Erikson, 1964a–c, 1977, 1979)*. In summary, Erikson proposed that from birth to one year children's core psychosocial development is around issues of trust and mistrust. Are the environment and the care-giving nurturing person(s) trustworthy? Does the child feel safe, relaxed, able to express need and expect those needs to be met?

The stage between the ages of one and three years old is to do with autonomy versus shame and doubt. Are children allowed to feel 'all right', intact people, or are they made to feel 'wrong', being patterned and thwarted by powerful adults?

The next stage, between the ages of three and five, is concerned with initiative versus guilt. Is the growing child's enterprise acceptable to the child and important adults?

Between six years old and puberty the major task is to do with industry, ability, initiative and achievement versus inferiority. Does the child feel valued, and that he or she has a contribution to make?

Each stage is built on the preceding one so a basic, firm foundation is of inestimable importance if children are to grow into healthy, mature adults. Children whose development has been impaired may be stuck, or fixated, at an earlier developmental stage until they have had the opportunity of working through it. A nurturing environment that is responsive to their needs throughout their childhood is necessary. When under stress and unable to cope, some children revert to a previous stage, a process known as regression (pp. 68–70) from which, given understanding and stable circumstances, they will normally regrow. Many of the children referred for play therapy need to go back to the first stage, and to experience and learn about trust. The play therapist can be sorely tried as the child tests out again and again whether the play therapist is trustworthy, reliable, consistent and caring. If the child can trust and love, autonomy may become an alternative battleground.

Sometimes classified as a neo-Freudian *(Phillips, 1988)*, D. W. Winnicott (1896–1971) was a child analyst who made a particular study of infants' relationships with their mothers in the first six months of life, and the ensuing application of his work such as the 'average expectable environment', 'good enough mothering', 'true self', 'false self', and the transitional object, has relevance to children and adults. Winnicott was one of the first practitioners to appreciate the value of therapeutic regression *(Davis and Wallbridge, 1983; Dockar-Drysdale, 1990; Winnicott, 1975, 1977, 1986)*, and developed the technique of 'therapeutic consultations' in which he had one, or occasional, lengthy interviews with the child, basing much of the work and communication around his squiggle game *(Winnicott, 1971b)*. His book *Playing and Reality (1971a)* was seminal.

Historical background to child-centred play therapy

- Anna Freud and Melanie Klein created their psychoanalytical schools of child analysis and child psychotherapy, based on the work of Sigmund Freud.
- Behavioural therapy became more widely known.
- Derived from the client-centred work of Carl Rogers, Virginia Axline developed child-centred play therapy.
- Family work became popular.
- Nowadays there is growing awareness of the therapeutic needs of many individual children.
- Child-centred play therapy (which has absorbed elements of psychoanalysis, object relations, behavioural and cognitive work) is based on person-centred theory and is increasingly one of the methods being developed, alongside family intervention, to help the child.

THE PERSON-CENTRED APPROACH

The person-centred approach

- People (children) strive to reach their potential, but can be thwarted by life experiences.
- Given conditions of acceptance, value, and respect, children can feel better about themselves, and their behaviour changes.
- Children are often powerless and pawns of adults, so parallel work with the child's family is important.
- The therapist encourages the child to lead the way towards healing by accepting the child, by reflecting rather than teaching, by being non-directive, and interpreting only rarely.
- The therapist encourages the child to find self-expression and self-value, anchoring therapy in reality by providing limits.

In the 1930s and 1940s Carl Rogers (1902–1987) sought an alternative to what were viewed by some people as the mechanistic excesses of behavioural therapy and the reductive pathological approach of psychoanalysis, and he turned to humanistic principles. He was attracted to the notion that, given a nurturing environment, individuals have within themselves the capacity to overcome or grow through their inner conflicts, and he developed the school known originally as non-directive, client-centred therapy, now as person-centred therapy *(Mearns and Thorne, 1988; Rogers, 1951, 1961, 1974, 1986; Thompson and Rudolph, 1988, pp. 65–82).*

> ... the individual has within himself or herself vast resources for self-understanding, for altering his or her self-concept, attitudes and self-directed behavior – and ... these resources can be tapped if only a definable climate of facilitative psychological attitudes can be provided.
> *(Rogers, 1986, p. 197)*

Person-centred therapy 'sees human beings ... as basically rational, socialized, forward-moving and realistic' *(Patterson 1980, p. 477)*, accepting that each individual has an innate drive towards growth and self-actualization (self-direction), is of inherent, unique, value and has a trustworthy, positive inner core *(Hobbs, 1986, p. 58)*. Self-actualization *(Maslow, 1976, pp. 44–9)* means that people have to have the opportunity to be self-realizing, to be true to themselves, to fulfil their potential; in other words, to develop self-esteem. Important people in their lives have to value them, and allow them reasonable self-determination.

Person-centred theorists contend that 'maladjusted' behaviour is often a response to a judgemental, critical, invasive environment (emotional, physical, spiritual and cognitive) in which needs are inconsistently met, or have not been met, by important carers *(Frick, 1971, p. 136; Meador and Rogers, 1979, p. 143; Nye, 1981, pp. 109, 112, Patterson, 1980, p. 477)*. With many troubled children their material and emotional environment has often been inconsistent, inadequate and unresponsive to their needs *(Rutter, 1975; Wolff, 1981)*, and mixed messages from adults also lead to considerable confusion.

> It is a fundamental thesis of the person-centred point of view that behaviour is not only the result of what happens to us from the external world but also a function of how we feel about ourselves on the inside.
> *(Thorne, 1984, p. 110)*

As *Wickes (1963, p. 78)* states ' ... in the child the transforming process can be arrested by nonacceptance of inner experiences'. In play therapy, the play therapist's approach offers the qualities of consistency, care and concern that may have been missing at formative stages in the child's life.

When children's urges and instincts are consistently or erratically thwarted or denied by people close to them, children may rationalize and feel that it is the child who is 'wrong', 'silly' or 'nasty'. In their attempt to gain adult approval they come to doubt, or even deny, the validity of their feelings *(Mearns and Thorne, 1988, p. 8; Miller, 1987)*, and this often results in 'acting out' or non-compliance. Such children may eventually operate from a false self *(Winnicott, 1986)*, thus jeopardizing their thrust towards self-actualization, and psychic and behavioural conflicts may flourish. To use an analogy: a growing plant can be deformed or stunted if light, water or nutrients are inadequate or if it has a confined space in which to grow. However, the plant can usually be successfully reared if more sympathetic improved conditions are applied early enough. Children are vulnerable to inadequate nurturing, and can be irretrievably damaged, though some retrospective repair work (such as is offered in play therapy) can sometimes help. Remedial work is aimed at making them feel better about themselves, and at restoring self-esteem (*Anderson, 1988; McKay and Fanning, 1987*).

Despite the concept of self-actualization having received some philosophical challenge (*Geller, 1982*), and the notion of non-directiveness having been disputed (*France, 1988, pp. 81–4; Halmos, 1965, pp. 90–105; Hayley, 1963, p. 7*), person-centred therapy is considered one of the major strands of humanistic theory (*Frick, 1971, p. xi*) and underpins, or is part of, several other counselling approaches (*Hales-Tooke, 1989; Merry, 1988; Rowan, 1987*). As Rogers' work developed, the transpersonal and intuitional aspects of interpersonal interaction became more important, and he revealed the additional awareness that results when therapists are in touch with their intuition (*Hales-Tooke, 1989; Rogers, 1986, p. 198; Rowan, 1987*).

Person-centred therapy does not rely on diagnostic labelling but is intended to help people explore, experience and trust their potential, encouraging clients to recognize and respond to the return of their natural growth impulses (*Smail, 1978, p. 28*). If it is accepted that children are inherently 'good' with the capacity to self-actualize, learning tasks and the accomplishment of developmental stages fall naturally into place within a child-centred framework. When children can be themselves and feel cared for in the therapeutic setting they stand a chance of caring about and valuing themselves (*Rogers, 1951, p. 207; Thorne, 1984, p. 121*), and their behaviour is likely to 'mature'. Children are helped to process what happens within sessions when the therapist identifies and reflects the child's behaviour and feelings, which are thus made more concrete. Gradually the child begins to control the processes, rather than being controlled by them.

Axline teased out the application of Rogers' work to a range of troubled children (*Axline 1964a–f; 1969; 1979a, b; Barlow, Strother and Landreth, 1985; Dorfman, 1951; West, 1983*). Axline explains (*1969, p. 15*):

Non-directive therapy is based upon the assumption that the individual has within himself, not only the ability to solve his own problems satisfactorily, but also this growth impulse that makes mature behavior more satisfying than immature behavior.

(See also Axline's eight principles, p. 154.)

- In play therapy, the play therapist
  - is trained in empathic responding
  - provides an environment in which the child can find self-expression
  - understands that play is a means of relationship, and provides information about the child's inner world
  - anchors play therapy in reality by providing limits
  - interacts in play with the child, if the child initiates this
  - reflects what the therapist perceives to be the child's feelings, as well as the child's actions
  - may answer direct questions from the child, if it seems emotionally congruent so to do.

- Therapeutic elements include
  - the relationship that develops between child and play therapist (the therapeutic alliance)
  - acceptance, understanding and therapeutic 'holding' that increase the child's self-esteem and sense of self
  - the child is helped to become free from unconscious drives and blocks resulting from poor life experiences.

'Optimal personality development is achieved when the organism's inherent tendency towards self-actualization is not markedly interfered with by experiences that force the individual to deny his thoughts, feelings and emotions' *(Johnson et al., 1986)*.

CHILD-CENTRED PLAY THERAPY AND THE FUTURE

Therapy needs to adapt to changing circumstances. 'Therapy' is not now just the province of white, western, fee-paying middle class people but nowadays is seen as having something useful to offer most people, including children, who have undergone trauma and difficulties, especially in their developmental years *(Webb, 1991)*. Sometimes these difficulties are one-off situations, sometimes long standing. Sometimes traumatized children remain with their parents; sometimes they have a number of carers, including being in children's homes. Therefore, therapeutic methods have to be developed that can respond to a variety of presenting problems, to a wide age range, and to children from different cultural backgrounds. Unfortunately there are constraints of time, money, and sufficient trained therapists.

Thus we need

- a variety of therapeutic paradigms that offer short and longer term individual work, group work (including sibling groups) and family work
- short-term focused therapeutic work
- child-centred play therapy
- a crisis response service
- assessment facilities
- research studies

ATTACHMENT AND LOSS

Exercise

- What did you feel, and do, about a recent serious loss or bereavement?
- What do you know about children's concepts and experiences of death and loss, at different developmental levels?
- What do you know about repeated personal loss?
- Pretend you are seven years old and that your beloved mother has unexpectedly disappeared
  - what do you feel?
  - what do you do to express your feelings?
  - what would help you feel better?
  - how would you have felt if you had hated your mother?

An understanding of attachment issues *(Aldgate, 1991; Fahlberg, 1982; Lendrum and Syme, 1992, pp. 3–13)* is necessary when working with troubled children '… attachment theory is a way of conceptualizing the propensity of human beings to make strong affectional bonds to particular others and of explaining the many forms of emotional distress and personality disturbance, including anxiety, anger, depression, and emotional detachment, to which unwilling separation and loss give rise' *(Bowlby, 1984, p. 27)*.

Bowlby's earlier view of the overriding importance of the child's early relationship specifically with the mother *(Bowlby, 1980, pp. 39–41)* has been subsequently modified and it is now understood that children can attach to figures other than their mother. The vital principle remains that children need to become attached to consistent, reliable, caring adults. Many troubled children have suffered privation (no opportunity to form affectional bonds), or deprivation (satisfactory early bonds were shattered and not suitably replaced *(Rutter, 1981)*). Traumatic life events are exacerbated for children who have experienced faulty attachment and unsatisfactory parenting, who have perhaps had multiple carers, and who may have lived in a 'chain of uncertainty' *(Aldgate, 1988, p. 49; Jewett, 1984, pp. 106–7)*.

> These children who had never experienced love, who had never belonged to anyone, and were never attached to anyone except on the most primitive basis of food and survival, were unable in later years to bind themselves to other people, to love deeply, to feel deeply, to experience tenderness, grief or shame to the measure that gives dimension to the human personality. *(Fraiberg, 1968, p. 293)*

Fitzgerald (1983, p. 25) suggests it is difficult to talk when not 'attached'. Do we sometimes say that children are being 'unco-operative' if they fail to talk to us?

Attachment and loss

- Satisfactory early attachment depends on the child having reliable, safe, consistent adult parental figures, plus an expectable environment.
- Children with healthy attachments have a better psychological and emotional prognosis.
- Children from chaotic, ever-changing, neglectful households may not have been able to attach, and may have difficulty in trusting and forming positive relationships. Some may be affectionless.
- Provided the child is now in a stable home and with caring adults, play therapy can be part of the remedial process to help the child to form loving relationships.
- Children have
  - less control than adults over the type and number of losses they experience
  - reduced cognitive capacity to process loss
  - feelings that are often ignored or rubbished
  - not always been told the truth about the loss.
- To deal with loss healthily, children need
  - trusted adults who model appropriate ways of expressing emotions and dealing with loss
  - to have their own feelings, fears and phantasies expressed and explored
  - to be told the truth.
- It is more difficult for children with faulty attachments to express feelings and to adjust healthily to loss.
- Many children referred for play therapy will have undergone major losses several times over.

Stages that a child might go through when experiencing loss

- Shock, protest, denial.
- Emotional anguish, searching, despair, anger, anxiety, guilt.
- Partial adjustment.
- Acceptance/resignation.

(Kübler-Ross, 1982; Machin and Samuels, 1993; Wells, 1988).

Children may be torn or paralysed, as they may not feel able to express grief, loss, fear, anger, or helplessness. Feelings of loneliness have to be hidden, curbed, denied, or eliminated through activity *(Segal, 1984, p. 591)* because the children are afraid of alienating their (prospective new) family *(Molin, 1988, p. 242)*. Subsequent loss may trigger previous unresolved loss, and this is compounded when children have faulty attachments and find it difficult to trust. Children's inability to control their situations can lead to helplessness and hopelessness *(Abramson et al., 1986)*, and feelings of desertion, confusion, and being overwhelmed, may lead to depression, worthlessness, guilt, or anger *(Segal, 1984, pp. 591–2)*. Children need the space and opportunity to grieve *(Marris, 1974, p. 27)*, express anger, and to have these feelings understood and accepted. Adults find it hard to allow children to mourn and feel sad *(Black, 1984, p. 41)*. 'Perhaps a denial of the suffering of the child client helps to quell the shadows of our own bewildering pain', recognized *Wardle (1975, p. 430)*.

Summary

Over the last few years there has been a broadening of boundaries, and many practitioners now recognize that they draw from more than one theoretical base. Play therapy is carving its own niche, drawing from the psychoanalytic, behavioural, gestalt and transpersonal schools, but resting mainly on the Rogerian person-centred approach. It will continue evolving as play therapists attend to the needs of troubled children. The majority of young people referred for play therapy has undergone multiple separations, and the chapter concludes with a discussion of attachment and loss.

Using the person-centred approach, the child often expresses his or her dilemma in symbolic play rather than in overt words, so the role of the unconscious and the importance of symbolism are outlined in the following chapter.

18

The unconscious and symbolism

I am deeply moved again and again at the discovery of how close the child's psyche is to spiritual and healing forces.

(Kalff, 1980, p. 65)

- In child-centred play therapy, the child decides how to use the session, and unconscious processes usually take over
- Therefore, awareness of
  - the unconscious
  - symbolism
  might help the play therapist to get beneath the surface of the sessions and understand a little more clearly what is happening.

THE UNCONSCIOUS

Exercise

- What is your definition of
  - the conscious?
  - the unconscious?
- We sometimes talk about children 'being in a world of their own'. What form of consciousness would you call this?
- What fictional stories can you recall that tell us about the unconscious of children?

Consciousness is awareness. Toby may be preoccupied with hunger; he is consciously aware of hunger which is a pressing, immediate state. A few minutes previously his cheek was scratched by the cat but, as his hunger became more immediate, the incident with the cat was temporarily forgotten, to be instantly recalled if something reminds him of the cat or his cheek. So some things are immediately conscious, in present awareness, and others are just below the surface but become conscious when given attention. A third level of the unconscious contains events and feelings that are repressed from consciousness, are hidden and cannot be brought to immediate recall; things that have caused discomfort (physically or emotionally) and have therefore been pushed out of awareness so that the person can adjust to living 'without the difficulty'. Toby had perhaps repressed some of the inconsistency and abuse he had received as a young child because mummy preferred a 'good boy' who did not complain. If something is repressed it does not cease to exist; the inner self is divided and a disturbance is created *(Harding,*

1973, p. 370), often exhibiting in physical or behavioural symptoms. The unconscious is 'alive' and, although not in awareness, makes its presence felt.

Sigmund Freud is credited with early explorations of the unconscious, tracing most human emotional malfunctions, most neuroses, back to infantile origins so that the unconscious was seen as a repository of early conflicts. Jung viewed the unconscious as a rich, fertile ground that, when understood and valued, could show the direction towards personal fulfilment. Seen this way, the unconscious becomes a promising tool allowing expression and resolution of inner conflicts. If the unconscious is thus used in an accepting therapeutic environment such as play therapy, redemption and release from the presenting symptoms caused by the child's inner conflicts may be effected, children become less at the mercy of their unconscious drives, and their behaviour usually improves.

A model of the unconscious, based on Jung

- Consciousness: things of which we are currently aware conveyed by our senses, feelings and thoughts.
- The personal unconscious: those things of which we are not presently aware, but which can be recalled.
- A deeper level of the personal unconscious contains repressions that are hard to bring into awareness, but can affect behaviour and emotions.
- The collective unconscious contains inherited predispositions, and resonates to myths and archetypes.

The Jungian child psychotherapist *Wickes (1963, pp. xvi–xvii)* wrote:

[Children] are very near to the unconscious, to the wisdom of thoughts that blow through them, to dreams that we have learned to forget; near to love and fear, to generosity and cruelty – to the direct experience of the opposites. They are near to the unconscious ... .

The unconscious communicates in images, symbols being the language of the unconscious *(Rushforth, 1981, p. 37)*. Where there is conflict, symbols often show the way towards resolution *(Neumann, 1954, p. 414)*.

Toby (p. 4):

Toby arrived early and looked quite smart this week. He went to the sandtray, dividing the vehicles between us and telling me to take mine away and play. Later he asked me to see the roads he had made. Some were maze-like, mostly with walls between. At one end of the sandtray was a dug-out bit with a small amount of water. Toby was repairing an upper road – apparently its infrastructure was unsafe. 'All the road's getting dug up – to make it better. Bombs keep blowing it up.' The fire engine and ambulance screeched along.

After going to the toilet, Toby was engrossed in some quiet dolls' house play. I could hear him say things like 'Better do downstairs today. Darling, come out. Is it dinner time yet, mummy? No. OK'.

Toby returned to the sandtray. 'I forgot the water' and he tipped some in. He made a hole in the bank by the water so that if vehicles fell in there was a way of getting them out. Some cars, including the ambulance, did sink. 'It's mended, all mended' as he made the bank more solid. 'The fatter you build it the harder to bash it down.' I was sent away to do my work. Toby was singing, and said he was enjoying school. He continued to make his structures more solid. 'Army's going to start soon. People die.' But he continued to make the top road safe. 'That looks good now, don't it?' I notice that the water had disappeared. 'I'm glad that water's going.' [Why's that?] 'We don't want the water in here, do we?' Three guns go into the ditch. 'He (the fourth gun) isn't a good driver.'

Toby looks at the clock. Suddenly, and urgently, the vehicles are put away and he flattens the sand. Toby sits on the table, explaining that this is his tree house, and I'm asked to place some biscuits by the 'trunk'.

Toby went to the home corner, took the baby doll and kissed it. 'She's going to bed soon.' He poured a drink out for himself and me. 'I'll make the baby's bottle in a minute. Pretend I'm the baby, right'. He filled two feeding bottles with orange squash, and took reserve jugs of water and squash. Toby got into bed, instructing me to feed him with the bottle. He asked for the dummy and sucked, slept, grizzled and gnawed a biscuit.

We then played shop and had a puppet show. He was the big black wolf who caught the little girl (me).

This was about half way through his play therapy, and the play therapist noted at the end of the above session:

1. Toby was much more confident, settled, happier, looking better this week.
2. Big change in the sand play. No huge cliffs, only a small amount of water that was absorbed by the sand. Some vehicles fell in the ditch, but were sort-of rescued. Lots of roads, the major one having a bad undersurface that needed re-doing. The road pattern had maze-like qualities, though the cul-de-sacs served as useful parking places so, although there was a road all round, the track was still puzzling.

(In previous sessions there had been mammoth disasters in the sandtray – cataclysms, earthquakes, floods, insurmountable obstacles. This time there were roads. Roads may be seen as the way through life – perhaps a bit circuitous in this case, but Toby did have a way through life, even if maze-like. Part of the road was in need of repair; the infrastructure that was being mended could stand for the unconscious that was now getting strengthened. Also the roads were possibly under attack, but were nevertheless there. Helpers (ambulance) were at hand, though could not be totally relied on not to get bogged down. After that, Toby felt safe enough to regress.)

3. Regression was extremely explicit. Previously I had had to care for the doll-baby or the Toby-baby, but increasingly he was able to express and nurture the baby part of himself.

4. The play appeared to have distinct phases. Toby looked at the clock, then flattened his sandtray and went into regression. The shop play and the puppet play seemed separate parts of the week's 'work'. We've had quite a lot of shop play before, and I can't recall this week's as being different. We've also had puppets before; he identified with the big bad wolf.

(This play was reasonably age-appropriate; he treated me fairly in the shop but, under the guise of a wolf, attacked me or what I stood for. Perhaps he was practising his nascent, inherent inner strength? Perhaps he still needed to be strong and snarly?)

SYMBOLISM

If workers are in tune with symbolism, they are more likely to enable and not, albeit unintentionally, stifle the expression and resolution of the child's needs as expressed by the unconscious. The language of symbolism is more subtle than certain dream dictionaries and elements of the popular press would have us believe. Although there may be some universal interpretations, symbolic language is unique to each individual, and symbols can have a plurality of meanings because they can combine or transcend opposites (*Ryce-Menuhin, 1988, p. 70*). What is a meaningful symbol for one child may not be so for the next, and play therapists must beware of transferring symbol interpretation from one person to another. The symbol only has meaning within the context of that specific child at that particular point in time (*Fromm, 1952, p. 27*), and during the course of play therapy a symbol can have more than one interpretation (*Jones, 1948, p. 97; White and Swainson, 1974, p. 187*). Dockar-Drysdale comments that communication is usually effective if the play therapist responds sensitively, using the same symbols as the child (*1990, p. 67*).

Exercise

- What are symbols?
- What are your symbols for
  - your inner child?
  - yourself?
  - your job?
  - your neighbour?
  - the prime minister?
- You are seven years old. Draw the symbols you would choose to describe yourself if you pretended you were a
  - car
  - flower
  - animal
  - food.

What is a symbol? The word derives from the Greek, meaning 'together: I throw' (*Macdonald, 1973, p. 1367*); Stevens (*1982, p. 242*) defined a symbol as: '...

a bridge connecting the known with the unknown, ego-consciousness with the unconscious'. With a sign there is an agreed link between it and what it stands for: a table is just that. A symbol stands for something other than itself *(Fiske, 1982; Jung, 1921, p. 601)*. In the extract on p. 200, the table stood for a tree house. Symbols, unlike signs, are alive, capable of change and growth, pregnant with creative meaning, evocative: they have the power to mediate experience, often of great intensity. In Toby's work the table was also a voyaging ship, a space ship, a kennel and a prison. The symbol, as Jung has shown, acts as transformer *(Jung, 1956)*.

Symbols communicate realities that may be too complex or too hidden for ordinary expression *(Cooper, 1978, p. 7)*. Children might summon up a lion in their play because they have seen one on television, in a book or at the safari park. The play might be seen as a straightforward expression of their interest in the lion, or their wish to communicate with someone about the lion. In this case, the lion is probably a sign. But if, through the lion, children want to express something of their own aggressive, strong, lordly nature, or if they are angry with a parent and want to 'gobble him or her up', then the lion might be symbolic. In psychotherapy, symbols serve an 'as if' function. Considered from the standpoint of realism, the symbol is not external truth, but is psychologically true *(Jung, 1956)*.

Klein (1955, p. 234) recognized the 'archaic language' of symbolism, observing that children's ability to use symbols enables them 'to transfer not only interests but also phantasies, anxieties and guilt to objects other than people'. Because of its ability to bring the conscious and unconscious elements of the psyche together, the symbol allows energies to flow from within 'in a new creative effort' *(Harding, 1973, p. 10)*. Children have often been admonished and told 'to behave', and this does not always yield the desired improvements, but an inner change is of a different order for it springs from and is grounded within the child, and is not merely a response to adult precepts.

Toby was going through a bad patch in the outer world:

Toby's aimless digging in the wet sandtray led to a river with precipitous banks running across the tray. 'No one could get out if they fell in the water.' He took one corner as his 'camp' which he defended with high walls, and constructed an elaborate prison, banks with spy holes, and a place where the wounded could be taken and reinforcements would wait. My camp was the other side of the river. We selected our soldiers and put them in position. Twice his Indians tricked my captains and imprisoned them, putting my forces at a disadvantage. A crocodile inhabited the river, making forays to snatch some of my people.

The play continued for a while, with Toby being the aggressor and me the victim. Then he added two planes and an ambulance. We poured more water into the river, which collapsed some of the banks, and Toby made the river bigger, excavating some of his land to form a house for the crocodile.

At this stage his forces and mine started to become friends rather than enemies. His plane became a magic bomber, and I was given a plane. The prisoners were released, people from both sides went swimming, and the alligator/crocodile became friendly.

The play therapist noted:

> The sandtray was important revealing, I felt, deep conflict (very deep river – water can symbolize emotions – and two opposing forces) his force, his energies having to outwit mine. The construction of the prison was elaborate. There was also a place to recover from battle trauma – so healing was a possibility – and reinforcements were available. After some time the forces and crocodile became friendly. The crocodile is seen by some authorities as a negative mother symbol and this tunes in with his constant bashing of me last session. *Cooper (1978, p. 44)* suggests that the crocodile can also symbolize fury and anger – which is about right for Toby just now. The loud music at the end was sustained and invasive – letting off steam, letting off aggression? For the first time he took biscuits away with him at the end of the session – something to do with deprivation, uncertainty and comfort? After the session I felt drained, angry, frustrated – and gobbled a large quantity of chocolate biscuits myself! It was possible I was picking up some of his very deep unhappy and insecure vibes.

If they are to have purpose, symbols should lead to resolution and, once expressed and accepted (not necessarily verbally, but implicitly by the play therapist), symbols have a redemptive function that can change the child's behaviour *(Martin, 1955, pp. 115, 120; von Franz, 1983, p. 254)* Almost any object or act can be symbolic *(Martin, 1955, p. 114)*. The Incredible Hulk can be used to express the child's wish for power (children who are either dominated by a powerful adult, or who, conversely, are given too much freedom and therefore fear their own aggression might play out their fears and phantasies with such figures). Another child, after painful and frightening hospital experiences, might bury persecuting doctors in the sand as he seeks to render them 'dead' and therefore to stop them assaulting him. Most children will be able to use play materials to express whatever is necessary. The phantasy element, including 'let's pretend,' is as important as object play with toys *(Fordham, 1978, p. 170)*. Sometimes 'let's pretend' play can seem more like rehearsing life skills but, if purposefully understood, its symbolic element is often important.

Adults may attribute a child's play to something seen on television, read in a book, or done at school. Of course exposure to such things cannot be denied, and symbols are influenced by the experiences of the conscious mind *(Whitmont, 1980, p. 118)* but children are confronted with hundreds of images in a normal day, so the play therapist will ask *'Why* did the child choose to play at HeMan (or Skeletor) *today?* What does this tell me about the child's inner needs at this point in time?', rather than dismiss it as 'He saw it on television'. There is some unconscious reason why the child picked on whatever it was *(Harding, 1973, pp. 378, 381)*.

Symbols

• Are a form of expression.
• Perform an 'as if' function. When I feel angry I feel 'as if' I were an angry lion.
• Have unique meaning for the individual who evoked the symbol.
• May have changing meanings, so can have more than one interpretation.
• Should be treated with respect.
• Beware learning symbolism from the popular press.

ARCHETYPAL IMAGES

• A Jungian concept, archetypes are unconscious underlying patterns prevalent in all societies and throughout history.

The study of archetypes is perhaps a bit specialized for some play therapists but, for workers with a Jungian background, archetypes are an important and interesting manifestation. It was Jung who, having studied the mythologies and religions of various cultures throughout the world, became aware that there are certain universally recurrent themes, known as archetypes, that crop up in all societies at all times. Archetypes are timeless and, as it were, stateless. *Jacobi (1971, p. 34)*, a contemporary of Jung, described archetypes as '… psychic manifestations of a biological, psychobiological, or ideational character, provided they are more or less universal and typical'. Archetypes characteristic of the adult process of psychic integration include the persona, shadow, animus and anima, wise woman, wise man and God *(Jacobi, 1959)*. For children, the archetype of the mother (good and bad) is often important; other archetypes appearing with some frequency are the hero, trickster, child, family, father and 'bad' person. Children may see these aspects more in terms of animals, insects, the supernatural (ghosts) or fairy tale figures (witches, kings, queens, stepmothers, princes and princesses).

The mother archetype is important and two-edged *(Neumann, 1955)*. '… on the one hand, the Great Mother is creative and loving, on the other,' she is destructive and ambivalent' *(Stevens, 1982, p. 90)*. *Fordham (1969, pp. 56, 58)* discusses the bad mother as portrayed by witches, ghosts and animals, and *Stevens (1982, p. 90)* includes the dragon, monster and sea-serpent.

Polly

Polly's mother left much to be desired and Polly was acutely ambivalent about her; on the one hand wanting her so that she could at least have a mother of sorts, and on the other hand yearning for consistent, loving mothering which at some level she realized she had missed (pp. 33–4).

> 'In bed, it's midnight. Be a ghost, be Dracula, be the devil … You be the witch.' … I have to turn her into a spider. Then she kills me several times by making 'psst' noises, and she says a daddy-long-legs is crawling up my legs. As we were near the end of the session, I turned myself into the good witch and made a spell that turned her into my good witch baby.

Three sessions later:

'Bedtime for you … I don't care if the ghosts get you. I'm a giant …' I, the ghost, am instructed to look for the baby, which Polly defends.... 'Shurrup you, Mr ghost. Shurrup. I know you're a silly ghost. Shurrup. Pretend you be Dracula now.'

Two weeks pass:

'Pretend you're the witch. Can't catch me for a bumble-bee'. [I can't catch you up there.] She continues 'Pretend this is a high building and you're a very small witch.' [I can't catch her. What shall I do?] 'Pretend you get me in the house. You can't catch me for a bumble-bee. You start crying.' I cry, exclaiming [She's beaten me, she's won.] 'Not eaten!' [No, beaten.] 'I come into your room. You don't know. You thought it was your friend. I get your baby. You don't know. When you see me get the baby you say "Put it down".' [Leave my baby alone] I remonstrate. 'No. Pretend I take it upstairs. You're not having your baby. Stinking – can I say that? – stinking witch. Very horrible. Pretend I take your baby away. You can't find it. You roar your head off. You screech.' [She's taken my baby away] I cry, making lots of loud angry noises, and she saves the baby.

After another fortnight:

We were making a birthday cake and she asked me to say [Mummy, there's a ghost]. 'Go away – shoo', she declares angrily, chasing the ghost, saying triumphantly 'It's dead'.

A bit later:

'Pretend you're dressed up as a witch. No, I'm the witch and you're the cat. You're the other witch.' She makes a telephone call to me, enquiring 'How are you?' [Very ill] I respond, in witchy tones. 'I'll make you better with my magic. I'll come to your house. This is the party now at my house. What would you like to eat?' [What have you got?] 'Witch pie – a few snails and slugs. I don't eat slugs. Don't you call me a dafthead.' She collects sand and sings 'Nice witch pie. It's got snakes, spiders, slugs, butterflies'. I remark that butterflies are too nice for witch pie. She cuts witch pie. 'Close the door, will you, my friend? Pretend I write Happy Birthday on the pie. It's yours. Your name?' [Witch Nelly.] 'Mine is Witch Polly. Pretend you're singing. You're singing really horrible.' She tells me my singing isn't horrible enough and I say it's the best I can do as a witch. 'Where's your cat? At home? Or on your broom? Can you show me where your broom is? Here's your cake. You tell me to have some more.' [I'll spit out the butterflies] I warn, perhaps getting a bit too enthusiastically into role. 'Have some more. It's the best I can do. Have some spider sauce on it. It might taste horrible. Let's go out for a witch walk.' She asks where my broomstick is and we ride on the playroom brush.

A week later:

'The fire's dead. We ain't got no warm.' Polly was making noises and I say [All sorts of funny noises. Perhaps it's the ghost?] She responds 'Don't make me scared. Bed – quick – for you, the ghost's coming', insistently. She wails, 'The ghost's coming. You better watch out. What's your name going to be?' [I don't know]' 'You say "The ghost has just burped" ', which I repeat.

Then I comment [That ghost is making funny noises. I'm frightened]. 'You say "It's Dracula, I'm frightened" '. [What's happening?] 'You rush into my house. You cry. You rush into my arms. It's only a cartoon.' [It's stopped], I say with relief. 'You're even more frightened.' [It's getting worse.] 'Pretend someone throws this [the feeding bottle] at you.' [Not at my face. I'm frightened.] 'You don't know someone's creeping round.'

She puts her cardigan over my head, instructing 'You're a ghost. You like the noise. You say "That's my friend Dracula".' [Hallo, Dracula, you're making a good noise.] 'Scare the people. Pretend it's night and we go down. Put on your cloak. Say "Put your cloak on, Dracula". I growlded [sic] at you. We fell out with each other. ' [I don't like you.] 'We're soon back together again . You turn into a nice man. Would you like to come down to my house where my friend is? Then you're a ghost. You're a nice man, but you're a ghost really. I'm Dracula really.' I ask what shall we do? 'Talk to him. Who is he?' I tell her he's my friend. 'He's Dracula. You say "How do you know he's Dracula?" '. Introductions are made and they recognize each other.

'You say "Let's go out haunting, my friend". By the nice friend, our fire. Will you look after my ghost-badge, fire? I'm not allowed to take it with me. This is my Dracula castle. This is a baby we've already bited. Shall we have some dinner before we go out? Shall we drink blood? What else?' [Pies?] 'Let's stamp feet – let's go somewhere stamping feet … . It's half time being Dracula.' [Can we stop?]' I injudiciously enquire. 'No, we've got a long time. You and the bloody Dracula-stopping.' … She spits out a bit of sand. 'That's the ashtray what we spit in. All right, Dracula?' [Yes.]

Notice how the dominance of the witch/ghost dwindles, eventually being defeated. Polly was no longer so much at the mercy of her negative-mother archetypes, and in her outer life was becoming more loveable.

Common archetypes in play therapy include
- the family
- mother, father, child, baby
- witch
- Dracula
- police
- robber
- hero
- trickster
- ghost
- monster
- giant
- fighting people
- food
- house
- baddy.

Andrew

Seven-year-old Andrew (p. 33) produced similar archetypes. In his first session he referred to a witch, ghost and two wise men. In session 4:

'I had a nightmare in my cupboard last night.' [Want to tell me about it?]' I enquire. 'I never really, it was my mum dressed up. Tricked me.'

Later:

'What's that witch?' and he tells me about a friend. 'Witches come into his bedroom. It's his mother dressed up and scares him. He doesn't know it's his mother. It looks like a witch in real life … My house is haunted with monsters. This man comes out of the kitchen every night. He's got one eye and green hair. He scares me. My mum told me. My uncle saw him come out of the kitchen one night. My uncle tried to shoot him, but he never did. He's a monster. Have you ever seen one?' [I might have.]

In previous chapters references have been made to Darth Vader, Incredible Hulk, HeMan, and Skeletor who can be seen as representing archetypal figures and, once alerted to the notion of archetypes, the interested play therapist will become aware that archetypes abound in myths and fairy tales *(Bettelheim, 1976; von Franz, 1980)*, and will perhaps perceive them with renewed insight when children introduce them into their play.

MANDALA

Exercise

A mandala often looks like a circular or square concentric pattern.

* Have fun! Draw and paint mandalas.
* Make some butterfly paintings. (Paint, fold the paper in half and press down. Open up the paper – and see what happens?)

A mandala is an ancient symbol appearing across the cultures *(Argüelles and Argüelles, 1972)* and, in varying ways, may be produced by children at a turning point in their therapy. Mandalas are usually concentric, counterbalanced designs, so some play therapists pay particular attention when children create patterns based on squares and/or circles, realizing that perhaps a 'breakthrough' in therapy is imminent.

[Mandalas] serve to produce an inner order – which is why, when they appear in a series, they often follow chaotic, disordered states marked by conflict and anxiety. They express the idea of a safe refuge, of inner reconciliation and wholeness. *(Jung, 1959, p. 384)*

Jung notes that they can prevent outbursts and disintegration, and are also symbols of the self *(Jung, 1956, p. 208n)*. Fordham *(1957, p. 132)* finds mandalas may be produced when the child is about to integrate a new element, or de-integrate (go to pieces in some way).

This may sound somewhat esoteric but, for the Jungian student, warrants further study. However, for some play therapists it is perhaps sufficient to realize that mandala-type configurations produced by children *may* herald some inner change which should subsequently become manifest in their outer lives. The play therapist would probably find it useful to make careful notes about mandalas, with sketches if appropriate, for later reference.

Two of Polly's and one of Toby's mandala paintings (Figs 8.9–8.11), produced at turning points in their play therapy, can be seen on p. 88.

Mandalas

- Are concentric, often circular, designs.
- Therapeutically, they may be created at times of change and integration.

DREAMS

Exercise

- Can you recall a dream or nightmare you had as a child? Paint or draw it.
- Speak to the different parts of the dream, and encourage them to talk to each other.
- Do the same with your current dreams.
- Discuss dreams with friends.
- Find out what children dream.

If children talk about, or are bothered by, dreams and nightmares, the worrying things often come from the child's unconscious and the child-centred play therapist could suggest that the child might like to paint the dream, or make a sandtray picture of it, or act it out – anything, really, to bring the dream into the light of day and express it. More detailed dreamwork should not be undertaken by play therapists unless they have specific training and experience *(Fordham, 1994, pp. 29–50; Oaklander, 1978, pp. 145–51; Smith, 1990; Wickes, 1977, pp. 256–90)*. Some children, particularly if they are abused at night or are drugged, may say they are dreaming whereas in fact they are recalling something that actually happened to them.

- Dreams and nightmares can be important
- Ask the child to show you the dream through drawing, sandtray, acting, puppets, or words.
- Pay attention to the feeling content of dreams.
- Without further training, be cautious of dreamwork.

Summary

In child-centred play therapy, the child is free to decide how to use the sessions, the 'choice' often being influenced by the resurgence of unresolved feelings, memories and events that have been repressed into the unconscious. As these precipitants are not in conscious awareness, they cannot be deliberately played out or discussed. However, they can be ventilated symbolically, symbols having the power to portray, mediate and transform. The play of some children is rich in archetypes that impart underlying experiences common throughout humanity. The relevance of the mandala is discussed, and we are reminded that some therapists may be trained to work with the unconscious that communicates in dreams.

Having unravelled something about the role of the unconscious and symbolism in the therapeutic process, in the final chapter we look at what is probably the most vital resource – ourselves – in particular, how we care for ourselves. We also say 'goodbye' to some of the children we have come to know in the preceding pages.

19

Valedictory: children
and play therapists

*Perhaps the most valuable gift we bring to work with children is our capacity to
remain vulnerable, whilst accepting our professional discipline and role.*
(Winnicott, 1984, p. 23)

- At the end of this book, it seems important to say 'goodbye' to the children
  who are at the heart of our endeavours
- Working with needy children can be extremely demanding, and play therapists
  are exhorted to take care of themselves so that they can give of their best

---

FAREWELL TO THE CHILDREN

I got a little sunbeam
And put it in my pocket,
So when the dark came
I had still got it

(Julian Levay, aged 7, 1979, p. 96)

Children who are troubled tend to hurt, often all over and inside, but they do
not always know why they hurt. All they can do is act out their hurt or
withdraw. For troubled children to be accepted, valued, encouraged to be
themselves, given opportunities to communicate in whatever way suits them,
respected despite the difficulties they know themselves to be in, given the
regular undivided attention of a sympathetic adult in a child-friendly environment – this is an experience called *play therapy*. It seems to work, because
youngsters feel better, family and school relationships improve, and children
such as Toby, Polly, Peter, Gemma and Andrew are freed to fulfil their potential,
though the experience can be painful for the play therapist *(Hoxter, 1983)*.

About six weeks after play therapy started, Gemma's foster mother
reported that Gemma (p. 33) was improving and was acting out less. Rather to
everyone's surprise, an adoptive placement was soon being sought, and
the frustrating part was waiting for a suitable family. If Gemma had had an
equable home background, play therapy could have been terminated after
about eight months, but it took nearly a year before her new adoptive family
was finalized. Shortly after going to her permanent family some of the previous
difficult behaviours returned, but this time were resolved much more quickly
as she tested out and healed the hurt within the context of her new permanent
family.

Andrew's play therapy (p. 33) lasted for five months and he had made considerable progress at school. He was no longer terrorizing the neighbour-hood, and work had been done with the family that helped stabilize his life-style. After play therapy, it was proposed that the social worker should undertake some life story work with Andrew, in particular helping him to unravel the foster home moves he had experienced in his early life. It was hoped, too, that Andrew's parents would talk to him about his mother's illness.

During play therapy Polly (pp. 33–4) improved and an adoptive family was sought. Play therapy with Polly could have been terminated after about eight months, but, as with Gemma, we were kept waiting for an adoptive placement to materialize. When it did, the placement did not work. This was not Polly's fault as she had done more than was required, but the adoptive parents had withheld vital personal information which soon jeopardized the placement. On the breakdown of what should have been her permanent family, traumatically for Polly, she was placed in a children's home, but soon gathered herself together and her next adoptive placement turned out satisfactorily.

Peter's performance improved in all areas of his life (p. 34). After about a year of play therapy, he moved to a small unit that specialized in preparing children for living in a family, and made a successful transition to a foster home.

CARING FOR THE PLAY THERAPIST

- Working with troubled children, especially in play therapy where they are sharing the wounded parts of themselves, can be shattering and draining.
- It behoves play therapists to
  - Ensure their holistic needs are met by paying attention to their own body, emo-tions, mind and spirit.
  - Work on their own painful issues in a supportive environment.
  - Take responsibility for re-creating themselves.
- The intact, fully functioning play therapist will give a better service to the child.

Working with the children we have already met is at times demanding, draining and exhilarating; stark case histories highlight the importance of care for the play therapist as well as for the child.

Frank is eight years old and for the past few months has been living in a children's home. He is lively, articulate, loves playing and thrives on attention. There are times, however, when he threatens to kill himself (he has been known to cut his wrists), ruins other children's possessions and throws his food at all and sundry. Until the age of seven Frank had had something like 23 changes of carer. As a young child he was severely physically and emotionally neglected; he was often left unattended in his own faeces and urine and that of the household dogs. He had several spells in hospital because of impaired development, returning to live with his mother, who more often than not had a different co-habitee, or a new baby, or might have moved to another semi-derelict property. Between times he would go into short-term foster care.

Susan, who is nine, is an intelligent, forthright girl. She usually looks immaculate and loves to wear good clothes. She cleans, polishes and tidies the house. She is wonderful with young children, having a particular affinity for those with handicaps. However, at times she has severe, almost uncontrollable tantrums; she bites, screams, kicks, hits and tries to strangle animals. She, too, has been removed from her mother and will never return. From an early age Susan had been forced to care for her younger brothers and sisters; she had been beaten by her mother's boyfriend and had been tied to the table leg if she would not do jobs such as peeling potatoes; she had been taunted and called dreadful names, had not been allowed to play with her friends. Susan had been placed in a foster home, but there was a change of policy and she returned to her mother. But this time Susan was older, and was soon reporting further physical abuse; she also disclosed that she had been sexually abused in the foster home.

Margie is six and her half-brother Fred is five. They were removed from their parents following sexual, physical and emotional abuse. It was known that the children had been sexually abused by several adults and teenagers of both sexes, and Margie's and Fred's behaviour could be bizarre. They would urinate and defaecate often secretly almost everywhere other than the toilet. They sexually molested each other, as well as other children and animals. Human and animal penises would be stroked, sucked and stuck into male and female body orifices, into which Margie and Fred would also insert sticks or cutlery. The children sobbed when they saw red meat, which they thought came from recently-killed children or pet animals. They could not bear macaroni or spaghetti because this reminded them of worms that had been put up their bottoms and that they had been made to eat. They had difficulty sleeping and would often chant during the night. Perhaps surprisingly, they coped reasonably well at school, though there would sometimes be complaints about inappropriate sexual touching and distractibility. There were times when Margie's eyes glazed and she 'froze', and she was over-protective of Fred.

In their professional lives play therapists come across children who have suffered deprivation, cruelty, abuse and loss in many forms including close relationships. In some ways these children are old for their years, having witnessed and experienced things that are difficult to imagine; in other ways they are immature and need to regrow the childhood that was denied them. Despite having similarities with torture victims (Goddard and Carew, 1988; Jones et al., 1987, pp. 260–2), many such children have a great innate thrust towards growth and wholeness. Once the child is protected, is in a reasonably nurturing and safe environment and has the right opportunities, the child's psyche can 'balance up', heal and compensate for gross deprivation and hideous experiences. The therapeutic task has to be multifaceted and holistic, and the role of the carers – whether in a family or residential setting – is paramount. Such children often require re-parenting and re-educating socially and emotionally, as well as academically. Usually they are performing below their potential academic ability and so require special attention at school. Psychotherapeutic assistance may also be desirable.

Children similar to David, Susan, Margie and Fred may be referred for play therapy *as part of* the healing process. There may be great pathos, anger and despair as raw emotions are faced and worked through. The play therapist can feel drained and buffeted by a kaleidoscope of feelings when he or she becomes the butt of the child's pain, confusion, hostility and aggression, and is treated as if he or she were the abuser or deserting parent.

Crompton (1990, p. 117) urges that 'in order to work effectively and to pay the cost, workers need training and preparation and the same kind of listening and respect they offer the children'. Play therapists have to be able to empathize with, feel into, accept and understand what the child is conveying, often wordlessly. Therefore workers have to be free and open within themselves to experience whatever needs to come up. It is important that they are receptive to unconscious and conscious aspects of the whole child – spiritual, emotional, physical, cognitive – so it is imperative that they pay attention to these aspects of themselves.

Sometimes workers exposed to the more sordid aspects of human experience become out of balance. Their bodies become tense, they may experience sleeping and/or eating difficulties, and often suffer from psychosomatic problems. Becoming emotionally drained, overwrought or burnt-out are hazards; and sex lives and close relationships may be adversely affected. Spiritually, play therapists can go to the depths, their faith apparently shattered, as they feel assailed from all sides with negativity and a spiritual vacuum. Cognitively, professionals may be nonplussed when usual norms no longer seem to apply and they become unable to communicate effectively; or they chatter inanely, sometimes inappropriately, as they try to make sense of what they are experiencing.

People working holistically need to take care of themselves and pay attention to their whole being. On the physical level they should undertake some sort of body work (for example yoga, massage, exercise, physical therapies, relaxation or workouts) and pay attention to diet, rest and recreation. Emotionally there is a need for satisfying relationships and experiences. Counselling or psychotherapy is mandatory for those play therapists engaged in the deeper levels of work. Paying attention to spiritual or philosophical needs seems vital too, be it through orthodox or New Age approaches, or merely establishing a world view; some play therapists dealing with the results of extreme human degradation find spiritual healing valuable in balancing up the depths. Cognitively there is a need to explore and understand the professional area of work, and to gather explanations, other views, other vistas, other idioms. Friends and peer support are important.

Play therapists, therefore, are encouraged to take responsibility for their own well-being in order to maintain themselves so that they can support the traumatized child. Workers who fail to care for their physical, spiritual, emotional and cognitive needs, both conscious and unconscious, are in danger of harming themselves and the children whom they strive to serve.

Exercise

- You are challenged to find time for, and do, something that
  - is good for your body
  - allows emotional outlet
  - your mind enjoys and finds satisfying
  - takes you further into your own quest for (inner) values.
- Enjoy holidays from work.
- Go kindly with yourself.

Play therapy can be absorbing, rewarding, taxing and frustrating. During the work the play therapist may be exposed to extremes of degradation and suffering, but there are also the supreme joys of achievement. An important part of the therapeutic equation is the personality and knowledge of the play therapist. We can never be perfect, but are duty bound to prepare ourselves as well as we can; second best is not good enough.

And a woman who held a babe against her bosom said, Speak to us of Children.
And he said: Your children are not your children.
They are the sons and daughters of Life's longing for itself.
They come through you but not from you.
And though they are with you yet they belong not to you.

You may give them your love but not your thoughts,
For they have their own thoughts.
You may house their bodies but not their souls,
For their souls dwell in the house of tomorrow, which you cannot visit, not even in your dreams.
You may strive to be like them, but seek not to make them like you.
For life goes not backward nor tarries with yesterday.
You are the bows from which your children as living arrows are sent forth.
The archer sees the mark upon the path of the infinite and He bends you with His might that His arrows may go swift and far.
Let your bending in the Archer's hand be for gladness;
For even as He loves the arrow that flies, so He loves also the bow that is stable.

(Gibran, 1980, pp. 20–3).

Appendix 1: recording schedules

People quite often ask 'How should I record a play therapy session?'. The following outlines might serve as a springboard for future practitioners to devise their own recording formats.

ONE-TO-ONE PLAY THERAPY

Place at the head of each session the name and age of the child, the date and number of the session.

(i) *Preliminary discussions*: Record preliminary discussions with referrer, child, carers, teachers, including the child's 'problem areas' as perceived by these people.

(ii) *First session*: process recording – a chronological account of what was done and said by play therapist and child, including non-verbal communication and feelings. Or, failing that, as detailed a recording as possible. After the write-up, the play therapist could highlight specific points; these are useful to bear in mind for the following session, for consultation discussions and for summarizing the work later (see iv–vi). (Occasional subsequent sessions might also benefit from process recording.)

(iii) *Sessional notes*: (new equipment might be noted) description of session, which may include the following:
   – chronological account
   – development of themes
   – verbal and non-verbal interactions
   – new or relevant material
   – feelings of worker and child.
   Any particular queries or quandaries? Anything to bear in mind for the next session?

(iv) *Initial summary*. Ideally, this will be written after the first four to six sessions.
   1. Child: name, date of birth, address, period under review: playworker.
   2. Problems at referral, and by whom referred.
   3. Child's background. Include information from initial interviews with carers, school, residential staff, social worker.
   4. Other significant people/workers. Names, designations, telephone numbers.
   5. Play therapy
      (a) structure – e.g. type of work, number and length of sessions, place
      (b) worker's initial assumptions/hypotheses, e.g. (i) theoretical understanding of how the child's situation is manifesting in her or his behaviour and (ii) predictive factors the worker may wish to test

      (c) process of intervention: (i) analysis of first session, (ii) how the child is responding to play sessions, (iii) what use the child is making of sessions, (iv) significant information emerging and (v) themes emerging.

  6. Have 'problems at referral' changed?

  7. Have any new significant areas emerged?

  8. Reasons for continuation/termination Do you need to alter the focus of the intervention?

  9. Summary. Signed. Date. Copies to ... .

(v) *On-going play therapy summaries*, e.g. 'second play therapy summary'. Every three or four months is about right for most ongoing summaries, i.e. once a term.

  1. Child: name, date of birth, address, period under review, playworker.

  2. Factual changes since the last summary.

  3. Play therapy
      (a) Number of sessions.
          Any change in basic structure?
      (b) Process of intervention: (i) how the child is responding, (ii) what use the child is making of sessions, (iii) significant information and (iv) themes.

  4. Review of the child's problems.

  5. Reasons for continuation/termination. Do you need to alter the focus of the intervention?

  6. Summary. Signed. Date. Copies to ... .

(vi) *Final play therapy summary.*

  1. Child: name, date of birth, address, period under review, play worker:

  2. Factual changes since last summary.

  3. Play therapy.
      (a) Number of sessions. Any basic change in structure?
      (b) Process of intervention: (i) how the child is responding, (ii) what use the child is making of sessions, (iii) significant information and (iv) themes.

  4. Review of child's problems.

  5. Reasons for termination.

  6. Overview of the work (including recommendations for future work, if appropriate). Signed. Date. Copies to ... .

ALTERNATIVE RECORDING SCHEDULES

Some workers might prefer an alternative sessional recording schedule that requires less writing.

(vii) Section I. A *mastercopy of play activities* for all sessions. This is subjective, but nevertheless gives an interesting overview, noting shifts in the material that is used, and making it easier to locate and follow through certain types of activity such as regression, sandtray or painting sequences. An example can be found below but it is expected that play therapists would decide on their own categories.

(viii) Section IIa. *Sessional recording.* Assuming that sessions last about an hour, a circle is divided into five minute (or 15 minute) segments. In the inner circle play therapists are invited to indicate whether they were involved with the child (yes/no, tick or cross). In the rest of the segment the child's activities should be noted, with expanding comments and verbatim quotes that can be continued in the spaces beyond the circle, and in Section III. The 'clock' allows each session to be seen at a glance. Section IIb contains a check list, showing the play therapist's and child's (inter)action.

Section III gives the opportunity to make notes on paintings, drawings, models, sandtray, dolls' house play, etc., with sketches or photographs if the work cannot be kept.

Section IV is intended to aid analysis of the session and the play therapist's role.

Activity	Session no.															
	1	2	3	4	5	6	7	8	9	10	11	12	13	14	15	16
planes																
boats																
land vehicles																
tanks																
"goodies" – soldiers																
"baddies" – soldiers																
weapons																
animals, wild								X			X					
farm																
domestic						X	X	X		X					X	X
village toys																
lego, construction toy								X	X	X	X					
jigsaw							X									
dolls' house				X				X						X		
dolls' house family				X				X						X		
dolls, cuddly toy				X				X		X						
food preparation	X	X	X	X	X		X		X	X	X		X		X	X
sand							X	X		X			X		X	X
water								X	X						X	X
home corner activities	X	X	X	X	X	X	X	X	X	X	X	X		X	X	X
baby	X	X	X	X	X	X	X	X	X	X	X	X	X	X	X	X
den	X	X	X	X	X	X	X	X	X	X	X	X	X	X	X	X
birth/death																
hide and seek				X		X		X			X				X	X
new house																
relationships	X	X	X	X	X				X				X			
role playing																
role reversal	X	X	X	X	X				X	X	X		X	X	X	
dressing up																
painting		X	X			X		X			X			X	X	
games																
music																
puppets																
telephone																
writing						X	X	X					X		X	
sex play																
special days				X	X		X	X				X			X	X
school		X														
police																
burglars																
hero																
bad man																
devil																
ghost														X	X	
dracula															X	
witch																
monster																
king/queen																
wise man																

Session I

Session IIa Sessional recording.

Fresh copies of Sections IIa, IIb, III and IV should be done each time.

Section III. *A more detailed account of certain aspects of the session*, e.g. sandtrays, paintings and drawings, dolls' house play.

Section IV. *Theoretical analysis and points for consultation*
1. What is/are the main features of the session?
2. How does the child's play relate to
   (a) the presenting problem(s)?
   (b) your own assessment?
3. In view of your analysis of the session, what points do you want to bear in mind for future sessions?
4. Is there anything you don't understand, or that worries you?
5. Are themes emerging? If so, what? And what is their significance?

RECORDING GROUPS

(ix) *Pre-group planning.* Much of this material is also covered in the checklist for the chapter on groupwork (pp. 142–3), and in Chapter 4 (Referrals).
   (a) Who are the leaders?
   (b) What are the aims and purposes of the group? Does it have a name?
   (c) What group theory(ies) are you using?
   (d) Who is the consultant? What are the arrangements for consultation?

(e) Do you have a suitable place, and equipment, for the group?

(f) What are the dates and times of sessions? How many sessions?

(g) What about escort arrangements?

(h) Who are the group members?

(i) What are the group leaders' personal expectations and how do they view their therapeutic roles?

(j) What pre-group meetings will you have?

(x) *Recording the sessions.* If using a written format, the simplest method is perhaps, after each session, to make notes on the session's aims, process and content, and on individuals within the group (including the group-workers). Post-session analysis could be based on Section IV, including an examination of the co-worker's relationship and roles. Additional or alternative aids to recording might be the sociogram, rating scales and chronogram *(Cox, 1973)*, but a full discussion of these is beyond the scope of this book. Some of the specialist texts suggest frameworks for recording a group *(e.g. Brown, 1986; Preston-Shoot, 1988)*.

(xi) *Group work summaries*

1. *Basic facts*
    name of group
    names of groupworkers
    period of the group (dates)
    number of children
    number of sessions
    location
    name of consultant
    number of consultancy sessions.

2. *Purpose of the group* State the reasons for the group's formation and its original goals.

3. *Group process issues* Major theories, issues, 'headlines', changes. Group development (refer to one of the theoretical group development models).

4. *Group members* Review of individual children's progress, or otherwise. Formalize any new specific goals for each/any member.

5. *External issues* Issues or concerns resulting from events or developments external to the group, e.g. significant changes in family situations, the playrooms not always being available.

6. *Co-working* Significant issues? Consider the link between the development of the co-working relationship and the life/development of the group. Any decisions regarding deliberate changes in the use of the working relationship?

7. *Groupwork methods* Comments regarding groupwork method(s). What has worked/not worked?

8. *Practical considerations* Any practical considerations such as venue, resources, transport?

9. *Continuation/termination* With reference to group developmental issues, consider the group's life until the next review, or describe the termination process and reasons for it.

10. *Revised goals* Review the original goals for the group in the light of the above. Are there any new or modified goals for the group as a whole for the next period of the group's life?
11. *Attendance chart.*
12. *Conclusions/summary* In the event of a final summary, give considerations of further work required, e.g. with individuals. Also considerations/issues concerning how future similar groups might be modified.
13. *Evaluation and follow-up* What are your plans for subsequent follow-up and evaluation? Names and designations of people writing the summary. Date. Copies to … .

Appendix 2: play equipment

Play therapy can take place in four types of room:

(a) Rooms designated as full-time playrooms with communal equipment.
(b) Rooms designated as full-time playrooms with some communal and some personal play materials.
(c) Part-time playrooms that serve another purpose, in which play materials might either be stored or might have to be brought in.
(d) Part-time playrooms where a portable play kit is necessary.

In all categories, play materials should reflect our multiracial society (*Ahmed et al., 1986*), and should be selected rather than accumulated.

COMMUNAL EQUIPMENT FOR FULL-TIME PLAYROOMS

Sandtray with tools (some playrooms have wet and dry sandtrays).
Sink (or watertray or baby bath).
Home corner with items such as table and chairs, play cooker and sink, cleaning equipment, kettle, multicultural pots and pans, crockery and cutlery, iron and ironing board, two telephones, cash register and toy money, shopping bag and purse.
Dolls of different nationalities – male, female, baby, teenage, with a selection of removable, washable clothes. Anatomically correct dolls may be suitable in certain cases.
Dolls' crib.
Life-sized baby doll (different racial groupings), nappies, baby accoutrements.
Feeding bottles, dummies and blankets.
Bed or child-sized crib.
Dolls' house, sturdy and of attractive design, including furniture for all rooms and a selection of miniature family dolls of different nationalities.
Puppets, preferably glove puppets that can be used in a variety of ways. The collection could include family groups, animals, phantasy and character figures, e.g. policeman, witch, devil, king, queen. Soft, furry animals appeal to all ages!
'World' toys such as small vehicles (ambulances, aeroplanes, breakdown trucks, cars, fire engines, lorries, police cars, rescue vehicles, ships, steamrollers, tractors, tanks, trains; buildings, fences, paths, road signs, trees; farm and wild animals; hospital ward; small human figures; fighting people; small domestic items; monsters; phantasy figures (*Lowenfeld, 1979, pp. 4–5*).
Big and little cuddly toys.

Paper, easel, paints, finger paints, crayons, scissors, glue, blackboard, chalks, blackboard rubber, clay, plasticine, play doh, string, Sellotape, portfolio for storing paintings.

Construction equipment such as bricks, blocks, Lego, Meccano, jigsaw puzzles.

Musical instruments (percussion are useful) reflecting the multiracial society.

Multicultural dressing-up clothes, which should be clean, attractive and invite imaginative play; long dresses and accessories; hats. Jewellery and shoes have their fascination. Face paints can help. Include a few things suitable for adults.

Equipment for aggressive play could include such items as guns, swords, skittles, darts, hammer pegs, balls, a punchball.

Scary toys, slime

Toys (or crockery) that can be broken (useful for certain children).

A small selection of books and table games for all ages (not all play therapists would require these).

Clock.

Polaroid camera with flash, and films.

Towels, tissues, Blue Tac, rag.

Big cushions, beanbags, rugs.

Child-sized tables and chairs.

There should be somewhere where the child can stand above the worker and also where the child can retreat and be (more or less) out of view. Some playrooms have a climbing frame or a raised deck with a den reached by a ladder; others have a sturdy table. The home corner, shop, or a table covered by a blanket can provide a quiet space.

Cups, biscuit box, etc., if food and drink are offered.

Refreshments.

Aprons and overalls.

First-aid kit.

Fire extinguisher and asbestos blanket.

Repair outfits, sewing kit.

Rubbish bin.

Portable fan heater.

Cleaning materials such as brushes, dustpan, duster, rag, mop and bucket.

Audiovisual equipment; one-way screen.

Play therapists will include other materials that they find useful.

If equipping a playroom for the first time, and if money is short, intending play therapists would probably acquire what they could from friends, colleagues, jumble sales, etc. However, make sure that 'rubbish' is not collected, and that the toys serve a therapeutic purpose with some relevance to the above list. Suggestions for basic equipment are:

sandtray with access to water

home corner items

dolls

feeding bottle, dummy, blanket
dolls' house furniture and play people
as many 'world' toys as can be acquired
cuddly toy
drawing and/or painting materials, play doh
guns, swords, scary toys, slime
punchball.

PART-COMMUNAL, PART-PERSONAL EQUIPMENT IN FULL-TIME PLAYROOMS

Communal toys might include:
sand and water trays
dolls' house
the basics of a home corner
blackboard and/or easel.

Each child would have an individual box, containing items such as: vehicles, fighting people, wild and domestic animals, houses and fences; paper, felt-tip pens, scissors, plasticine, string; paints; dolls' house family and furniture; feeding bottle; telephones; puppets; gun.

PART-TIME PLAYROOMS THAT SERVE ANOTHER PURPOSE

Ideally, play materials would be stored in lockable cupboards in the room. Alternatively they might be in lockable cupboards just outside, or in mobile furniture such as trolleys.

PORTABLE PLAY KITS

A couple of bags or boxes might contain the same sort of items as the individual boxes above, plus some puppets, place settings and pots and pans. A container of sand and a portable dolls' house would be useful.

References

Abramson, L. Y., Alloy, L. B. and Metalsky, G. I. (1986), 'The hopelessness theory of depression: Does the research test the theory?', in *Social Cognition and Clinical Psychology: A Synthesis*, L.Y. Abramson (ed.), Guilford Press, New York.

Adams, P. L. (1982), *A Primer of Child Psychotherapy*, Little, Brown & Co., Boston, MA.

Adcock, M., Lake, R. and Small, A. (1988), 'Assessing children's needs', in *Direct Work with Children: A Guide for Social Work Practitioners*, J. Aldgate and J. Simmonds (eds), pp. 25–35, B.T. Batsford and British Agencies for Adoption and Fostering, London.

Ahmed, S., Cheetham, J. and Small, J. (eds) (1986), *Social Work with Black Children and Their Families*, B.T. Batsford and British Agencies for Adoption and Fostering, London.

Aldgate, J. (1988), 'Work with children experiencing separation and loss. A theoretical framework', in *Direct Work with Children: A Guide for Social Work Practitioners*, J. Aldgate and J. Simmonds (eds), pp. 36–48, B.T. Batsford and British Agencies for Adoption and Fostering, London.

Aldgate, J. (1991), 'Attachment theory and its application to childcare social work – An introduction', in *Handbook of Theory for Practice Teachers in Social Work*, J. Lishman (ed.), pp. 11–35, Jessica Kingsley, London.

Aldgate, J., Simmonds, J., Daniel, P., Martin, G. and Pigott, V. (1988), 'Aspects of work with emotionally damaged children', in *Direct Work with Children: A Guide for Social Work Practitioners*, J. Aldgate and J. Simmonds (eds), pp. 49–61, B.T. Batsford and British Agencies for Adoption and Fostering, London.

Allan, J. (1988a) *Inscapes of the Child's World, Jungian Counseling in Schools and Clinics*, Spring Publications, Dallas, TX.

Allan, J. A. B. (1988b), 'Serial drawing: A Jungian approach with children', in *Innovative Interventions in Child and Adolescent Therapy*, C. E. Schaefer (ed.), pp. 98–131, John Wiley, New York.

Allen, F. H. (1947), *Psychotherapy with Children*, Kegan Paul, Trench, Trubner & Co., London.

Allen, F. H. (1964), 'The beginning phase of therapy', in *Child Psychotherapy: Practice and Theory*, M. R. Haworth (ed.), pp. 101–5, Basic Books, New York.

Alvarez, A. (1988), 'Beyond the unpleasure principle: Some preconditions for thinking through play', *Journal of Child Psychotherapy*, **14**(2), pp. 1–13.

American Psychiatric Association (1980), *Diagnostic and Statistical Manual of Mental Disorders (DSMIII)*, American Psychiatric Association, Washington, DC.

Amster, F. (1964), 'Differential uses of play in treatment of young children', in *Child Psychotherapy: Practice and Theory*, M. R. Haworth (ed.), pp. 11–19, Basic Books, New York.

Anderson, J. (1988), *Thinking, Changing, Rearranging*, Metamorphous Press, Portland.

Argüelles, J. and Argüelles, M. (1972), *Mandala*, Shambala, London.

Ariel, S. (1992), *Strategic Family Play Therapy*, John Wiley.

Ariès, P. (1986), *Centuries of Childhood*, Penguin, Harmondsworth.

Arlow, J. A. and Kadis, A. (1979), 'Finger painting in the psychotherapy of children', in *The Therapeutic Use of Child's Play*, C. Schaefer (ed.), pp. 329–43, Jason Aronson, New York.

Astor, J. (1991), 'The emergence of Michael Fordham's model of development: A new integration in analytical psychology', in *Extending Horizons. Psychoanalytic Psychotherapy with Children, Adolescents and Families*, R. Szur and S. Miller (eds), pp. 405–22, Karnac Books.

Ault, R. L. (1983), *Children's Cognitive Development*, Oxford University Press, New York and Oxford.

Axline, V. M. (1964a), 'Nondirective therapy', in *Child Psychotherapy: Practice and Theory*, M. R. Haworth (ed.), pp. 34–9, Basic Books, New York.

Axline, V.M. (1964b), 'The eight basic principles', in *Child Psychotherapy: Practice and Theory*, M.R. Haworth (ed.), pp. 93–4, Basic Books, New York.

Axline, V.M. (1964c), 'Establishing rapport', in *Child Psychotherapy: Practice and Theory*, M.R. Haworth (ed.), pp. 95–101, Basic Books, New York.

Axline, V.M. (1964d), 'Accepting the child completely', in *Child Psychotherapy: Practice and Theory*, M.R. Haworth (ed.), pp. 239–42, Basic Books, New York.

Axline, V.M. (1964e), 'Recognition and reflection of feelings' in *Child Psychotherapy: Practice and Theory*, M.R. Haworth (ed.), pp. 262–4, Basic Books, New York.

Axline, V.M. (1964f), *Dibs: in Search of Self. Personality Development in Play Therapy*, Penguin, Harmondsworth.

Axline, V.M. (1969), *Play Therapy*, Ballantine Books, New York.

Axline, V.M. (1979a), 'Play therapy procedures and results', in *The Therapeutic Use of Child's Play*, C. Schaefer (ed.), pp. 209–18, Jason Aronson, New York.

Axline, V.M. (1979b), 'Play therapy as described by children', in *The Therapeutic Use of Child's Play*, C. Schaefer (ed.), pp. 517–33, Jason Aronson, New York.

Bandler, D. (1987), 'Working with other professionals in an in-patient setting', *Journal of Child Psychotherapy*, 13(2), pp. 81–9.

Bannister, A. (1989), 'Healing action–action methods with children who have been sexually abused', in *Child Sexual Abuse: Listening, Hearing and Validating the Experiences of Children*, H. Blagg, J.A. Hughes and C. Wattam (eds), Longman, Harlow.

Barker, P. (1981), *Basic Family Therapy*, Granada, London.

Barlow, K., Strother, J. and Landreth, G. (1985), 'Child-centered play therapy: Nancy from baldness to curls', *The School Counselor*, 32(5), pp. 347–56.

Barrett, C.L., Hampe, L.E. and Miller, L. (1978), 'Research on psychotherapy with children', in *Handbook of Psychotherapy and Behavior Change: An Empirical Analysis*, S.L. Garfield and A.E. Bergin (eds), pp. 411–35, John Wiley, New York.

Beail, N. (1989), 'I had a nightmare', *Community Living*, 2(3), pp. 18–20.

Beck, A.T., Rush, A.J., Shaw, B.F. and Emery, G. (1985), *Cognitive Therapy of Depression*, Basic Books, New York.

Beiser, H.R. (1979), 'Play equipment', in *The Therapeutic Use of Child's Play*, C. Schaefer (ed.), pp. 423–34, Jason Aronson, New York.

Benson, J.F. (1987), *Working More Creatively with Groups*, Tavistock, London.

Bentovim, A. and Boston, P. (1988), 'Sexual abuse – basic issues – characteristics of children and families', in *Child Sexual Abuse Within the Family*, A. Bentovim, A. Elton, J. Hildebrand, M. Tranter, and E. Vizard (eds), pp. 16–39, Wright, London.

Berry, J. (1971), 'Helping children directly', *British Journal of Social Work*, 1(3), pp. 315–32.

Berry, J. (1972), *Social Work with Children*, Routledge & Kegan Paul, London.

Bettelheim, B. (1976), *The Uses of Enchantment. The Meaning and Importance of Fairy Tales*, Penguin, Harmondsworth.

Bixler, R.H. (1964), 'Limits are therapy', in *Child Psychotherapy: Practice and Theory*, M.R. Haworth (ed.), pp. 134–47, Basic Books, New York.

Bixler R.H. (1982), 'Case transfer in play therapy', in *Play Therapy: Dynamics of the Process of Counseling with Children*, G.L. Landreth (ed.), pp. 247–53, Charles C. Thomas, Springfield, IL. Reprinted from *Journal of Clinical Pathology*, 1946, 2, pp. 274–8.

Black, D. (1984), 'Sundered families. The effect of loss of a parent', *Adoption and Fostering*, 8(2), pp. 38–43.

Boston, M. (1983a), 'Technical problems in therapy', in *Psychotherapy with Severely Deprived Children*, M. Boston and R. Szur (eds), pp. 58–66, Routledge & Kegan Paul, London.

Boston, M. (1983b), 'The Tavistock workshop: An overall view', in *Psychotherapy with Severely Deprived Children*, M. Boston and R. Szur (eds), pp. 1–10, Routledge & Kegan Paul, London.

Boston, M. (1987), *Issues encountered in work with adoptive and foster families*, Lecture at Mapperley Hospital, Nottingham, on 6 November 1987.

Boston, M. (1989), 'In search of a methodology for evaluating psychoanalytic psychotherapy with children', *Journal of Child Psychotherapy*, 15(1), pp. 15–46.

Boston, M. (1991), 'The splitting image: A research perspective', in *Extending Horizons. Psychoanalytic Psychotherapy with Children, Adolescents and Families*, R. Szur and S. Miller (eds), Karnac Books.

Boston, M. and Lush, D. (1993), 'Can child psychotherapists predict and assess their own work? A research note', *ACPP Review and Newsletter*, **15**(3), pp. 112–9.

Boston, M. and Lush, D. (1994), 'Further considerations of methodology for evaluating psychoanalytic psychotherapy with children: Reflections in the light of research experience', *Journal of Child Psychotherapy*, **20**(2), pp. 205–29.

Bottome, P. (1946), *Alfred Adler: Apostle of Freedom*, Faber & Faber, London.

Bowlby, J. (1980), *Attachment and Loss, Vol. 3. Loss: Sadness and Depression*, Hogarth Press and the Institute of Psycho-analysis, London.

Bowlby, J. (1984), 'The making and breaking of affectional bonds', in *In Touch with Children*, BAAF (ed.), pp. 27–40, British Agencies for Adoption and Fostering.

Bowyer, R. B. (1970), *The Lowenfeld Technique*, Pergamon Press, Oxford.

Brady, C. A. and Friedrich, W. N. (1982), 'Levels of intervention: A model for training in play therapy', *Journal of Clinical Child Psychology*, **11**(1), pp. 39–43.

Braithwaite, C. (1986), 'Art always reveals the truth, but not necessarily the whole truth', *Community Care*, **622**, pp. 15–17.

Brammer, L. M. (1979), *The Helping Relationship: Process and Skills*, Prentice-Hall, Englewood Cliffs, NJ.

Branthwaite, A. and Rogers, D. (1985), *Children Growing Up*, Open University Press, Milton Keynes.

Bray, M. (1984), *Children's Hours – A Special Listen*, Children's Hour Charity Trust, 79 Long Acre, London WC2E 9NG.

Bray, M. (1986), 'Communicating with young children', *Childright*, **31**, pp. 18–20.

Bray, M. (1991), *Poppies on the Rubbish Heap. Sexual Abuse: The Child's Voice*, Canongate, Edinburgh.

Brown, A. (1979), *Groupwork*, Heinemann Educational, London.

Brown, A. (1986), *Groupwork*, Gower, Aldershot.

Brown, J.A.C. (1964), *Freud and the Post-Freudians*, Penguin, Harmondsworth.

Brummer, N. (1988), 'White social workers/black children: Issues of identity', in *Direct Work with Children*, J. Aldgate and J. Simmonds (eds), pp. 75–86, B.T. Batsford and British Agencies for Adoption and Fostering, London.

Cardiff Social Work Resource Centre (undated), *Communicating with Children: Therapeutic Techniques for Working with Children and Young People*, School of Social Work, Cardiff University (booklet and video).

Carkhuff, R. R. and Berenson, B. G. (1967), *Beyond Counseling and Therapy*, Holt, Rinehart & Winston, New York.

Cass, J. (1971), *The Significance of Children's Play*, B.T. Batsford, London.

Catholic Children's Society (1983), *Finding Out About Me*, Purley.

Cattanach, A. (1994), *Play Therapy. Where the Sky meets the Underworld*, Jessica Kingsley, London.

Chethik, M. (1989), *Techniques of Child Therapy: Psychodynamic Strategies*, Guilford Press, New York.

Chetwynd, T. (1982), *A Dictionary of Symbols*, Paladin, London.

Cirlot, J. E. (1971), *A Dictionary of Symbols*, Routledge & Kegan Paul, London.

Cohen, D. (1993), *The Development of Play*, Croom Helm, London.

Connell, H. M. (1985), *Essentials of Child Psychiatry*, Blackwell Scientific, Melbourne.

Cooper, J. C. (1978), *An Illustrated Encyclopedia of Traditional Symbols*, Thames & Hudson, London.

Copley, B. and Forryan, B. (1987), *Therapeutic Work with Children and Young People*, Robert Royce, London.

Cox, M. (1973), 'The group therapy interaction chronogram', *British Journal of Social Work*, **3**(2), pp. 243–56.

Cox, M. V. (1993), *Children's Drawings of the Human Figure*, Lawrence Erlbaum, Hove.

Crompton, M. (1980), *Respecting Children: Social Work with Young People*, Edward Arnold, London.

Crompton, M. (1990), *Attending to Children: Direct Work in Social and Health Care*, Edward Arnold, London.

Currant, N. (1985), 'The expansive educational value of puppets', *Academic Therapy*, 21(1), pp. 55–60.

Dalley, T. (1984), *Art as Therapy: An Introduction to the Use of Art as a Therapeutic Technique*, Tavistock, London.

Dalley, T., Case, C., Schaverien, J., *et al.* (1987), *Images of Art Therapy: New Developments in Theory and Practice*, Tavistock, London.

D'Ardenne, P. and Mahtani, A. (1989), *Transcultural Counselling in Action*, Sage, London.

Dartington Social Research Unit (1995), *Child Protection and Child Abuse: Recent Research Findings and Their Implications*, HMSO, London.

Davis, C. M. (1990), 'What is empathy, and can empathy be taught?', *Physical Therapy*, 70(11), pp. 707–11.

Davis, M. and Wallbridge, D. (1983), *Boundary and Space: An Introduction to the Work of D.W. Winnicott*, Penguin, Harmondsworth.

Davison, G. C. and Neale, J. M. (1982), *Abnormal Psychology: An Experimental Clinical Approach*, John Wiley, New York.

Daws, D. and Boston, M. (eds) (1981), *The Child Psychotherapist and Problems of Young People*, Wildwood House, London.

De Mause, L. (1974), *The History of Childhood*, Souvenir Press, London.

Deblinger, E., McLeer, S. V., Atkins, M. S., *et al.* (1989), 'Post-traumatic stress in sexually abused, physically abused, and non-abused children', *Child Abuse and Neglect*, 13(3), pp. 403–8.

Dennison, S. T. (1989), *Twelve Counseling Programs for Children At Risk*, Charles C. Thomas, Springfield, IL.

Despert, J. L. (1964), 'Using the first interview as a basis for therapeutic planning', in *Child Psychotherapy: Practice and Theory*, M. R. Haworth (ed.), pp. 110–14, Basic Books, New York.

Di Giuseppe, R. A. (1981), 'Cognitive therapy with children', in *New Directions in Cognitive Therapy: A Casebook*, G. Emery, S. D. Hollon, and R. C. Bedrosian (eds), pp. 50–67, Guilford Press, New York.

Dockar-Drysdale, B. (1990), *The Provision of Primary Experiences: Winnicottian Work with Children and Adolescents*, Free Association Books, London.

Dockar-Drysdale, B. (1993), *Therapy and Consultation in Child Care*, Free Association Books, London.

Dockar-Drysdale, B. E. (1968), 'The process of symbolization observed among emotionally deprived children in therapeutic school', in *Disturbed Children: Papers on Residential Work*, 2, R. J. N. Todd (ed.), Longman, London.

Donovan, D. M. and McIntyre, D. (1990), *Healing the Hurt Child. A Developmental–Contextual Approach*, Norton & Co.

Dorfman, E. (1951), 'Play therapy', in *Client-centered Therapy*, C. R. Rogers (ed.), pp. 235–77, Constable, London.

Doyle, C. (1990), *Working with Abused Children*, Macmillan Education, Basingstoke and London.

Driver, E. and Droisen, A. (eds) (1989), *Child Sexual Abuse: Feminist Perspectives*, Macmillan Education, Basingstoke.

Durfee, M. B. (1979), 'Use of ordinary office equipment', in *The Therapeutic Use of Child's Play*, C. Schaefer (ed.), pp. 401–11, Jason Aronson, New York.

Dwivedi, K. N. (ed.) (1993a), *Group Work with Children and Adolescents. A Handbook*, Jessica Kingsley, London.

Dwivedi, K. N. (1993b), 'Coping with unhappy children who are from ethnic minorities', in *Coping with Unhappy Children*, V. Varma (ed.), Cassell, London.

Dwivedi, K. N. , Lawton, S. and Hogan, S. (1993), 'Structural and organizational aspects', in *Group Work with Children and Adolescents. A Handbook*, K. N. Dwivedi (ed.), Jessica Kingsley, London.

Dyke, S. (1987), 'Saying "No" to psychotherapy: Consultation and assessment in a case of sexual abuse', *Journal of Child Psychotherapy*, 13(2), pp. 65–79.

Egan, G. (1982), *The Skilled Helper*, Brooks/Cole, Monterey.

Ellis, A. and Grieger, R. (eds) (1977), *Handbook of Rational–Emotive Therapy*, Springer, New York.

Erickson, G.D. and Hogan, T.P. (eds) (1972), *Family Therapy: An Introduction to Theory and Techniques*, Brooks/Cole, Monterey.

Erikson, E. H. (1964a), 'Toys and reasons', in *Child Psychotherapy: Practice and Theory*, M. R. Haworth (ed.), pp. 3–11, Basic Books, New York.

Erikson, E. H. (1964b), 'The initial session and its alternatives', in *Child Psychotherapy: Practice and Theory*, M. R. Haworth (ed.), pp. 106–10, Basic Books, New York.

Erikson, E. H. (1964c), 'Clinical observation of play disruption in young children', in *Child Psychotherapy: Practice and Theory*, M. R. Haworth (ed.), pp. 264–76, Basic Books, New York.

Erikson, E. H. (1977), *Childhood and Society*, Triad/Granada.

Erikson, E. H. (1979), 'Play and cure', in *The Therapeutic Use of Child's Play*, C. Schaefer (ed.), pp. 475–85, Jason Aronson, New York.

Escalona, S. (1964), 'Some considerations regarding psychotherapy with psychotic children', in *Child Psychotherapy: Practice and Theory*, M. R. Haworth (ed.), pp. 50–8, Basic Books, New York.

Evans, C. (1978), *Psychology: A Dictionary of the Mind, Brain and Behaviour*, Arrow Books, London.

Fahlberg, V. (1982), *Attachment and Separation*, British Agencies for Adoption and Fostering, London.

Fahlberg, V. (1988), 'Re-parenting sexually abused children', British Agencies for Adoption and Fostering seminar (6 June 1988), London.

Fancher, R. E. (1973), *Psychoanalytic Psychology: The Development of Freud's Thought*, W. W. Norton, New York.

Faust, J. and Burns, W. (1991), 'Coding therapist and child interaction: Progress and outcome in play therapy', in *Play Diagnosis and Assessment*, C. E. Shaefer, K. Gitlin and A. Sandgrund (eds), pp. 663–73, John Wiley.

Federation, S. (1986), 'Sexual abuse: treatment modalities for the younger child', *Journal of Psychosocial Nursing*, 24(7), pp. 21–4.

Fine, L. J. (1979), 'Psychodrama', in *Current Psychotherapies*, R.J. Corsini *et al.* (eds), pp. 428–59, F. E. Peacock, Itasca, IL.

Finke, H. (1947), 'Changes in the expression of emotionalised attitudes in six cases of play therapy', unpublished master's thesis, University of Chicago, referred to in Guerney (1983a).

Fischer, J. (1978), *Effective Casework Practice: An Eclectic Approach*, McGraw-Hill, New York.

Fiske, J. (1982), *Introduction to Communication Studies*, Methuen, London.

Fitzgerald, J. (1983), *Helping Children When They Must Move*, British Agencies for Adoption and Fostering, London.

Flekkøy, M. G. (1991), *A Voice for Children. Speaking Out as their Ombudsman*, Jessica Kingsley, London.

Fordham, F. (1966), *An Introduction to Jung's Psychology*, Penguin, Harmondsworth.

Fordham, M. (1957), *New Developments in Analytical Psychology*, Routledge & Kegan Paul, London.

Fordham, M. (1969), *Children as Individuals*, Hodder & Stoughton, London.

Fordham, M. (1978), *Jungian Psychotherapy: A Study in Analytical Psychology*, John Wiley, Chichester.

Fordham, M. (1994), *Children as Individuals*, Free Association Books, London.

Fox, L. (1982), 'Two value positions in child care', *British Journal of Social Work* 12(3), pp. 265–90.

Fraiberg, S. H. (1968), *The Magic Years: Understanding and Handling the Problems of Early Childhood*, Methuen, London.

France, A. (1988), *Consuming Psychotherapy*, Free Association Books, London.

Freud, A. (1959), *The Psycho-analytic Treatment of Children*, Hogarth Press and the Institute of Psycho-analysis, London.

Freud, A. (1980), *Normality and Pathology in Childhood*, Hogarth Press and the Institute of Psycho-analysis, London.

Frick, W. B. (1971), *Humanistic Psychology: Interviews with Maslow, Murphy and Rogers*, Charles E. Merrill, Columbus, OH.

Friedrich, W. N. (1990), *Psychotherapy of Sexually Abused Children and Their Families*, Norton & Co., New York.

Froebel, F. (1974; first published in English 1887), *The Education of Man*, Kelly, Clifton.

Fromm, E. (1946), *The Fear of Freedom*, Kegan Paul, Trench, Truber & Co., London.

Fromm, E. (1952), *The Forgotten Language*, Gollancz, London.

Furth, G. M. (1982), 'The use of drawings made at significant times in one's life,' in *Living with Death and Dying*, E. Kübler-Ross (ed.), pp. 63–94, Souvenir Press, London.

Gardener, H. (1980), *Artful Scribbles: The Significance of Children's Drawings*, Norman, London.

Gardner, R. A. (1979), 'Mutual storytelling technique', in *The Therapeutic Use of Child's Play*, C. Schaefer (ed.), pp. 313–21, Jason Aronson, New York.

Gath, A. (1985), 'Recognition and treatment of emotional abuse', *Update*, pp. 445–52.

Gavshon, A. (1989), 'Playing: its role in child analysis', *Journal of Child Psychotherapy*, 15(1), pp. 47–62.

Gazda, G. M. (1978), *Group Counseling: A Developmental Approach*, Allyn & Bacon, Boston, MA.

Geller, L. (1982), 'The failure of self-actualization theory: A critique of Carl Rogers and Abraham Maslow', *Journal of Humanistic Psychology*, 22(2), pp. 56–73.

Gibran, K. (1980), *The Prophet*, Pan, London.

Gil, E. (1991), *The Healing Power of Play. Working with Abused Children*, Guilford Press, New York.

Gillespie, A. (1986), 'Art therapy at the Familymaker's project', *Adoption and Fostering*, 10(1), pp. 19–23.

Gillmore, R. D. (1991), 'Termination in psychotherapy with children and adolescents', in *Saying Goodbye. A Casebook of Termination in Child and Adolescent Analysis and Therapy*, A. G. Schmukler (ed.), The Analytic Press, Hillsdale, NJ.

Ginott, H. G. (1961), *Group Psychotherapy with Children: The Theory and Practice of Play Therapy*, McGraw-Hill, New York.

Ginott, H. G. (1964a), 'Problems in the playroom', in *Child Psychotherapy: Practice and Theory*, M. R. Haworth (ed.), pp. 125–30, Basic Books, New York.

Ginott, H. G. (1964b), 'The theory and practice of "therapeutic intervention" in child treatment', in *Child Psychotherapy: Practice and Theory*, M. R. Haworth (ed.), pp. 148–58, Basic Books, New York.

Ginott, H. G. (1968), 'Group therapy with children', in *Basic Approaches to Group Psychotherapy and Group Counseling*, G. M. Gazda (ed.), Charles C. Thomas, Springfield, IL.

Ginott, H. G. (1982a), 'Play therapy: The initial session', in *Play Therapy: Dynamics of the Process of Counseling with Children*, G. L. Landreth (ed.), pp. 201–16, Charles C. Thomas, Springfield, IL, reprinted from *American Journal of Psychotherapy* (1961), 15, pp. 73–8.

Ginott, H. G. (1982b), 'A rationale for selecting toys in play therapy', in *Play Therapy: Dynamics of the Process of Counseling with Children*, G. L. Landreth (ed.), pp. 145–51, Charles C. Thomas, Springfield, IL, reprinted from *Journal of Consulting Psychology* (1960), 24, pp. 243–6.

Glassman, U. and Kates, L. (1990), *Group Work: A Humanistic Approach*, Sage, Newbury Park, CA.

Goddard, C. and Carew, B. (1988), 'Protecting the child: Hostages to fortune', *Social Work Today*, 20(16), pp. 12–14.

Goldenson, R.M. (ed.) (1984), *Longman Dictionary of Psychology and Psychiatry*, Longman, New York.

Goldstein, J., Freud, A., Solnit, A.J., and Goldstein, S. (1986), *In the Best Interests of the Child*, Free Press, New York.

Gondor, L.H. (1964), 'Use of fantasy communications in child psychotherapy', in *Child Psychotherapy: Practice and Theory*, M.R. Haworth (ed.), pp. 374–83, Basic Books, New York.

Guerney, L.F. (1983a), 'Client-centered (non-directive) play therapy', in *Handbook of Play Therapy*, C.E. Schaefer and K.J. O'Connor (eds), pp. 21–64, John Wiley, New York.

Guerney, L.I. [*sic*] (1983b), Play therapy conference, North Texas State University, Denton, April 1983, reported in K. Barlow, J. Strother and G. Landreth (1985), 'Child-centered play therapy: Nancy from baldness to curls', *The School Counselor*, 32(5), pp. 347–56.

Guerney, L.F. (1984), 'Play therapy in counseling settings', in *Child's Play: Developmental and Applied*, T.D. Yawkey and A.D. Pellegrini (eds), pp. 291–321, Lawrence Erlbaum, Hillsdale, NJ.

Gumaer, J. (1984), *Counseling and Therapy for Children*, Free Press, New York.

Hales-Tooke, J. (1989), 'Feeling and meaning in client–centred therapy', *Counselling*, 67, pp. 9–13.

Hall, L. and Lloyd, S. (1989), *Surviving Child Sexual Abuse*, Falmer Press, Lewes.

Halmos, P. (1965), *The Faith of the Counsellors*, Constable, London.

Hardiker, P. and Barker, M. (eds) (1981), *Theories of Practice in Social Work*, Academic Press, London.

Harding, E.M. (1973), *Psychic Energy: Its Source and Transformation*, Princeton University Press/Bollingen, New Jersey.

Harmon, M. (1976), *Got To Be Me*, Argus, Niles, IL.

Harter, S. (1983), 'Cognitive-developmental considerations in the conduct of play therapy', in *Handbook of Play Therapy*, C.E. Schaefer and K.J. O'Connor (eds), pp. 95–127, John Wiley, New York.

Haugaard, J.J. and Reppucci, N.D. (1988), *The Sexual Abuse of Children*, Jossey-Bass, San Francisco, CA.

Hawkey, L. (1979), 'Puppets in child psychotherapy', in *The Therapeutic Use of Child's Play*, C. Schaefer (ed.), pp. 359–72, Jason Aronson, New York.

Hawkins, P. and Shohet, R. (1989), *Supervision in the Helping Professions: An Individual, Group and Organizational Approach*, Open University Press, Milton Keynes.

Haworth, M.R. (ed.) (1964), *Child Psychotherapy: Practice and Theory*, Basic Books, New York.

Haworth, M.R. (1990), *A Child's Therapy: Hour by Hour*, International Universities Press, Madison.

Haworth, M.R. and Keller, M.J. (1964), 'The use of food in therapy', in *Child Psychotherapy: Practice and Theory*, M.R. Haworth (ed.), pp. 330–8, Basic Books, New York.

Hayley, J. (1963), *Strategies of Psychotherapy*, Grune & Stratton, New York.

Heap, K. (1985), *The Practice of Social Work with Groups: A Systematic Approach*, Allen & Unwin, London.

Heincke, C.M. and Strassmann, L.M. (1975), 'Toward more effective research in child psychotherapy' *American Academy Child Psychiatry*, 14, pp. 561–88.

Hellendoorn, J. (1988), 'Imaginative play technique in psychotherapy with children', in *Innovative Interventions in Child and Adolescent Therapy*, C. Schaefer (ed.), pp. 43–67, John Wiley, New York.

Hellersberg, E.F. (1964), 'Children's growth in play therapy', in *Child Psychotherapy: Practice and Theory*, M.R. Haworth (ed.), pp. 168–76, Basic Books, New York.

Hendrick, H. (1990), 'Constructions and reconstructions of British childhood: An interpretive survey, 1800 to the present', in *Constructing and Reconstructing Childhood: Contemporary Issues in the Sociological Study of Children*, A. James and A. Prout (eds), pp. 35–59, Falmer Press, Lewes.

Herbert, M. (1975), *Problems of Childhood*, Pan, London.

Herbert, M. (1981), *Behavioural Treatment of Problem Children*, Academic Press, London.

Hobbs, T. (1986), 'The Rogers interview', *Changes*, 4(4), pp. 254–8.

Holgate, E. (ed.) (1972), *Communicating with Children: Collected Papers*, Longman, London.

Horne, A. (1989), 'Sally: A middle group approach to early trauma in a latency child', *Journal of Child Psychotherapy*, 15(1), pp. 79–98.

Houston, G. (1984), *The Red Book of Groups*, Rochester Foundation, 8 Rochester Terrace, London NW1 9JN.

Houston, G. (1990), *Supervision and Counselling*, The Rochester Foundation, 8 Rochester Terrace, London NW1 9JN.

Hoxter, S. (1981), 'Play and communication', in *The Child Psychotherapist and Problems of Young People*, M. Boston and D. Daws (eds), pp. 202–31, Wildwood House, London.

Hoxter, S. (1983), 'Some feelings aroused in working with severely deprived children', in *Psychotherapy with Severely Deprived Children*, M. Boston and R. Szur (eds), pp. 125–32, Routledge & Kegan Paul, London.

Hoyles, M. (1989), *The Politics of Childhood*, Journeyman, London.

Hudson, B.L. and Macdonald, G.M. (1986), *Behavioural Social Work: An Introduction*, Macmillan, Basingstoke.

Humphries, S., Mack, J. and Perks, R. (1988), *A Century of Childhood*, Sidgwick & Jackson, London.

Hurlock, E. (1978), *Child Development*, McGraw-Hill, Tokyo.

Irwin, E.C. (1983), 'The diagnostic and therapeutic use of pretend play', in *Handbook of Play Therapy*, C. E. Schaefer and K.J. O'Connor (eds), pp. 148–73, John Wiley, New York.

Irwin, E.C. (1991), 'The use of a puppet interview to understand children' in *Play Diagnosis and Assessment*, C.E. Schaefer, K. Gitlin and A. Sandgrund (eds), pp. 617–40, John Wiley.

Isaacs, S. (1948), *Childhood and After*, Routledge & Kegan Paul, London.

Iwaniec, D. (1955), *The Emotionally Abused and Neglected Child*, John Wiley, Chichester.

Jackson, L. and Todd, K.M. (1964), 'Play as expression of conflict' in *Child Psychotherapy: Practice and Theory*, M.R. Haworth (ed.), pp. 314–21, Basic Books, New York.

Jacobi, J. (1959), *The Psychology of C. G. Jung*, Routledge & Kegan Paul, London.

Jacobi, J. (1971), *Complex Archetype Symbol*, Princeton University Press/Bollingen Series LVII, New Jersey.

Jacobs, M. (1993), *Still Small Voice. A Practical Introduction to Counselling in Pastoral and Other Settings*, Society for Promoting Christian Knowledge, London.

James, A. and Prout, A. (eds) (1990), *Constructing and Reconstructing Childhood: Contemporary Issues in the Sociological Study of Children*, Falmer Press, Lewes.

James, B. (1989), *Treating Traumatized Children. New Insights and Creative Interventions*, Lexington Books, Lexington, MA.

Jennings, S. (1993), *Playtherapy with Children: A Practitioner's Guide*, Blackwell Scientific, Oxford.

Jennings, S. and Minde, A. (1993), *Art Therapy and Dramatherapy. Masks of the Soul*, Jessica Kingsley, London.

Jewett, C. (1984), *Helping Children Cope with Separation and Loss*, Batsford Academic and Educational with British Agencies for Adoption and Fostering, London.

Johnson, J., Rasbury, W. and Siegel, L. (1986), *Approaches to Child Treatment*, Pergamon Press.

Johnson, K. (1989), *Trauma in the Lives of Children*, Macmillan Education, Basingstoke.

Jones, D.N., Pickett, J., Oates, R., and Barbor, P.R.H. (1987), *Understanding Child Abuse*, Macmillan Education, Basingstoke.

Jones, D.P.H. (1986), 'Individual psychotherapy for the sexually abused child', *Child Abuse and Neglect*, 10, pp. 377–85.

Jones, E. (1948), *Papers on Psycho-analysis*, Baillière, Tindall & Cox, London.

Jung, C.G. (1921), *Psychological Types*, Collected Works 6, Routledge & Kegan Paul, London.

Jung, C. G. (1954), *The Development of Personality*, Collected Works 17, Routledge & Kegan Paul, London.

Jung, C. G. (1956), *Symbols of Transformation*, Collected Works 5, Routledge & Kegan Paul, London.

Jung, C. G. (1959), *The Archetypes of the Collective Unconscious*, Collected Works 9, 1, Routledge & Kegan Paul, London.

Jung, C. G. (1961), *Freud and Psychoanalysis*, Collected Works 4, Routledge & Kegan Paul, London.

Jung, C. G. (1964), *Man and His Symbols*, Picador, London.

Jung, C. G. (1966), *The Practice of Psychotherapy*, Collected Works 16, Princeton University Press, Princeton, NJ.

Kalff, D. M. (1980), *Sandplay: A Psychotherapeutic Approach to the Psyche*, Sigo Press, Santa Monica, CA.

Katz, R. L. (1963), *Empathy*, Free Press, London.

Kelly, G. A. (1955), *The Psychology of Personal Constructs*, Vols 1 and 2, Norton, New York.

Kempe, R. S. and Kempe, C. H. (1978), *Child Abuse*, Open Books, London.

Kilgore, L. C. (1988), 'Effect of early childhood sexual abuse on self and ego development', *Social Casework*, April, pp. 224–30.

Klein, M. (1932), *The Psycho-analysis of Children*, Hogarth Press and The Institute of Psycho-analysis, London.

Klein, M. (1955), 'The psychoanalytic play technique', *American Journal of Orthopsychiatry*, **25**, pp. 223–37, reprinted in *The Therapeutic Use of Child's Play*, C. Schaefer (ed.) (1979), pp. 125–40, Jason Aronson, New York.

Konopka, G. (1968), 'Effective communication with adolescents in institutions', in *Children in Care*, R. J. N. Todd (ed.), Longman, Green & Co., London.

Kübler-Ross, E. (1982), *Living with Death and Dying*, Souvenir Press, London.

La Fontaine, J. (1990), *Child Sexual Abuse*, Polity Press, Cambridge.

Landreth, G. L. (ed.) (1982), *Play Therapy: Dynamics of the Process of Counseling with Children*, Charles C. Thomas, Springfield, IL.

Lanyado, M. (1989), 'Variations on the theme of transference and counter-transference in the treatment of a ten-year-old boy', *Journal of Child Psychotherapy*, **15**(2), pp. 85–101.

Lau, A. (1984), 'Transcultural issues in family therapy', *Journal of Family Therapy*, **6**, pp. 91–112.

Lebo, D. (1979), 'Toys for nondirective play therapy', in *Therapeutic Use of Child's Play*, C. Schaefer (ed.), pp. 435–47, Jason Aronson, New York.

Lebo, D. (1982), 'The development of play as a form of therapy: from Rousseau to Rogers', in *Play Therapy: Dynamics of the Process of Counseling with Children*, G. L. Landreth (ed.), pp. 65–73, Charles C. Thomas, Springfield, IL, reprinted from *American Journal of Psychiatry* (1955), **112**, pp. 418–22.

Lebo, D. and Lebo, E. (1957), 'Aggression and age in relation to verbal expression in non-directive play therapy', *Psychological Monographs*, **71**, p. 449.

Lendrum, S. and Syme, G. (1992), *Gift of Tears. A Practical Approach to Loss and Bereavement Counselling*, Routledge.

Lennox, D. (1982), *Residential Group Therapy for Children*, Tavistock, London.

Levay, J. (1979), 'The sunbeam', in *Those First Affections*, T. Rogers (ed.), Routledge & Kegan Paul, London.

Lewis, C. R. (1985), *Listening to Children*, Jason Aronson, New York.

Liddell, H. G. and Scott, R. (1940), *Greek–English Lexicon*, Clarendon Press, Oxford.

Long, S. (1986), 'Guidelines for treating young children', in *Sexual Abuse of Young Children: Evaluation and Treatment*, K. MacFarlane, J. Waterman *et al.* (eds), pp. 220–44, Holt, Rinehart & Winston, London.

Lowenfeld, M. (1935), *Play in Childhood*, Gollancz, London.

Lowenfeld, M. (1979), *The World Technique*, George Allen & Unwin, London.

Lowenfeld, V. and Brittain, W. L. (1964), *Creative and Mental Growth*, Macmillan, New York.

Lush, D. (1977), 'The child guidance clinic', in *The Child Psychotherapist and Problems of Young People*, M. Boston and D. Daws (eds), pp. 63–85, Wildwood House, London.

Lusk, R. and Waterman, J. (1986), 'Effects of sexual abuse on children', in *Sexual Abuse of Young Children: Evaluation and Treatment*, K. MacFarlane and J. Waterman (eds) *et al.*, pp. 101–18, Holt, Rinehart & Winston, London.

Macdonald, A. M. (1973), *Chambers Twentieth Century Dictionary*, Constable, Edinburgh.

Machin, L. and Samuels, W. (1993), *Working with Young People in Loss Situations*, Longman.

Maier, H. W. (1978), *Three Theories of Child Development*, Harper & Row, New York.

Manor, O. (1988), 'Preparing the client for social groupwork: an illustrated framework', *Groupwork*, **2**, pp. 100–14.

Marcus, I. M. (1979), 'Costume play therapy', in *The Therapeutic Use of Child's Play*, C. Schaefer (ed.), pp. 373–82, Jason Aronson, New York.

Marris, P. (1974), *Loss and Change*, Routledge & Kegan Paul, London.

Martin, P. W. (1955), *Experiment in Depth*, Routledge & Kegan Paul, Boston.

Maslow, A. H. (1954), *Motivation and Personality*, Harper & Row, New York.

Maslow, A. H. (1976), *The Farthest Reaches of Human Nature*, Penguin, Harmondsworth.

McKay, M. and Fanning, P. (1987), *Self-esteem*, New Harbinger, Oakland, CA.

McMahon, L. (1992), *The Handbook of Play Therapy*, Tavistock and Routledge.

Meador, B. D. and Rogers, C. R. (1979), 'Person-centered therapy', in *Current Psychotherapies*, R. J. Corsini *et al.* (eds), pp. 131–84, Peacock Publishers, Itasca, IL.

Mearns, D. and Thorne, B. (1988), *Person-centred Counselling in Action*, Sage, London.

Merry, T. (1988), *A Guide to the Person-centred Approach*, The Association for Humanistic Psychology in Britain, London.

Millar, S. (1968), *The Psychology of Play*, Penguin, Harmondsworth.

Miller, A. (1987), *The Drama of Being a Child and the Search for the True Self*, Virago, London.

Mitchell, J. (1981), 'Letters from a kangaroo: a third object technique for working with the young child', *British Journal of Social Work*, **11**(2), pp. 189–201.

Mitchell, R. R. and Friedman, H. S. (1994), *Sandplay Past, Present and Future*, Routledge & Kegan Paul, London.

Molin, R. (1988), 'Treatment of children in fostercare: Issues of collaboration', *Child Abuse and Neglect*, **12**(2), pp. 241–50.

Moreno, J. L. (1946), *Psychodrama, Vol. I*, Beacon House, New York.

Moreno, J. L. (1959), *Psychodrama, Vol. II*, Beacon House, New York.

Moreno, J. L. (1969), *Psychodrama, Vol. III*, Beacon House, New York.

Mosak, H. H. (1979), 'Adlerian psychotherapy', in *Current Psychotherapies*, R. J. Corsini *et al.* (eds), pp. 44–94, Peacock Publishers, Itasca, IL.

Moustakas, C. E. (1953), *Children in Play Therapy: A Key to Understanding Normal and Disturbed Emotions*, McGraw-Hill, New York.

Moustakas, C. E. (1959), *Psychotherapy with Children: The Living Relationship*, Ballantine Books, New York.

Moustakas, C. E. (1964), 'The therapeutic process', in *Child Psychotherapy: Practice and Theory*, M.R. Haworth (ed.), pp. 417–19, Basic Books, New York.

Moyles, J. R. (1994), *The Excellence of Play*, Open University Press, Buckingham.

Nader, K. and Pynoos, R. S. (1991), 'Play and drawing techniques as tools for interviewing traumatized children' in *Play Diagnosis and Assessment*, C.E. Schaefer, K. Gitlin and A. Sandgrund (eds), pp. 375–90, John Wiley, New York.

Naitove, C. E. (1982), 'Arts therapy with sexually abused children', in *Handbook of Clinical Intervention in Child Sexual Abuse*, S.M. Sgroi (ed.), pp. 269–308, Lexington Books, Lexington, MA.

Neumann, E. (1954), *The Origins and History of Consciousness*, Pantheon, New York.

Neumann, E. (1955), *The Great Mother*, Routledge & Kegan Paul, London.

Newson, E. (1983), 'Play therapy: an alternative language for children and their social workers', *Foster Care*, December, pp. 16–17.

Newson, J. and Newson, E. (1979), *Toys and Playthings in Development and Remediation*, Penguin, Harmondsworth.

Nickerson, E. T. (1973), 'Psychology of play and play therapy in classroom activities', *Educating Children*, Spring.

Nickerson, E. T. and O'Laughlin, K. S. (1983), 'The therapeutic use of games', in *Handbook of Play Therapy*, C. E. Schaefer and K. J. O'Connor (eds), pp. 174–87, John Wiley, New York.

Nye, R. D. (1981), *Three Psychologies: Perspectives from Freud, Skinner and Rogers*, Brooks/Cole, Monterey, CA.

Oaklander, V. (1978), *Windows to Our Children*, Real People Press, Utah.

O'Connor, K. J. (1991), *The Play Therapy Primer. An Integration of Theories and Techniques*, John Wiley.

Patterson, C. H. (1980), *Theories of Counseling and Psychotherapy*, Harper & Row, New York.

Patterson, C. H. (1986), *Theories of Counseling and Psychotherapy*, Harper & Row, New York.

Payne, H. (ed.) (1993), *Handbook of Inquiry in the Arts Therapies. One River, Many Currents*, Jessica Kingsley, London.

Peters, U. H. (1985), *Anna Freud: A Life Dedicated to Children*, Weidenfeld & Nicolson, London.

Phillips, A. (1988), *Winnicott*, Fontana, London.

Phillips, R. D. (1985), 'Whistling in the dark? A review of play therapy research', *Psychotherapy*, 22(4), pp. 752–60.

Piaget J. (1962), *Play, Dreams and Imitation in Childhood*, Routledge & Kegan Paul, London.

Piaget, J. and Inhelder, B. (1969), *The Psychology of the Child*, Basic Books.

Pincus, A and Minahan, A. (1973), *Social Work Practice: Model and Method*, Peacock Publishers, Itasca, IL.

Pollock, L. A. (1983), *Forgotten Children: Parent–Child Relations from 1500 to 1900*, Cambridge University Press.

Preston-Shoot, M. (1988), 'A model for evaluating groupwork', *Groupwork*, 2, pp. 147–57.

Pringle, M. K. (1980), *The Needs of Children*, Hutchinson, London.

Qvortrup, J. (1990), 'A voice for children in statistical and social accounting. A plea for children's rights to be heard' in *Constructing and Reconstructing Childhood. Contemporary Issues in the Sociological Study of Children*, A. James and A. Prout (eds), Falmer Press, Lewes.

Rank, O. (1936), *Will Therapy*, Knopf, New York.

Redgrave, K. (1987), *Child's Play: 'Direct Work' with the Deprived Child*, Boys' and Girls' Welfare Society, Cheadle.

Reed, J. P. (1975), *Sand Magic. Experience in Miniature: A Non-verbal Therapy for Children*, JPR Publishers, New Mexico.

Reid, K. (1988), 'But I don't want to lead a group!', *Groupwork*, 2, pp. 124–34.

Reisman, J. M. (1973), *Principles of Psychotherapy with Children*, John Wiley, New York.

Rich, J. (1968), *Interviewing Children and Adolescents*, Macmillan, London.

Rogers, C. R. (1951), *Client-centered Therapy*, Constable, London.

Rogers, C. R. (1957), 'The necessary and sufficient conditions of therapeutic personality change', *Journal of Consulting Psychology*, 21, pp. 95–103.

Rogers, C. R. (1961), *On Becoming a Person: A Therapist's View of Psychotherapy*, Constable, London.

Rogers, C. R. (1974), 'Remarks on the future of client-centered therapy', in *Innovations in Client-centered Therapy*, D.A. Wexler and L.N. Rice (eds), John Wiley, New York.

Rogers, C. R. (1986), 'Client-centered therapy', in *Psychotherapist's Casebook*, I. L. Kutash and A. Wolf (eds), pp. 197–208, Jossey-Bass, San Francisco, CA.

Rosenthal, L. (1956), 'Child guidance', in *The Fields of Group Psychotherapy*, S. R. Slavson (ed.), pp. 215–32, International Universities Press, New York.

Ross, P. (1991), 'The family puppet technique: For assessing parent–child interaction patterns', in *Play Diagnosis and Assessment*, C. E. Schaefer, K. Gitlin and A. Sandgrund (eds), John Wiley, New York.

Rousseau, J.-J. (1925), *Emile*, Dutton, New York.

Rowan, J. (1987), A *Guide to Humanistic Psychology*, The Association for Humanistic Psychology in Britain, London.

Rushforth, W. (1981), *Something is Happening*, Turnstone, Wellingborough.

Rutter, M. (1975), *Helping Troubled Children*, Penguin, Harmondsworth.

Rutter, M. (1981), *Maternal Deprivation Reassessed*, Penguin, Harmondsworth.

Ryan, T. and Walker, R. (1993), *Life Story Work*, British Agencies for Adoption and Fostering, London.

Ryce-Menuhin, J. (1988), *The Self in Early Childhood*, Free Association Books, London.

Ryce-Menuhin, J. (1992), *Jungian Sandplay. The Wonderful Therapy*, Routledge.

Sainsbury, E. (ed.) (1994), *Working with Children in Need. Studies in Complexity and Challenge*, Jessica Kingsley, London.

Salo, F. (1990), ' "Well, I couldn't say no, could I?" Difficulties in the path of late adoption', *Journal of Child Psychotherapy*, **16**(1), pp. 75–91.

Sandler, J., Kennedy, H., and Tyson, R. L. (1980), *The Technique of Child Psychoanalysis: Discussions with Anna Freud*, Hogarth Press, London.

Sandström, C. I. (1979), *The Psychology of Childhood and Adolescence*, Penguin, Harmondsworth.

Saphira, M. (1985), *The Sexual Abuse of Children*, Ponsonby, Auckland.

Schaefer, C. (ed.) (1979), *The Therapeutic Use of Child's Play*, Jason Aronson, New York.

Schaefer, C. E. (1985), 'Play therapy', *Early Child Development and Care*, **19**(1/2), pp. 95–108.

Schaefer, C. E. (ed.) (1988), *Innovative Interventions in Child and Adolescent Therapy*, John Wiley, New York.

Schaefer, C. E. and O'Connor, K. J. (eds) (1983), *Handbook of Play Therapy*, John Wiley, New York.

Schaefer, C. E. and Reid, S. E. (eds) (1986), *Game Play. Therapeutic Use of Childhood Games*, John Wiley, New York.

Schaefer, C. E., Gitlin, K. and Sandgrund, A. (eds) (1991), *Play Diagnosis and Assessment*, John Wiley, New York.

Schiffer, M. (1952), 'Permissiveness versus sanction in activity group therapy', *International Journal of Group Psychotherapy*, **2**, pp. 255–61.

Schorsch, A. (1979), *Images of Childhood*, Mayflower Books, New York.

Segal, H. (1979), *Klein*, Fontana, Glasgow.

Segal, R. M. (1984), 'Helping children express grief through symbolic communication', *Social Casework*, **65**(10), pp. 590–9.

Sgroi, S. M. (ed.) (1982), *Handbook of Clinical Intervention in Child Sexual Abuse*, Lexington Books, Lexington, MA.

Shaw, J. (1987), 'Let us seek to inspire and encourage clients through a holistic approach', *Social Work Today*, **18**(43), pp. 16–17.

Simmonds, J. (1988), 'Social work with children: Developing a framework for responsible practice', in *Direct Work with Children: A Guide for Social Work Practitioners*, J. Aldgate and J. Simmonds (eds), pp. 1–21, B.T. Batsford and British Agencies for Adoption and Fostering, London.

Sinason, V. (1988), 'Dolls and bears: from symbolic equation to symbol. The significance of different play materials for sexually abused children and others', *British Journal of Psychotherapy*, **4**(4), pp. 349–63.

Singer, J. L. (1973), *The Child's World of Make-believe: Experimental Studies of Imaginative Play*, Academic Press, New York.

Skynner, R. (1976), *One Flesh: Separate Persons*, Constable, London.

Slavson, S. R. (1979), 'Play group therapy', in *The Therapeutic Use of Child's Play*, C. Schaefer (ed.), pp. 241–52, Jason Aronson, New York.

Smail, R. J. (1978), *Psychotherapy: A Personal Approach*, Dent, London.

Smalley, R. (1971), 'The functional approach to casework practice', in *Theories of Social Casework*, R.W. Roberts and R.H. Nee (eds), University of Chicago Press, Chicago, IL.

Smith, M. (1990), 'Out of sight not out of mind', *Social Work Today*, **21**(27), pp. 30–1.

Smith, P. B. (1980), *Group Processes and Personal Change*, Harper & Row, London.

Stainton Rogers, W. and Roche, J. (1994), *Children's Welfare and Child's Rights. A Practical Guide to the Law*, Hodder & Stoughton, London.

Stevens, A. (1982), *Archetypes: A Natural History of the Self*, Routledge & Kegan Paul, London.

Striker, S. and Kimmel, E. (1978), *The Anti-colouring Book*, Hippo Books, London.

Swainson, M. (1978), 'Symbolism in the growth process', *Self and Society*, **6**(6), pp. 182–7.

Swanson, F. L. (1970), *Psychotherapists and Children: A Procedural Guide*, Pitman, New York.

Thomas, G. V. and Silk, A. M. J. (1990), *An Introduction to the Psychology of Children's Drawing*, New York University Press, New York.

Thompson, C. L. and Rudolph, L. B. (1988), *Counseling Children*, Brooks/Cole, Pacific Grove, CA.

Thorne, B. (1984), 'Person–centred therapy', in *Individual Therapy in Britain*, W. Dryden (ed.), Harper & Row, London.

Truax, C. B. and Carkhuff, R. R. (1967), *Toward Effective Counseling and Psychotherapy: Training and Practice*, Aldine, Chicago, IL.

Tustin, F. (1981), 'Psychotherapy with psychotic children', in *The Child Psychotherapist and Problems of Young People*, M. Boston and D. Daws (eds), pp. 232–50, Wildwood House, London.

United Nations (1989), *The UN Convention on the Rights of the Child*, United Nations, New York.

Valente, L. and Fontana, D. (1993), 'Research into dramatherapy theory and practice. Some implications for training', in *Handbook of Inquiry into the Arts Therapies. One River, Many Currents*, H. Payne (ed.), Jessica Kingsley, London.

van der Kooij, R. and Hellendoorn, J. (eds) (1986), *Play – Play Therapy – Play Research*, Swets North America, Berwyn; Swets & Zeitlinger, Lisse.

van der Post, L. (1976), *Jung and the Story of Our Time*, Penguin, Harmondsworth.

Vargo, B., Stavrakaki, C., Ellis, J. and Williams, E. (1988), 'Child sexual abuse: Its impact and treatment', *Canadian Journal of Psychiatry*, **33**(6), pp. 468–73.

Vinturella, L. and James, R. (1987), 'Sand play: A therapeutic medium with children', *Elementary School Guidance and Counseling*, **21**(3), pp. 229–38.

von Bertalanffy, L. (1948), *General Systems Theory*, Braziller, New York.

von Franz, M.-L. (1980), *The Psychological Meaning of Redemption Motifs in Fairy Tales*, Inner City Books, Toronto.

von Franz, M.-L. (1983), *Shadow and Evil in Fairytales*, Spring, Dallas.

Walker, L. E. A. and Bolkovatz, M. A. (1988), 'Play therapy with children who have experienced sexual assault', in *Handbook on Sexual Abuse of Children*, L. E. A. Walker (ed.), pp. 249–69, Springer, New York.

Walrond-Skinner, S. (1976), *Family Therapy. The Treatment of Natural Systems*, Routledge & Kegan Paul, London.

Wardle, M. (1975), 'Hippopotamus or cow: not communicating about children', *Social Work Today*, **6**(14), pp. 428–32.

Waterhouse, S. (1987), *Time For Me*, S. Waterhouse, 34 Bell Lane, Byfield, Northamptonshire.

Webb, N. B. (1989), 'Supervision of child therapy: Analyzing therapeutic impasses and monitoring counter–transference', *The Clinical Supervisor*, **7**(4), pp. 61–76.

Webb, N. B. (ed.) (1991), *Play Therapy with Children in Crisis. A Casebook for Practitioners*, Guilford Press, New York.

Wells, J. (1989), 'Powerplays – considerations in communicating with children', in *Child Sexual Abuse: Listening, Hearing and Validating the Experiences of Children*, H. Blagg, J. A. Hughes and C. Wattam (eds), Longman, Harlow.

Wells, R. (1988), *Helping Children Cope with Grief*, Sheldon Press.

West, J. (1983), 'Play therapy with Rosy', *British Journal of Social Work*, **13**(6), pp. 645–61.

West, J. (1990a), 'Children "in limbo" ', *Adoption and Fostering*, **14**(2), pp. 11–15.

West, J. (1990b), 'Play work and play therapy: Distinctions and definitions', *Adoption and Fostering*, **14**(4), pp. 31–7.

Whitaker, D. S. (1985), *Using Groups to Help People*, Routledge & Kegan Paul, London.

White, R. and Swainson, M. (1974), *Seven Inner Journeys*, Spearman, London.

Whitmont, E. C. (1980), *The Symbolic Quest: Basic Concepts of Analytical Psychology*, Barrie & Rockliff, London.

Wickes, F. G. (1963), *The Inner World of Choice*, Coventure, London.

Wickes, F. G. (1977), *The Inner World of Childhood*, Coventure, London.

Will, D. and Wrate, R. M. (1985), *Integrated Family Therapy: A Problem-centred Psychodynamic Approach*, Tavistock, London.

Willock, B. (1983), 'Play therapy with the aggressive, acting-out child', in *Handbook of Play Therapy*, C. E. Schaefer and K. J. O'Connor (eds), pp. 387–411, John Wiley, New York.

Wilson, K., Kendrick, P. and Ryan, V. (1992), *Play Therapy. A Non-directive Approach for Children and Adolescents*, Baillière Tindall, London.

Winnicott, C. (1984), 'Face to face with children', *In Touch with Children*, pp. 19–23, British Agencies for Adoption and Fostering, London.

Winnicott, D. W. (1971a), *Playing and Reality*, Penguin, Harmondsworth.

Winnicott, D. W. (1971b), *Therapeutic Consultations in Child Psychiatry*, Basic Books, New York.

Winnicott, D. W. (1975), *Through Paediatrics to Psycho-analysis*, Hogarth Press and The Institute of Psycho-analysis, London.

Winnicott, D. W. (1977), *The Piggle: An Account of the Psychoanalytic Treatment of a Little Girl*, Penguin, Harmondsworth.

Winnicott, D. W. (1986), *Home is Where We Start From: Essays by a Psychoanalyst*, Penguin, Harmondsworth.

Wolff, S. (1981), *Children Under Stress*, Penguin, Harmondsworth.

Wolff, S. (1986), 'Child psychotherapy', in *An Introduction to the Psychotherapies*, S. Bloch (ed.), pp. 222–51, Oxford University Press, Oxford.

Wolman, B.B. (ed.) (1973), *Dictionary of Behavioural Science*, Macmillan, London.

Woltmann, A. G. (1964), 'Psychological rationale of puppetry', in *Child Psychotherapy: Practice and Theory*, M. R. Haworth (ed.), pp. 395–9, Basic Books, New York.

Wood, A. (1988), 'King Tiger and the roaring tummies. A novel way to help young children and their families change', *Journal of Family Therapy*, **10**, pp. 49–63.

Woodhead, M. (1990), 'Psychology and the cultural construction of children's needs', in *Constructing and Reconstructing Childhood: Contemporary Issues in the Sociological Study of Children*, A. James and A. Prout (eds), Falmer Press, Lewes.

Wright, D. M., Moelis, I. and Pollack, L. J. (1976), 'The outcome of individual psychotherapy: Increments at follow-up', *Journal of Child Psychology and Psychiatry*, **17**, pp. 175–85.

Yates, A. (1990), 'Eroticized children' in *Handbook of Sexology. Vol VII. Childhood and Adolescent Sexology*, E. M. Perry (ed.), pp. 325–34, Elsevier, Amsterdam.

Yawkey, T. D. and Pellegrini, A. D. (eds) (1984), *Child's Play: Developmental and Applied*, Lawrence Erlbaum, Hillsdale, NJ.

Yura, M. T. and Galassi, M. D. (1982), 'Adlerian usage of children's play', in *Play Therapy: Dynamics of the Process of Counseling with Children*, G. L. Landreth (ed.), pp. 130–6, Charles C. Thomas, Springfield, IL, abridged from *Journal of Individual Psychology*, **30**, pp. 194–201 (1974).

Zimrin, H. (1986), 'A profile of survival', *Child Abuse and Neglect*, **10**(3), pp. 339–49.

Author Index

Subject Index